Rosalba Carriera

Illuminating Women Artists: The Eighteenth Century

The *Illuminating Women Artists* series is being published at a critical moment in contemporary culture. It marks a significant intervention within the broader movement underway among scholars, museums, collectors and the wider world of cultural heritage to make evident the contributions of women artists and place them in the context of both their times and the continuing history of art. Each book is written by a leading specialist in the field of art history and will appeal to audiences from the academic sphere to the general public. Beautifully illustrated, the volumes collectively offer an unprecedented visual contextualisation of the lives and works of their subjects. In several cases the books are the first full monograph on the artist in question.

Books in the sub-series *Illuminating Women Artists: The Eighteenth Century* critically reappraise the lives and works of female artists in Europe from the late seventeenth to the early nineteenth century. Many of the women represented by the volumes were celebrated professional artists in their own eras, yet their names and works have not been passed down continually in the history of art. As the first series dedicated to correcting this omission, the books interweave established conclusions with new discoveries to reframe how women's artistic production is approached and understood.

Rosalba Carriera

ANGELA OBERER

GETTY PUBLICATIONS
LOS ANGELES

Published in the United States of America by Getty Publications, Los Angeles
1200 Getty Center Drive, Suite 500
Los Angeles, California 90049-1682
getty.edu/publications

Distributed in the United States and Canada by the University of Chicago Press

Printed in China

ISBN 978-1-60606-860-1
Library of Congress Control Number: 2022947760

Published simultaneously in the United Kingdom by Lund Humphries
Huckletree Shoreditch
Alphabeta Building
18 Finsbury Square
London EC2A 1AH
UK
lundhumphries.com

Copy edited by Julie Gunz
Project managed and designed by Crow Books
Set in Adobe Caslon Pro

Front cover: Rosalba Carriera, *A Muse*, mid-1720s, pastel on paper, 31 × 26 cm (12 3⁄16 × 10 ¼ in.), J. Paul Getty Museum, Los Angeles

Back cover: Rosalba Carriera, *Portrait of Sir James Gray*, 1744–5, pastel on paper, 56 × 45.8 cm (22 1⁄16 × 18 1⁄16 in.), J. Paul Getty Museum, Los Angeles

Contents

Series Foreword

Illuminating Women Artists: The Eighteenth Century was conceptualised at a pivotal moment in contemporary life, when the call to dismantle structural bias was taking on a new urgency. As social justice movements, such as #MeToo, #BlackLivesMatter and #TransLivesMatter, exposed assumptions about gender, race and sexual identity, academic research has been infused with a new energy around these topics. Although approaches to, and even the very applicability of, identity categories as they are defined today vary in regard to the past, early modernity and the contemporary moment share a desire to contend with the power structures that have repressed individuals and groups, albeit in historically distinct ways. Books in the *Illuminating Women Artists* series advance a specific aspect of this study – the feminist academic enterprise – by making evident various ways that women negotiated, and sometimes resisted, structural constraints in the sphere of the visual arts.

The series is indebted to feminist art-historical studies that were first produced in the 1970s in response to the broader women's rights movements of that time. This foundational scholarship aimed to disrupt the traditional academic focus on early modern male artists by writing their female counterparts into the discipline of art history. Since then, feminist scholarship has worked to investigate gender norms which created different conditions for women and men who sought to practise art. That scholarship has demonstrated that women were ambitious, successful and fully embedded in artistic practice on a variety of levels, and were not merely marginal to the story of masculine creation and triumph that has yet to be seriously decentred in art history.

Illuminating Women Artists: The Eighteenth Century considers women artists within their social, cultural, temporal and geographic contexts. In particular it shows how women in Europe worked under a variety of challenging conditions from the late seventeenth century into the early nineteenth. This 'long eighteenth century' was an era defined by radical transformations in thought, culture, society and politics brought about by the philosophical movement known as the Enlightenment, the rise (and sometimes the fall) of expansionist ambitions of colonialism and empire, wars and revolutions. Questions about the nature and ideal role of women in society were at the heart of the most pressing cultural, philosophical, political and social debates of this period. Women authors and artists played a key role in those debates and challenged normative structures in important ways. They were also products of the social structures of their place and time, such as gender, class and race. These structures contributed to the formation of women's identities and to their conceptions about others. Thus acculturated into dominant cultural attitudes, women artists were often complicit in supporting social hierarchies of class and race. They themselves derived from a spectrum of social classes – artisan, merchant, professional or patrician. So far none have come to light that can be identified as anything other than racially white.

Societal limitations disadvantaged most women who aspired to a life in the visual arts. For example, women were excluded from the formal training open to male artists through art academies or guilds, and therefore they sought private instruction elsewhere, often from relatives, both male and female, but also in the private studios of established artists. Marriage and motherhood could contribute to a lapse in artistic production. Presumably for this reason, some women did not marry until they were fully established as professional artists, or they did not marry at all. Being unmarried presented challenges of its own, as women in this period had virtually no civil or political rights, and they generally needed a supportive male relative to act on their behalf in legal and business matters. Some men did train, and/or supportively promote, their daughters or wives as artists, which also aggrandised the family and improved its financial standing through patronage and sales.

Women who were professionally successful and their artistic production critically acclaimed, were nonetheless often evaluated according to gender stereotypes. Yet, certain women independently challenged, and circumvented or broke, restrictive gender protocols to enable prolific art production. In the process, they revised those protocols and influenced the history of art. Some established their own professional studios, publicly exhibited their works and trained pupils, both female and male, who in turn established themselves as professionals in studios of their own. Some produced images for prestigious European courts and churches. Others were involved with scientific enquiry, producing illustrations for research and publications in the fields of natural history, medicine or entomology. Women held official posts as royal botanical illustrators, court portraitists or drawing teachers. Some were members of art academies or guilds. Many more – hundreds by the end of the eighteenth century – had no official affiliations, but availed themselves of expanding opportunities to exhibit their work at public exhibitions and commercial venues. Thanks to a burgeoning art market and a taste for collecting art, women were able to produce work for patrons and customers across a broad social spectrum, from the most elite classes (kings, queens, aristocrats) to the more middling sorts. These women in the aggregate produced works that varied widely in artistic media and in subject and genre, including narrative subjects from history, mythology and literature, as well as sacred themes, portraiture and still life.

Five decades of sustained research have transformed our understanding of early modern women artists. *Illuminating Women Artists: The Eighteenth Century* takes stock of this work through books that offer state-of-the-question analyses of their subjects. These peer-reviewed volumes interweave established conclusions with new discoveries investigated through emerging modes of analysis to reframe our understanding of the lives, artistic production and works of art by European women. Books in this series make a substantive case for women's presence in aesthetic culture, and trace the complex circumstances that conditioned their making of art, their careers and their lives. Together the books reveal the varied ways in which women of the long eighteenth century skilfully and often successfully navigated restricting gender norms to stake out productive lives as artmakers and develop innovative approaches to the works they produced. The volumes offer an unprecedented contextualisation of the lives and works of their subjects, to whom in some cases a monograph has not previously been dedicated.

Marilyn Dunn, Loyola University Chicago
Melissa Hyde, University of Florida

Acknowledgements

This book would not have been possible without the help and support I received during the research for the first version of my book on Rosalba Carriera. My deep gratitude goes to Melissa Hyde, whose detailed and constructive comments in my initial project were enormously helpful. Without her believing in my research and offering rigorous, necessary criticism combined with excellent advice, nothing would have followed.

I am also immensely grateful to fellows, friends and colleagues who have always encouraged and sustained me and who have helped me to prepare the first manuscript in English. Special thanks go to Patricia Rucidlo, who read many chapters more than once, toning down some of my convoluted Germanic syntax as much as possible, and to Martino Traxler, who translated most of the Italian passages into English.

My greatest debt is to Robin Larsen and to Ann Pollak. Robin has always believed in this project and supported me by pre-editing the first manuscript. Her much-needed corrections and thoughtful, original suggestions were of enormous help. Without Ann's final polishing of the text for this version, for which I am enormously grateful, I would have not been able to send the manuscript to Lund Humphries.

I cannot express enough thanks to the art lover Neil Jeffares. His professional feedback and his constructive criticism have allowed me to correct mistakes previously published. His sophisticated comments on women writers, and art made by 'women, poor, disabled or other minorities' (see 'Fairness, Candour & Curiosity – From Finance to Art History', on https://neiljeffares.wordpress.com), and his unique intuition will remain an inspiration. May this book inspire him in the face of any kind of *défaillance*.

Many thanks as well to his colleague Cavaliere Xavier F. Salomon, whose impeccable work at the *Burlington Magazine* has unquestionably helped to improve the quality of the prestigious journal.

I am very grateful for the peer reviewers' detailed comments and recommendations that helped enormously to improve my manuscript.

For professional support and friendly guidance, I would like to thank Erika Gaffney. Without her always gentle attitude and careful supervision, this book would not have turned out the same. Julie Gunz has also been exceptional. What would I have done without her help! Heartful thanks also to the series editors Marilyn Dunn and Melissa Hyde, who accepted this book to be part of the Lund Humphries series *Illuminating Women Artists*.

Finally, I would like to acknowledge with endless gratitude the patience, support and love with which Ernesto has accompanied me on this journey.

Preface

Rosalba Carriera (1673–1757) started her life as a painter at a time of significant growth in the number of professional female artists in Europe. While during the Renaissance and Mannerist periods only 35 women are known to have pursued this profession, by the Baroque, the number had increased to 200.[1] In the eighteenth century the situation further improved. As De Girolami Cheney et al. put it: 'In a [...] stylish atmosphere of enlightened enquiry, more women would pursue their own professional careers than had previously been seen. This is especially true in the fine arts. The eighteenth century was accordingly the great transitional period for women artists.'[2]

In the eighteenth century, the mere mention of Carriera's first name was enough to evoke an enthusiastic response in Italy, Germany, France and England. 'Not without due cause is Signora Rosalba valued as an ornament of Italy, and Europe's foremost female artist';[3] 'She fills Europe with her works'; '[Rosalba is] one of the brightest lights in painting that your Italy has ever given us';[4] '[...] the glory of her sex'; 'the most talented female artist of our century'.[5] Her international reputation and fame grew to the point that the father of Johann Wolfgang von Goethe (1749–1832), Johann Caspar Goethe, and the French artist, engraver and writer Charles-Nicolas Cochin (1715–90) referred to her simply as 'Signora Rosalba' or 'Mademoiselle Rosalba'.[6] It had long since become unnecessary to add her surname in order to identify her.

Nevertheless, the artist who was more celebrated in her day than any female painter before her has today almost disappeared from view. She is barely known outside a relatively small circle of art lovers and connoisseurs. Only in Venice, her birthplace, does she still enjoy a certain degree of fame, but beyond the lagoon, she has all but sunk into oblivion. This is even more surprising if we take into consideration the vast numbers of works that Carriera produced during her lifetime. The artist's first catalogue raisonné, published by Bernardina Sani in 1988, which the author later expanded and updated to reflect the latest research in a 2007 edition,[7] includes 425 pastels and miniatures. While various paintings attributed to Carriera are no longer considered to be authentic works, numerous other examples by her hand have been discovered, for which reason a revised and an updated catalogue raisonné is urgently needed. The same is true for a more profound analysis of the vast majority of her works, which remains a desideratum for research.

Considering furthermore that 2023 celebrates the 350th anniversary of Rosalba Carriera's birth, I am all the more delighted that Lund Humphries and the series editors Marilyn Dunn and Melissa Hyde have offered to include this outstanding painter in their series *Illuminating Women Artists*.

This book is a richly illustrated distillation of *The Life and Work of Rosalba Carriera (1673–1757) – The Queen of Pastel*, a longer study I published in 2018 with Amsterdam University Press with the idea to introduce Carriera to a wider public. It examines her oeuvre and creative processes and constructs a personal, as well as professional, history of this unique female painter. It documents the difficulties, complications and consequences that arose then, or that more generally can also arise today, when a woman decides to become an independent artist. It further includes an analysis of the interplay between society's expectations, generally accepted codes for gendered behaviour, and one single female painter's astute strategies for achieving success as well as autonomy in her professional life as a famed artist.

Fundamental questions I raise again are: What kind of artist was Carriera? How did she manage to build up her career? How did she run her business and organise her own workshop? What are the specific characteristics of her paintings? Which external and internal factors helped her achieve success? Addressing these various questions, this book offers an opportunity to gain a deeper understanding of Carriera as an outstanding portraitist, an erudite history painter, and an artist who regularly produced erotic and eroticising images.

I am equally enthusiastic about the decision taken by the Gemäldegalerie in Dresden, the museum that owns the largest collection of Carriera works in the world, to celebrate the 350th anniversary with an exhibition devoted to the artist. The curator, Dr Roland Enke, is just as excited to be able to put together the first show on the Venetian celebrity that Dresden has ever had.

My hope is, therefore, that Rosalba Carriera's work presented in this book together with the exhibition in Dresden will contribute to the recovery and the acknowledgement of her outstanding career. 'The White Rose of Venice', one of the most intriguing, most surprising, and most overlooked women artists in modern times, deserves to be well known again after her reputation has sadly dwindled for more than two centuries.

Introduction

Venice at the Dawn of the Eighteenth Century

Rosalba Carriera was born into a city that had established itself as the most successful republic in Italy but was facing a period of decline during its last century of independence before its end in 1797. The opening of new trade routes to the East had already started to impact adversely on the Republic's foreign trade by the end of the Venetian 'Golden Age' at the close of the sixteenth century, and the loss of its holdings in Turkey, Greece and the East during the first 20 years of the eighteenth century dramatically reduced the extent of the Republic's dominions.

Changes in the local social structures occurred in tandem with the economic and political decline. The numbers of Venetian nobility were drastically shrinking, creating significant problems for the ruling class. The Venetian state, which was governed exclusively by members of the nobility, had to find large numbers of new men; and these newcomers were not always welcomed or highly esteemed. At the same time, poverty was expanding exponentially. The number of citizens defined as poor and subsidised by the state grew from 445 in 1586 to a potentially threatening 17,956 in 1760, and as high as 23,015 in 1787. One-sixth of the population was sustained by officially administered charity.[1]

Despite these threats *La Serenissima* (the most serene), as Venice was then known, remained a richly flowering cultural hub. By the end of the seventeenth century, music, painting and the decorative arts were blooming once again, and celebrations, processions and festivals such as the months-long carnival were increasingly numerous and important to the Republic. With its dances, bullfights, acrobatic displays, wrestling and boxing tournaments and fireworks, the colourful and entertaining masquerades, the Venetian carnival became one of the biggest attractions (fig.1). And although the various celebrations camouflaged a troublesome reality, they also amused and gratified a steadily growing, unparalleled number of travellers who came to Venice to see the spectacular city in the lagoon with its splendid art and architecture. The visitors also came to indulge in the world of luxury and libertinism which was well known far beyond the city's borders. In the seventeenth century as many as 20,000 courtesans, concubines and prostitutes were to be found in Venice, a surprisingly high number considering that the city's population was estimated to be around 160,000. Moreover, during the seventeenth and eighteenth centuries, over 130 gaming houses – '*casinos*', which took their name from the Venetian word for small house – sprang up around the city promising a particular type of excitement and entertainment (fig.2). The first coffee houses, the so-called *botteghe da caffè*, were also part of the public amusement, opening up

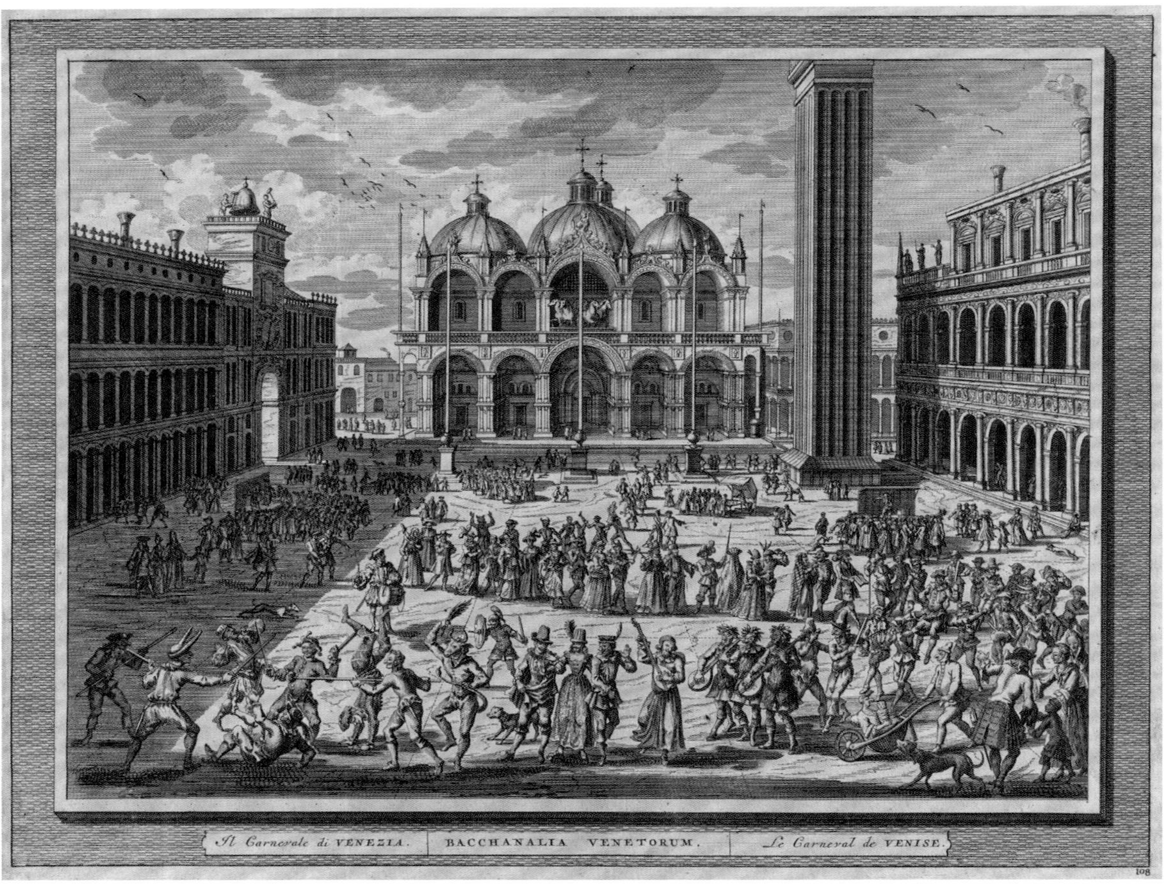

1 *The Carnival of Venice*, 1722, engraving, from *Thesaurus Antiquitatum et Historiarum Italiae*, vol.IX, 32 × 41.8 cm (12 ⅝ × 16 ⅜ in), The Metropolitan Museum of Art, New York

at the end of the seventeenth century. They became so popular that they numbered 213 by 1763.[2]

At the same time, the intellectual and artistic culture in Venice turned back to its roots, with significant results. As a reflection of the importance of theatre to Venetian culture and society, some 14 theatres were operating by the beginning of the eighteenth century, with at least eight of them open throughout the entire year. From October to February, as well as from Ascension Day (40 days after Easter) to mid-June and during September, several public opera houses, open to entertain Venetians and foreigners alike, had turned the city into Europe's undisputed capital of musical drama.

The visual arts also recovered after a century of stagnant conformity and indecisiveness. Painters like Sebastiano Ricci (1659–1734) and Giovanni Battista Piazzetta (1682–1754) embellished churches, official palaces and private homes with history paintings that enjoyed international fame. Giovanni Battista Tiepolo (1696–1770) enjoyed an outstanding career as a fresco-painter decorating walls and ceilings in and outside of Venice, a telling example of which is this sketch which was made in the 1760s as a model for

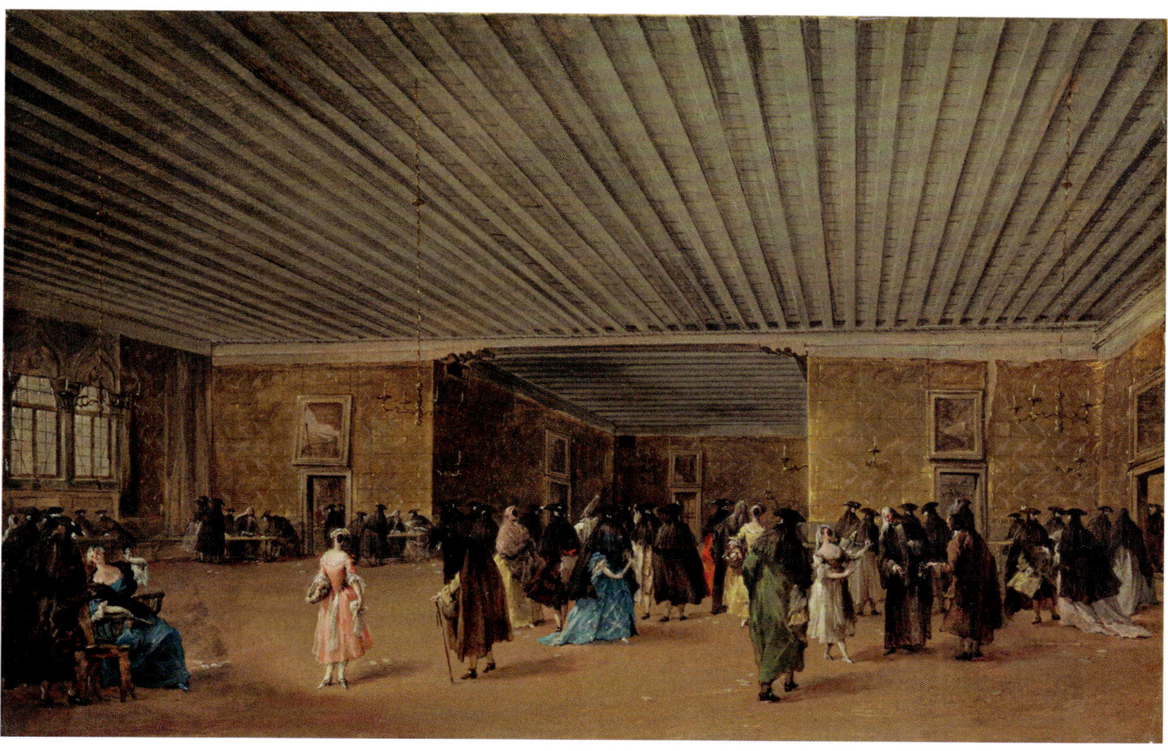

2 Francesco Guardi, *The Ridotto Pubblico at Palazzo Dandolo*, *c.*1765–8, oil on canvas, 34 × 50.8 cm (13 3/8 × 20 in), The Metropolitan Museum of Art, New York

the decoration of the ceiling of a room next to the throne room of the Royal Palace in Madrid (fig.3). In this *Apotheosis of the Spanish Monarchy* the enthroned figure of Spain is being crowned by Mercury while Apollo arrives holding a royal sceptre in his right hand and his lyre in the left. Jupiter commands the proceedings from above. The painter resolved the challenges of perspective and foreshortening for this image that was to be seen from below, thus testifying to his exceptional capabilities which resulted in his international success.

Pietro Longhi (1702–85) instead chose a different approach to art, portraying intimate scenes from Venetian contemporary social and private life. In *The Faint*, an elegant lady pretends to swoon in order to upset a table of cards after an unfortunate hand in a gambling session (fig.4). She is seen sinking into a chair while servants and friends rush to support and help her. Longhi gained a far-reaching reputation for aptly representing the fashion, the manners and decadence of his era through a gentle form of digestible social criticism, meant to entertain.

Cityscapes represented another genre for which Venetian art became famous. The picturesque renderings of characteristic views of Venice such as *Piazza San Marco*, by Giovanni Antonio Canal, called Canaletto (1697–1768) or *The Grand Canal above the Rialto* by Tiepolo's brother-in-law Francesco Guardi (1712–93) contributed directly to the visual production of the Grand Tour (figs 5 and 6).[3] These types of paintings fulfilled the expectations of the grand tourists and were perfect gifts to take home along with the memories of an unforgettable journey, of having lived whatever their idea was of the 'Venetian experience'.

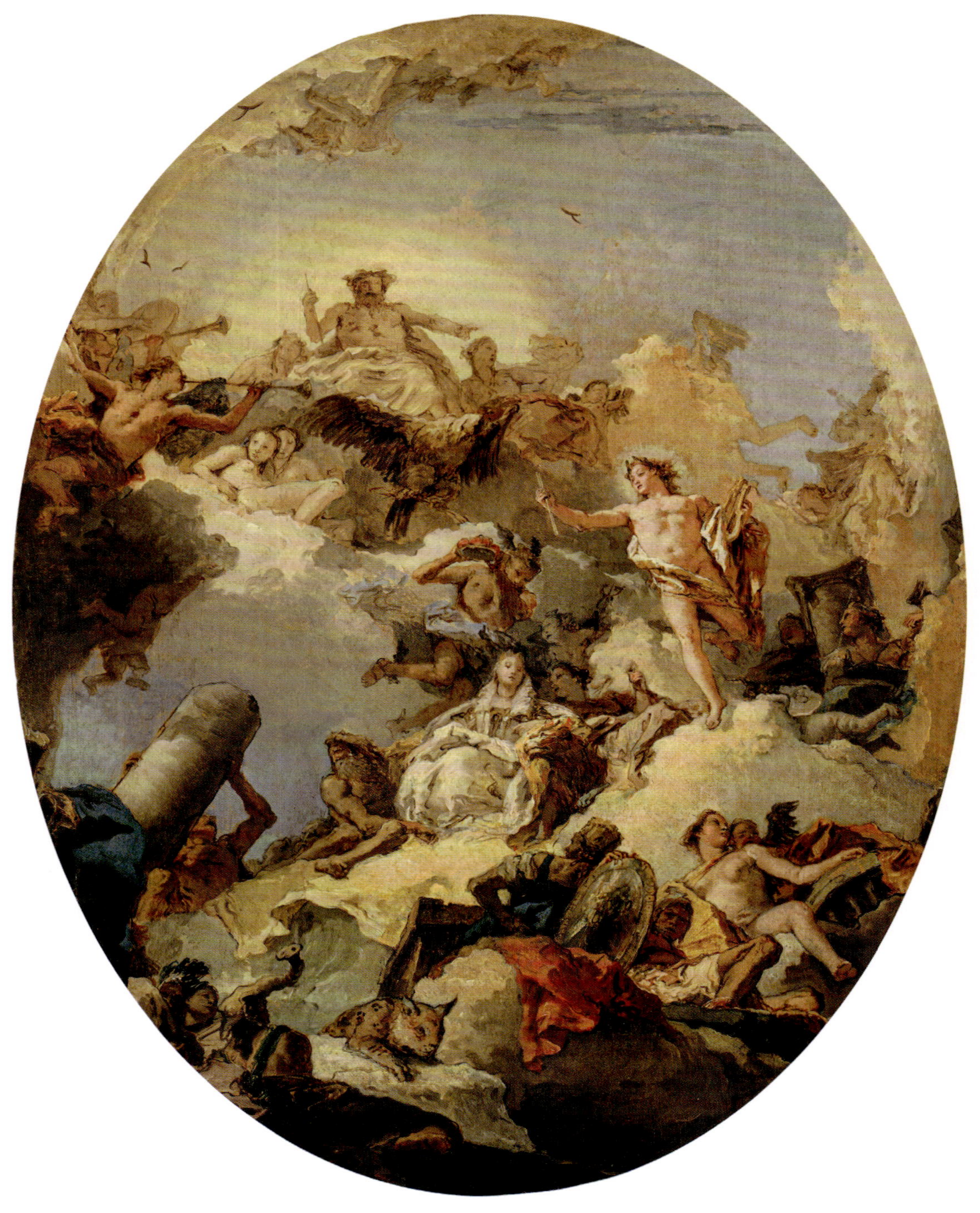

3 Giovanni Battista Tiepolo, *The Apotheosis of the Spanish Monarchy*, 1760s, oil on canvas, 84 × 69 cm (33 × 27 1/4 in), The Metropolitan Museum of Art, New York

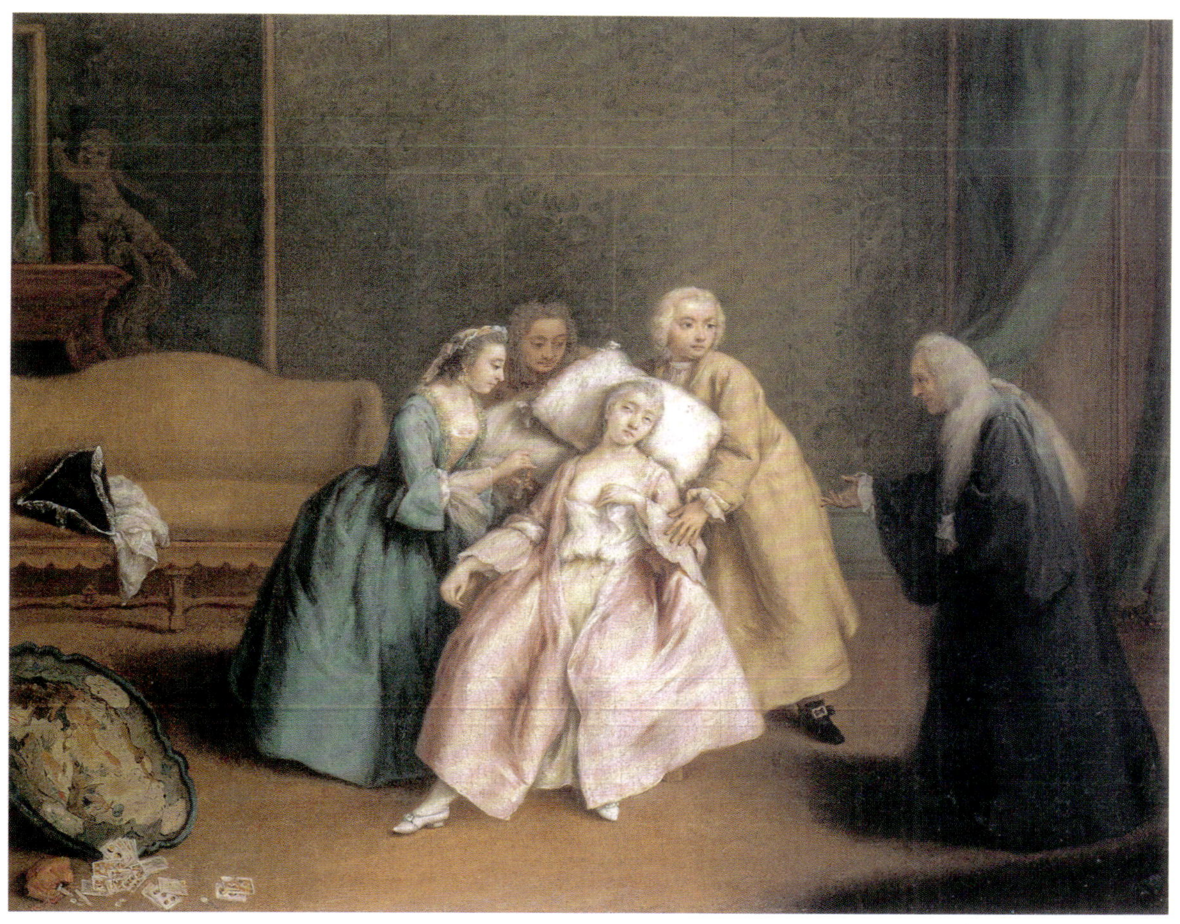

4 Pietro Longhi, *The Faint*, *c.*1744, oil on canvas, 50 × 61.7 cm (19 ¾ × 24 ¼ in), Samuel Kress Collection, The National Gallery of Art, Washington DC

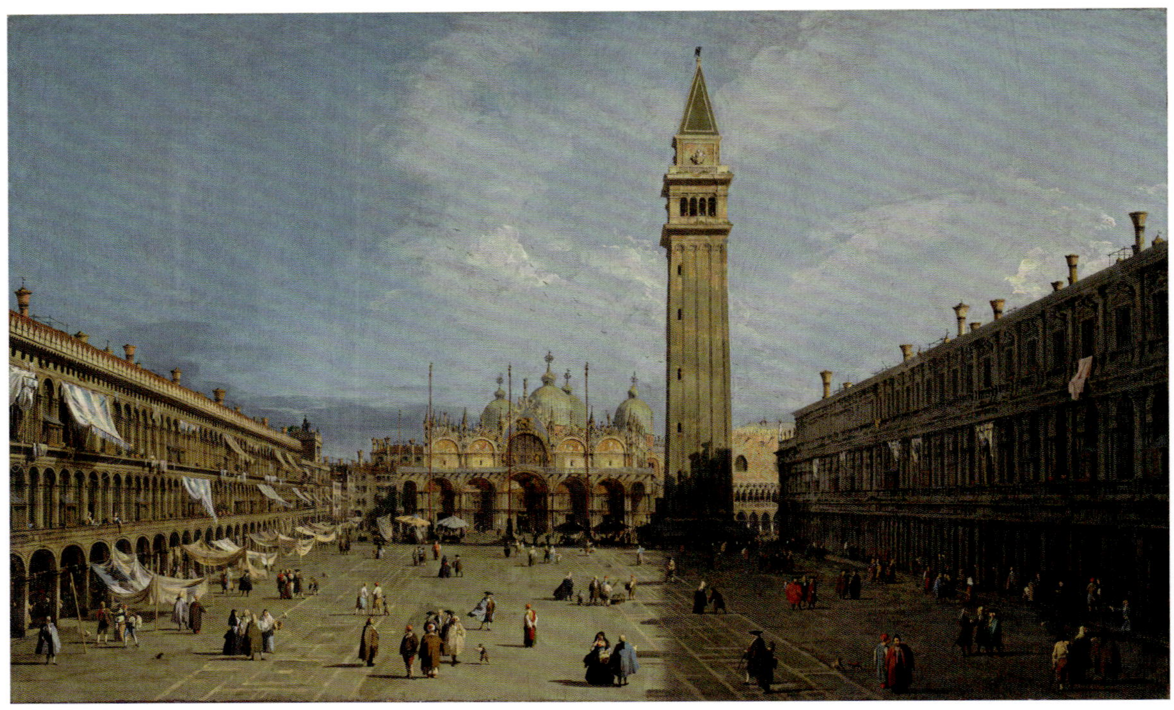

5 Canaletto, *Piazza San Marco*, late 1720s, oil on canvas, 68.8 × 112.4 cm (27 × 44¼ in), The Metropolitan Museum of Art, New York

6 Francesco Guardi, *The Grand Canal above the Rialto*, late 1760s, oil on canvas, 53.3 × 85.7 cm (21 × 33¾ in), The Metropolitan Museum of Art, New York

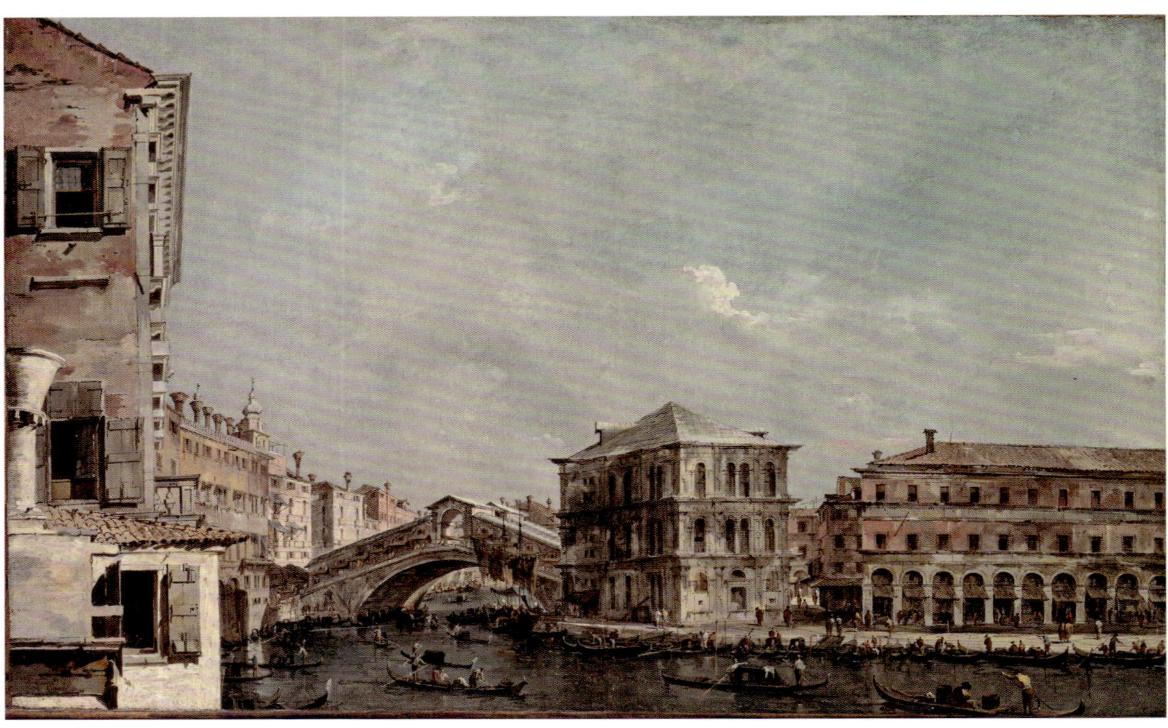

The successes of women as protagonists on Venice's cultural stage were just as exceptional. 'The prominence of women artists, poets, translators, *salonnières,* and journalists in Venice was indeed one of its distinctive characteristics.'[4] And many foreign visitors were well aware of this particular aspect of the city. Other than Rosalba Carriera, among the female painters in Venice during the seventeenth and eighteenth centuries who need to be mentioned is Giulia Lama (1681–1747) who was a history painter, and one of the first women known to draw and study the nude from live models. Elisabetta Lazzarini (1662–1729), sister and pupil of Gregorio Lazzarini (1655–1730), and the flower painter Margherita Caffi (*c.*1650–1710), who worked for the Medici in Florence as well as for the Habsburgs in Madrid and Innsbruck, are just two other names to add to the list of gifted and talented women in Venice who managed to establish careers as artists.

I

The Beginning of Carriera's Artistic Career

CARRIERA'S WORLD *EN MINIATURE*

On 12 January 1673, Alba Foresti (1655–1738) gave birth in Venice to her first child. Alba and her husband Andrea Carriera (1645–1719) decided to christen the girl with the names 'Rosalba and Zuanna' (Giovanna) as stated on the baptismal certificate. Unbeknownst to the new parents, their firstborn would grow up to become arguably the most influential woman artist of Italy, and the most renowned female painter in all of Europe in the eighteenth century.

On 7 October 1675, just over two and a half years after her first child, Alba gave birth to another girl, Giovanna, whom friends and family called 'Neneta' or 'Zanina'. The historical documentation states that Giovanna, like her older sister, was also baptised as Rosalba Zuanna. This unusual duplication of names stemmed from the fact that the firstborn was so ill as a small child that her parents feared she would die, so they elected to give their second daughter the same name.[1] Another two years later, on 10 September 1677, a third daughter, Anzola (Angela) Cecilia, was born; she was nicknamed 'Anzoletta'.

Andrea Carriera, the artist's father, was a lawyer who worked for the Venetian Republic, while little is known about her mother, Alba, except that she dedicated her leisure time to the production of lace and embroidery. Together the couple ensured that all of their children received an excellent education; along with needlework and lace production, which was considered to be part of any female education, the girls were tutored in Latin, French and music. Rosalba and Giovanna were also known to have been well versed in the classics and contemporary poetry.

Little is known about the first two decades of Carriera's life. As a young woman, she set up her workshop, where she produced her first artworks and instructed her sisters in painting. Teaching younger siblings was a common practice in artists' families since the Renaissance, which reflected the traditional role allocated to the oldest daughter. She was meant to take responsibility alongside the parents for her younger brothers and sisters. It was not long before Rosalba became the one to whom not only her sisters but also both parents always deferred. Rosalba's privileged position within the family is suggested by one of the early documents regarding her life. It states that the family moved in 1700 from the Rio di San Barnaba to a house on the Grand Canal in the San Vio quarter, next to the Ca' Venier dei Leoni, which today is the seat of the Guggenheim Museum (fig.7). Soon after moving in, the main occupant's name on the contract was altered from Alba Carriera to Rosalba Carriera.[2] While the ambitious artist was working on building her career, she apparently had also begun overseeing the general administration of the household.

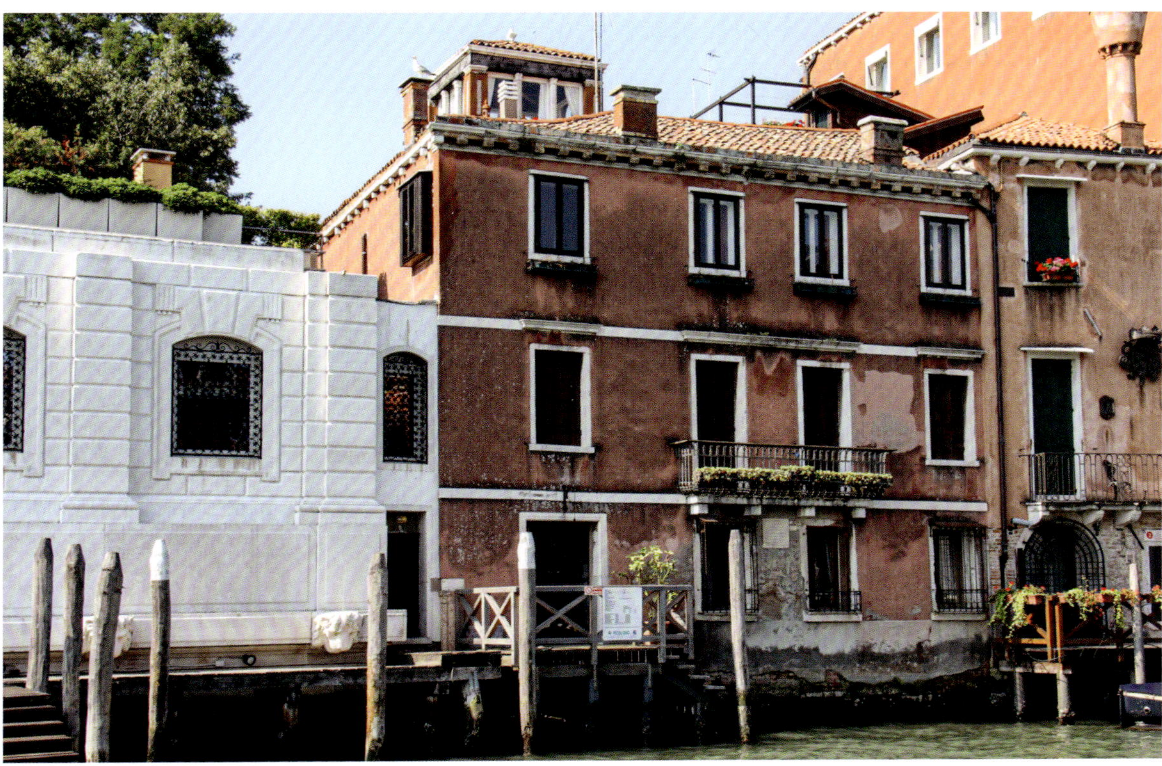

7 Carriera's house on the Grand Canal

Young women were unable to take lessons from a master within a painter's workshop, and therefore most of the female artists known until the eighteenth century learned their trade from their father, brother or another family member, or took private lessons. Carriera's start was considerably more difficult since she had no direct relative still alive who was a painter. There had been an artist in the family: her grandfather, Pasqualino Carriera, but he can be excluded as her teacher, because he died before she was born. Indeed, it is not known either how or when she embarked on her artistic career. The only indication regarding her beginnings can be found in an early biography of the painter by Antoine-Joseph Dézallier d'Argenville (1680–1765) in his *Abrégé de la vie des plus fameux peintres* (*Brief Lives of the Most Famous Painters*):

> Inspiration pierced through the small amusements of youth, which really began to bore her. She took it upon herself to copy a figure that her father had designed for the heading of a sonnet; a friend, who learned to draw from a foreign painter, made her master see the drawing that Rosalba had made; his astonishment was extreme; he glimpsed there the excellence to which she would arrive one day. This master encouraged her to continue, and gave her several of his drawings to copy: it is thus that auspicious beginnings give proof of the great artist.[3]

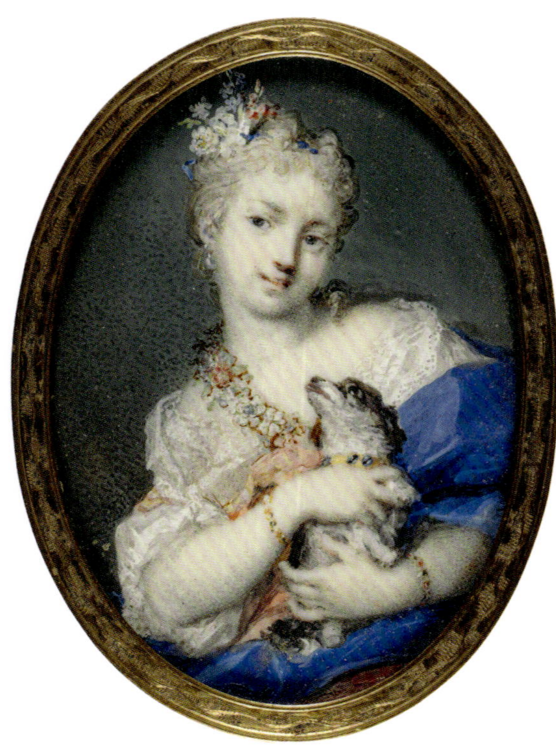

8 Rosalba Carriera, *Woman with a Dog*, 1710–20, watercolour on ivory, 7.5 × 5.5 cm (2 ⅞× 2 ⅛ in), The Cleveland Museum of Art, OH

Dézallier d'Argenville's observations include two significant details: first, it was a female friend ('une amie' in French) who first noticed her talent; and second, it was 'inspiration', an unprecedented notion for a woman artist, that prompted Carriera to turn away from her childish pastimes to the more intellectual pursuit of art.[4] And while her teacher has never been identified by name, it is likewise possible that Carriera was primarily a prodigious autodidact.

The first known artworks that Carriera produced were lids of *tabatières*, snuffboxes for tobacco, and other types of miniatures, an art form that had evolved from illuminated manuscripts and gained popularity among the aristocracy starting in the sixteenth century. A vast production of handbooks and treatises accompanied the growing fascination with these pictures *en miniature.* From France and England, the practice arrived in Italy as well, and by the end of the seventeenth century, the small-scale paintings had become a trans-European idiom of intimacy.[5]

Although it is still uncertain how or through whom Carriera was introduced to this specific technique, or whether she ever read any treatises about it, she soon became a veritable expert in the genre. These small paintings proved particularly attractive as their production entailed extreme artistic and artisanal skill and great delicacy of execution to capture and portray a person's features and character, or to depict a mythological or pastoral scene in such minute detail.

The vast majority of miniatures were portraits of loved ones, family members or friends, with one of the latter presumably represented in Carriera's painting showing a woman with a dog (fig.8). But celebrities or royalty could also be represented in this form. Like pieces of jewellery, their particular, extremely personal value for their owners turned them into deeply sentimental artefacts. Whether serving as amorous tokens, or as a means of communication between lovers, family or friends, these 'portrait objects' became for each owner a 'topos of affective private engagement',[6] bordering at times on the sublimation of a fetish.

Given their size, miniatures were often enclosed in precious containers of gold and silver, decorated with diamonds or other precious stones. Their owners would carry and wear them like jewellery, pairing the treasured materials with sentimental value. Particularly clear crystal or glass covered and protected the fragile miniatures, such as seen in this example in the Cleveland Museum of Art (fig.9).

The miniatures produced by Carriera were set either in gilded frames or other expensive mountings, or into the lids of *tabatières*, which Carriera called

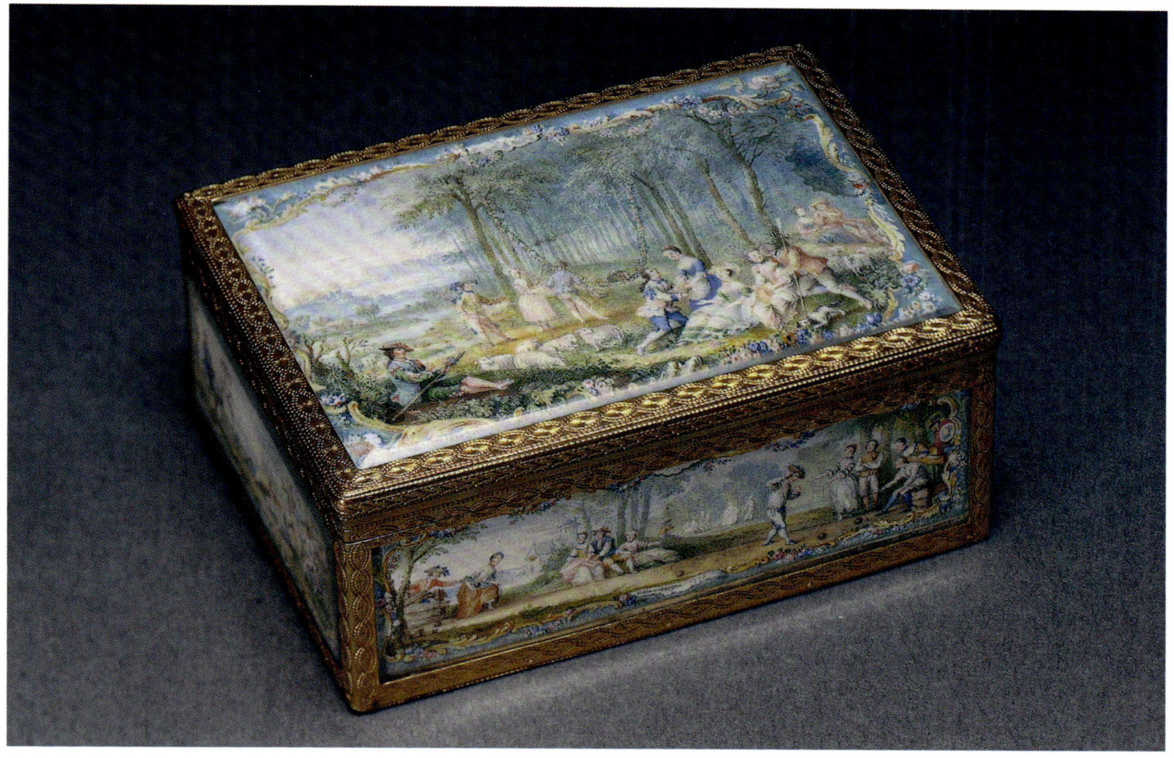

9 Jean Ducrollay (goldsmith) and Louis Nicolas von Blarenberghe (painter), Snuffbox, 1753–4, gold and glass with miniatures, 3.4 × 5.6 cm (1 ¼ × 2 ¼ in), The Cleveland Museum of Art, OH

10 Jean George, Snuffbox with miniature, *c.*1763–4, gold, silver, copper decorated with diamonds, 4 × 7.1 cm (1 ⅝ × 2 ¾ in), The Rijksmuseum, Amsterdam

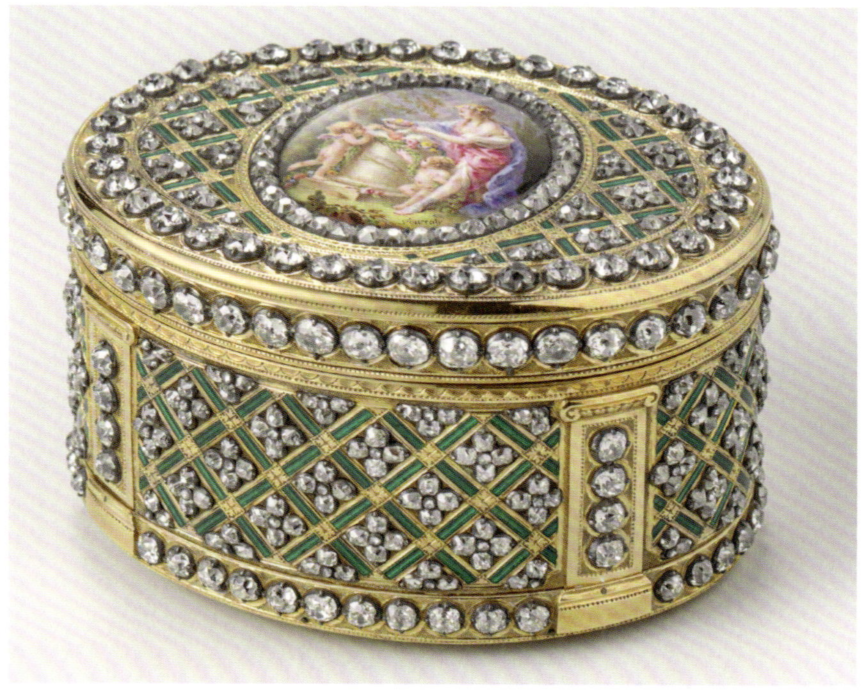

fondelli. The latter had become immensely popular during the seventeenth century not only as tobacco holders but also as decorative trappings and valuable collectors' items (fig.10). Passing literally from hand to hand, the snuffboxes were part and parcel of the political and social scene throughout Europe.

Although the popularity of miniatures paired with the Rococo period's widespread appreciation for refined objects and small-scale works of art in general – according to the *tant plus petit, tant plus beau* (the smaller, the more beautiful) principle[7] – Carriera's decision to focus on this genre surely depended on other reasons. First, it gave her slightly easier access to the artistic profession. Her contemporaries would regard this activity as a typically female genre which thus did not risk her reputation. At the same time, it is reasonable to presume her decision was effectively a clever strategy to forge ahead without the fear of serious rivalry. As noted by Vincenzo Maria Coronelli (1650–1718) in his traveller's book from 1697, *Guida de' Forestieri per succintamente osservare tutto il più riguardevole nella Città di Venetia* (*Foreigners' Guide for Succinctly Observing the Most Impressive Aspects of the City of Venice*), there were only seven miniature painters in the city apart from Carriera and her sister Giovanna, most of whom are almost completely unknown today.[8]

Specialising in miniatures, therefore, meant occupying an almost empty niche in Venice. And just as important, Carriera's pursuit of the miniature genre meant she did not have to compete with those artists who earned their living as history painters, executing altarpieces or frescoes for the local churches and palaces. With miniature painters seen as not meeting the same intellectual and technical standards as history painters who worked on an easel or in fresco, they were not deemed part of the central art establishment, and thus had a lower profile. Carriera's male colleagues, therefore, most likely never perceived her or her small-scale works as a professional threat.[9] On the contrary, some of her male colleagues might have even appreciated her role as a magnet for the multitude of tourists who would come to meet the exceptional artist, commission a miniature portrait and on departure take the easily transportable work of art home with them as either a memento or a display of material wealth. In a city where foreigners at the beginning of the eighteenth century numbered between 30,000 and 40,000, which included residents and travellers, it was an enormous advantage to produce easily portable art right on the spot.[10] Being small in size, such paintings could also be sent by post or courier service at a reasonable price after her clients had left the city.

Concentrating on miniature, and later pastel, paintings offered yet another advantage in the form of certain practical conveniences, especially when contrasted with oil and fresco painting or sculpture.[11] Carriera never had to strain herself physically; she avoided exposure to chemicals with strong and unpleasant odours; and her clients got their paintings without seemingly endless and tiresome sittings.

Carriera's miniatures were typically oblong, oval-shaped ivory plates, whose size varied from about 5.5 to roughly 15 cm (2 ¼–5 ¾ in). Her figures are usually depicted in a simple view of either the head and shoulders or of a half-figure in front of an unadorned background. The sitters normally turned their heads in the opposite direction of their bust, as can be seen in the miniature depicting a man in armour (fig.11).

From a technical perspective, Carriera was also, importantly, the first artist to recognise the promising qualities of ivory as a medium for the tiny and intimate paintings. During her lifetime, she was the sole artist who made the use of this material popular internationally. Though its water-repellency presented difficulties, ivory proved particularly attractive due to its exotic origins, its scarcity, and the resulting preciousness of artefacts produced from it. Moreover, its semi-transparent quality made it possible to produce particular light effects by leaving some parts of the miniature unpainted, usually sections of the flesh tones of the face, hands or other parts of the body of pale-skinned sitters.[12]

CARRIERA AND HER EROTIC MINIATURES

Although the market for erotic literature and visual arts was growing at the end of the seventeenth century, it remained a problematic sphere for female artists. Yet, when Carriera sent a miniature depicting a Venus to Louis Vatin at the start of the eighteenth century, the French art collector responded on 10 September 1701: 'I feel again the violence of a curious desire, my charming mute with coral lips, on the shore of a stream, of a liquid crystal, your divine attractions I will enjoy.'[13] Vatin's surprisingly direct and personal account of the kind of desire the little painting evoked is even more astonishing considering that he was addressing a woman. Historic records such as this provide ample proof of acknowledgement of and praise for Carriera's erotic paintings.

Erotic subjects – whether in mythological disguise, tied to Arcadian visions or veiled behind literary quotations – appear predominantly in Carriera's miniatures, and this is probably no coincidence when considering that the delicate, tiny artworks were mainly intended for private viewing. Given their small format, the works could be easily hidden from the general public, thereby avoiding any confrontation over possibly controversial images. Together with books and prints they constituted a major medium for piquant and arousing art.[14]

The Bayerisches Nationalmuseum in Munich owns a beautiful example of Carriera's erotic painting that depicts a young girl in a garden. In addition to mythological scenes, images of rural subjects such as shepherdesses, peasants and farm girls in pastoral disguise were part of a popular subject matter at the time. Carriera produced numerous variations of the same theme, with the composition and the artful pose of her Arcadian subjects modified only minimally. Her females are typically outfitted in countrified costumes and straw hats, complemented by baskets holding fruit or vegetables. Nevertheless, there is much more to discover behind and beyond the initial appearance of innocence in her miniatures.

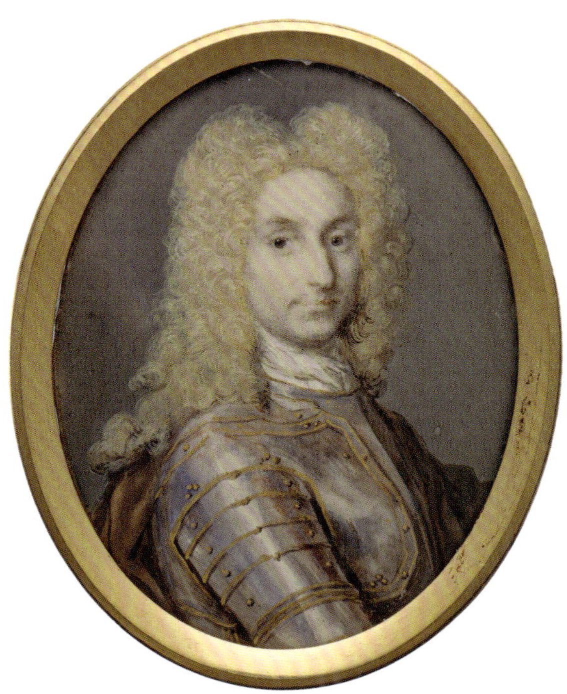

11 Rosalba Carriera, *Portrait of a Man*, *c.*1710, tempera on ivory, 7.6 × 5.9 cm (3 × 2 ¼ in), The Metropolitan Museum of Art, New York

At first glance, the painting in Munich (fig.12) merely illustrates an ordinary, healthy, robust-looking, full-breasted girl in countrified costume who turns towards the onlooker in a graceful and elegant pose. She is wearing a straw hat decorated with fresh flowers and holds a basket full of apples and grapes that she has just picked. Directly behind her is another basket overflowing with more ripe and shiny apples. A tree towers on the other side of a wall in the background, suggesting the existence of another prolific garden. The girl looks directly at the spectator with a hint of a smile while her right hand reaches for the grapes in her basket; her straw hat casts a light shadow over her blue eyes. The viewer gets an overall impression of blooming nature, rich harvest and

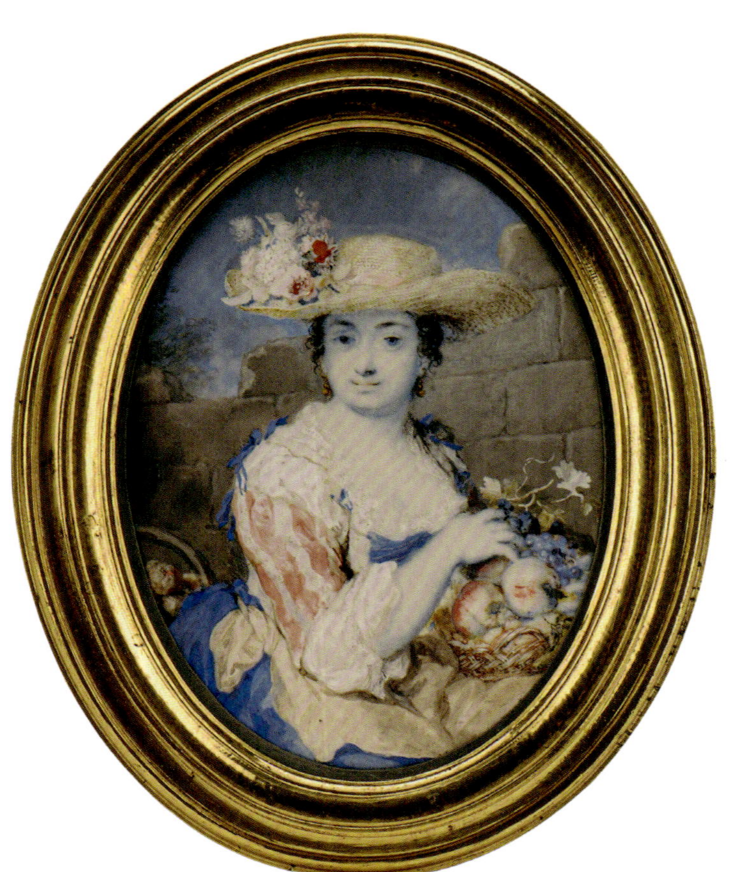

12 Rosalba Carriera, *Young Girl as a Gardener*, 1709, watercolour and gouache on ivory, 10 × 7.6 cm (3 ⅞ × 3 in), Bayerisches Nationalmuseum, Munich

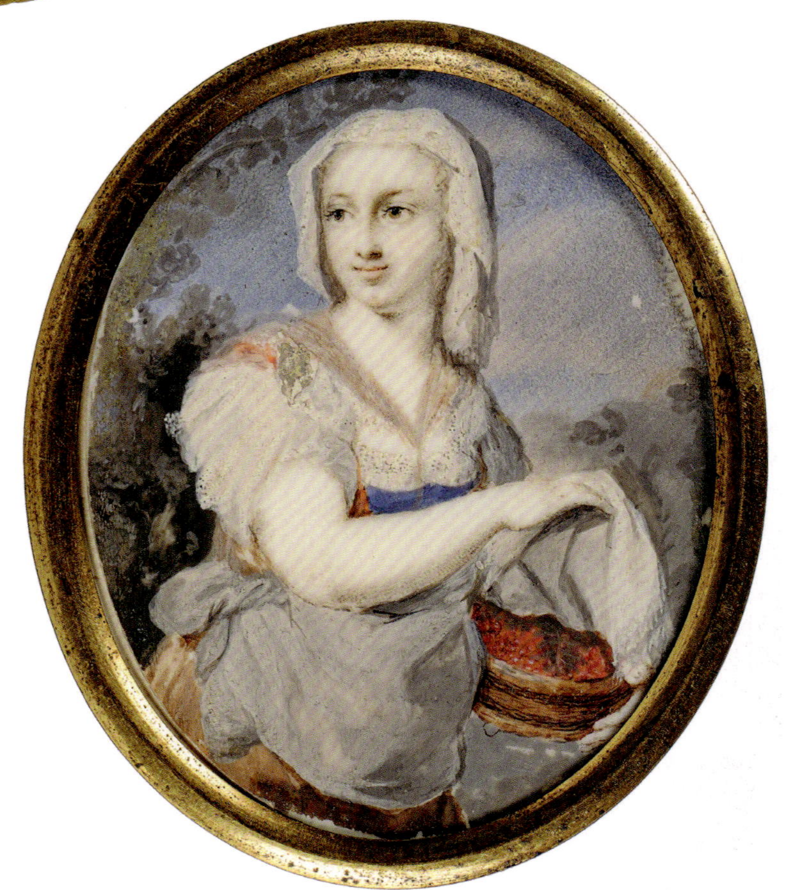

13 Rosalba Carriera, *Girl with a Basket of Strawberries*, 1700–1710, watercolour and gouache on ivory, 8.4 × 6.9 cm (3 ¼ × 2 ¾ in), Museo degli Argenti, Palazzo Pitti, Florence

boundless fertility in this artwork, where the colours of the fruit correspond to the colours of her dress as if they were one inextricable entity.

Accepting the general notion of fecundity in terms of female sexuality, the girl's attributes add up to covertly depicted sexual innuendo. Even if the allusions are controlled and hidden in this scene of a young, neat farm girl, her accessories can be decoded as disguised metaphors for lovemaking. Bonnets, like straw hats or aprons and baskets, can be interpreted as references to the female sex, to the vagina, or by extension to the womb that needs to be inseminated.[15] The apple is a fruit indicating temptation, and consequently original sin, in the context of Christian symbolism. In this miniature, Carriera followed in the tradition of the Renaissance, depicting the apple, among various suggestive fruits, as an object of desire to mean not only love but also an erotic charge.[16] Grapes have sexual connotations as well. According to Ovid's *Metamorphoses* (Book 6), for example, Dionysus transformed himself into bunches of false grapes to possess a young woman. Flowers, on the other hand, can be understood as a symbol of vanity, especially in combination with young, beautiful women, and a reminder of the short-lived existence of both the blossom and the youth and beauty of human beings.

Once these symbols are applied to an interpretation of Carriera's work, the message is clear. Her version of a young gardener can be seen by innocent eyes as an idyllic depiction of a healthy young woman bringing fruit, whereas, to an astute observer, the miniature is ripe with sexual allusions. While the young woman reaches for the flagrantly symbolic grapes in the basket, the above-mentioned womb to be inseminated, the apples also remind us of their sexual charge. The flowers are, on the one hand, aesthetically pleasing and they favourably balance the pictorial composition; on the other hand, they symbolically complete the miniature's message of ephemeral beauty; and even more directly, the flowers will decay just as the woman will soon be deflowered. The loss of the woman's virginity is indicated by the wall in the background, with one block of the massive stones having already fallen and the remainder of the barrier likely to collapse soon and give access to another prolific garden.

The miniature of a girl with a basket of strawberries is another example of the subject matter Carriera painted regularly: mythological scenes, images of rural shepherdesses and gardeners (fig.13). In this case, the key to reading the miniature again lies in the basket and the fruit. Since the Renaissance, strawberries have been associated with virgin's blood, visually and metaphorically. Shakespeare, for example, used the metaphor in his sonnet 'Venus and Adonis' (460) where he stated: 'Or as the berry breaks before it staineth'. Furthermore, the plant itself is a part of the generic rose family, the flower most frequently connected with love and desire.[17] Carriera's girl is uncovering the bright red strawberries in her basket previously protected by a white piece of cloth, a gesture that corresponds to her losing her virginity. To convey the full intensity of this miniature's erotic charge we might remember that Elizabethan gardeners considered the strawberry as 'the purest of fruits, the treble-leafed straw-berry plant bore a red fruit from its initially white flower'.[18]

An example of Carriera's work on a mythological theme is *Venus and Cupid* (fig.14), a miniature currently held at the National Gallery of Denmark in Copenhagen. This miniature shows the seated goddess of love and beauty embracing her son who is standing next to her playing with a bird on a leash. Venus, barely covered, is longingly looking at the bird while she is tickling the nipple of her left breast between the ring finger and pinkie of her right hand, a gesture that adds to the depiction's erotic charge. Cupid, on the other hand, is apparently unaware of his mother's delight, and follows the flight of his companion with a smile on his face.

In depicting Venus in the company of Cupid, Carriera followed the general iconography of the goddess of love as it had been known inside and

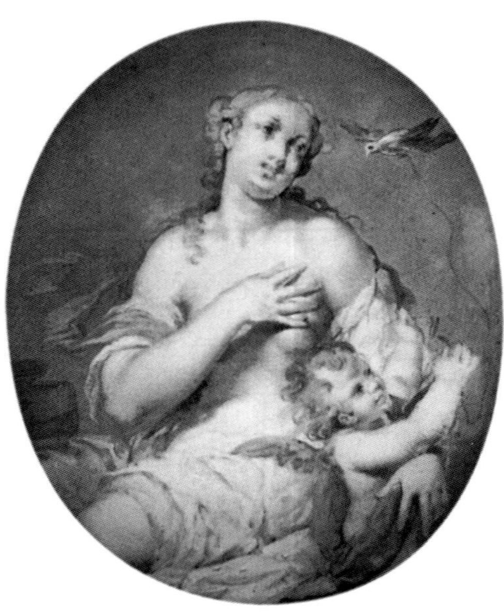

14 Rosalba Carriera, *Venus and Cupid*, 1707–11, watercolour and gouache on ivory, 10.3. × 8.5 cm (4 × 3½ in), National Gallery of Denmark, Copenhagen

outside of Italy since the Renaissance. Even so, the addition of the rather unusual bird on a string is a striking departure from tradition. In his work *Iconologia* (first published in 1593, and then in 1603), Cesare Ripa (*c.*1555–1622) suggests one explanation of what the bird may represent. Ripa's personification of 'Controlled Love' (*Amor Domato*) shows a seated Cupid with his feet resting on his bow and quiver, an hourglass in his right hand, and a thin and emaciated bird on the index finger of his left hand.[19] It is Venus's son, instead of her, who is in control of love as symbolised by the bird. Considering that Ripa's book had 'a significant impact in artistic circles, serving as a visual encyclopaedia and recipe book on how to depict certain images, whether allegorical [...] or personifications',[20] it is plausible that Carriera drew inspiration from Ripa's work for her Venus and Cupid. But even if the *Iconologia* was not the source of her bird on the string, Carriera could have counted on a current general understanding of the bird as a widely used emblem of male sexuality, the phallus and sexual intercourse. Even today, the Italian word *uccello* (bird) is used as a euphemism for the male member.[21]

Carriera's miniature can be read as an allusion to an event occurring just before Venus fell in love with Adonis. It is the moment of her infatuation with the hunter after one of Cupid's arrows had scratched her breast – maybe the breast that Carriera titillatingly emphasised. As a result of this 'accident', Venus disarmed Cupid, as portrayed in numerous paintings since the Renaissance. But Carriera did something different. She interpreted the story with great artistic freedom, inventing a scene for which she had no visual precedent, but which Ovid describes with the following words:

> For while the boy, Cupid, with quiver on shoulder, was kissing his mother, he innocently scratched her breast with a loose arrow. The injured goddess pushed her son away: but the wound he had given was deeper than it seemed, and deceived her at first. Now captured by mortal beauty, she cares no more for Cythera's shores, nor revisits Paphos surrounded by its deep waters, nor Cnidos, the haunt of fish, nor Amathus, rich in minery: she even forgoes the heavens: preferring Adonis to heaven.[22]

Translating the Ovidian description into a comprehensible visual depiction, Carriera expressed Venus's enthusiasm through physical longing, as highlighted by the goddess's stroking of the nipple of her breast, turning the scene into a painting about erotic delight. Ovid's text and the miniature have one fact in common: Venus has no control of her emotions or her desires. In Carriera's painting, the longing goddess is enchanted by what she craves, but she has no power to control the flight of the bird. It is her son who holds the leash, just as he keeps the bird on his finger in Ripa's personification of 'Controlled Love'. Whereas the containment of

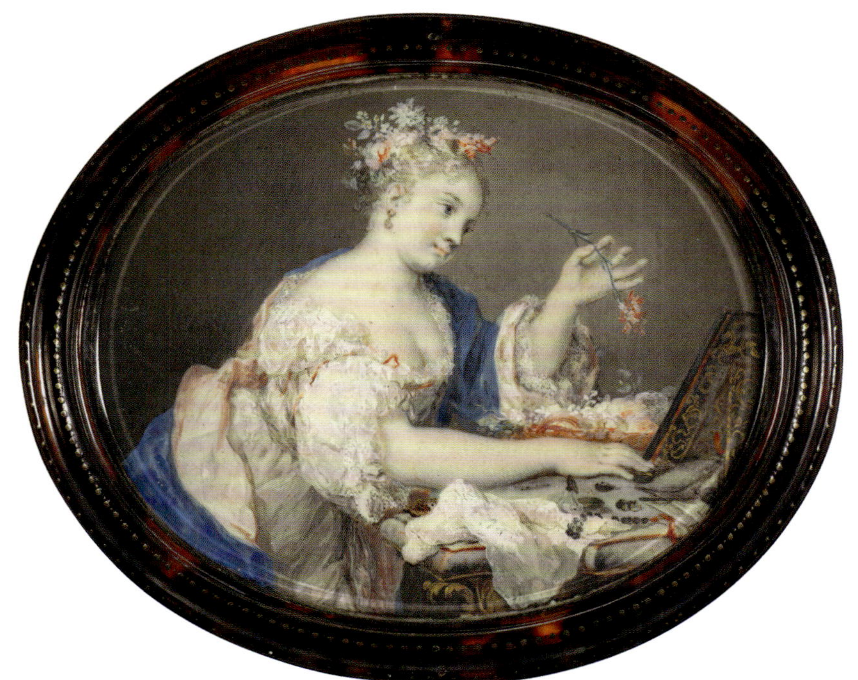

15 Rosalba Carriera, *Lady Putting Flowers in her Hair*, *c.*1710, watercolour and gouache on ivory, 8.6 × 10.5 (3⅜ × 4⅛ in), The Cleveland Museum of Art, OH

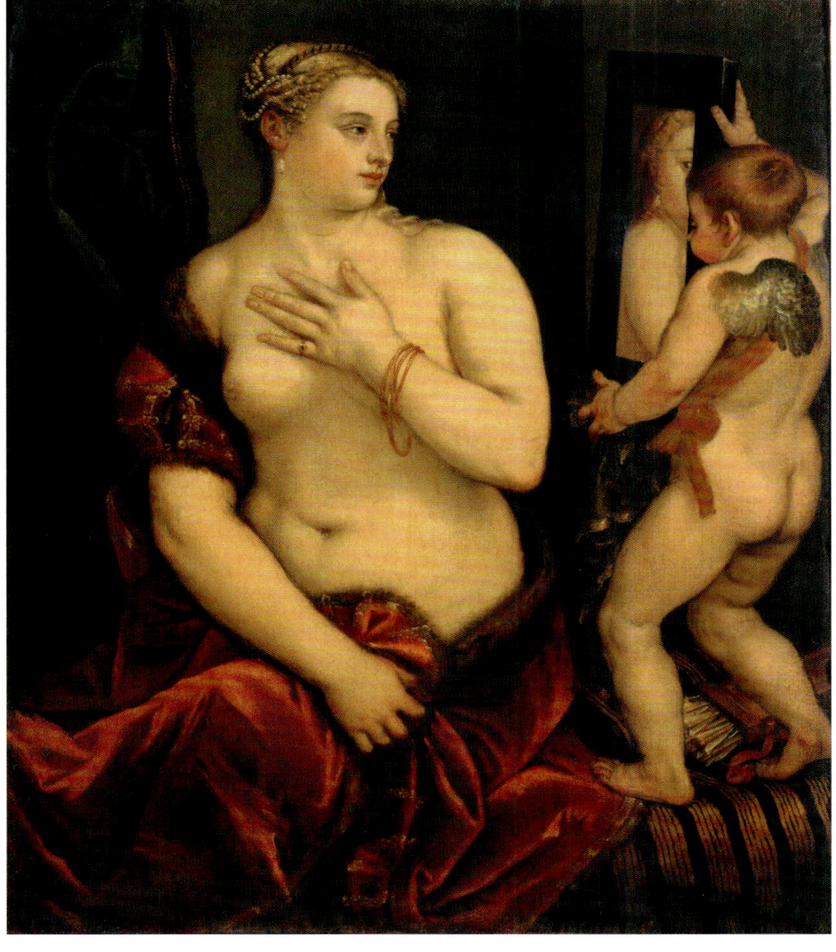

16 After Titian, *Venus with a Mirror*, 1500–1741, oil on canvas, 131 × 93.5 cm (51⅝ × 36¾ in), Staatliche Kunstsammlungen, Gemäldegalerie Alte Meister, Dresden

sexuality is metaphorically embedded in birds shown in cages in numerous Dutch paintings, Carriera lets Cupid hold it on a leash.[23] The latter could also be read as a version of the ribbon which is a standard symbol of the indomitable power to bind lovers together.[24] The fact is that it is he who can permit the bird to fly or not, just as it is he who can shoot arrows of the type he chooses or not. Thus, he has the capacity to interfere, and meddle in his mother's love affairs, as the above-mentioned myth of Venus and Adonis shows.

A particularly beautiful miniature by Carriera at the Cleveland Museum of Art (fig.15) is one of a smaller group of the artist's oeuvre depicting genre scenes. In this artwork, the painter departed from her usual format of a vertical oval shape while drawing on the famous iconographic tradition of the 'Lady (or Venus) at her Toilet'. This theme was especially popular during the Renaissance in Venice with artists like Giovanni Bellini (*c.*1435–1516) and later in numerous works by Paris Bordon (*c.*1500–1571) and Paolo Veronese (1528–88) or like this example, based on a painting by Titian (1488/90–1576) (fig.16).

Carriera shows a beautiful young lady at her fancy dressing table, looking into an ornate mirror that is carefully propped up on the table in front of her. Spread over the table in artful disarray are the accoutrements of an elegant lady's toilette: fashionable accessories like pieces of jewellery, a perfume bottle, hair sticks, a handkerchief underneath which an unidentified object, maybe a tortoise shell, is visible, as well as a small bag for cosmetics or jewellery. A basket with flowers, what seem to be two sheets of paper, possibly a letter, and what looks like a magnifying glass are also among the objects put on display. With a hint of a smile, the young lady has raised her left hand in which she delicately holds a flower between the index finger and thumb, perhaps intending to add it to the decoration in her hair. She is shown in her white, diaphanous décolleté chemise with lace-trimmed sleeves, with a bright blue garment hanging as if it might slip off her body except that she has inserted her left arm into the sleeve. Her marble-white skin, as accentuated by the marble table underneath her arm, highlights the elegance of her demeanour.

More careful scrutiny of the painting reveals seductive innuendo in the woman's outfit, her gesture, and the table's display of erotically coded objects. Is the woman depicted in the act of dressing or undressing? Has she just taken off half of the blue garment or has she not finished putting it on? Is she adding another flower to her hair, or is she slowly taking the flowers out of her hair, one by one? And what about the symbolism of the various objects placed around her?

Although it was fashionable in the eighteenth century for ladies to decorate their hair with flowers, the act of doing so was rarely presented in paintings, thereby suggesting that Carriera added a symbolic subtext. If the flower in the lady's left hand is what it resembles, namely, a columbine stalk, the painting's message shifts from a judgement upon vanity to one characteristic of an erotic charge, as the columbine flower is symbolic of the game of seduction, love and sexuality. In antiquity, it was a plant linked to phalli, but it was also associated with Venus. The red version of the columbine was deemed to inflame passion.[25] Furthermore, the *deshabillé* of the woman's boudoir, its *désordre* or '*négligence*, that delicate indecency disguised as inattention',[26] can be read as an allusion to love and seduction. If what seems to be paper on the right of the miniature really represents a letter, it might be interpreted as an announcement of the arrival of the lady's lover, as had been depicted in so many other paintings in which women stare pensively at their mirror image with a letter lying at their side.

Looking again at the scene, one realises that it portrays a woman in contemporary clothes whose setting would be a space familiar to any spectator in the eighteenth century: a boudoir filled with everyday objects. At first, it seems to depict a simple genre scene. But within its pictorial invention is an encoded erotic charge, a sexual discourse hidden from innocent eyes. While the young woman is immersed in her own narcissistic observation of her looks in the mirror which is turned away from the spectator, the onlooker performs the same intense act of looking at what she is indulging in, but does so from a slightly different angle. Only visible from behind, the mirror on the right is a clear, long-standing emblem of vanity which, like flowers, is a memento mori and is used here with an erotic twist. She observes herself as the spectator does, in close-up. The miniature calls for the spectator's participation to complete a 'viewer-created narrative'[27] that plays upon a rhetoric of interaction and voyeurism. Only the fantasy of the onlooker can anticipate the girl's actions and, in an act of complete immersion, can ponder the outcome.

Placing the young lady close to the picture plane, Carriera offers the spectator physical proximity to the woman, which can become even more intimate by bringing the miniature as near as possible to the eye. The silky softness of her elegant garment, the fluffiness of the handkerchief with refined, crisp lace casually placed on the edge of her dressing table, and the tactility of the flowers all seem to exhale pure sensuality.

This haptic aspect of miniatures is even more pronounced in one of the most fascinating miniatures Carriera ever produced. It is kept in the Royal Collection Trust and depicts *Françoise-Marie, Duchesse d'Orléans, as Amphitrite* (fig.17).[28]

Françoise-Marie de Bourbon, Mademoiselle de Blois (1677–1749), was one of seven children whom Louis XIV (1638–1715) had with his mistress Françoise-Athénaïs de Rochechouart, better known as Madame or Marquise de Montespan (1640–1707). On 18 February 1692, Françoise-Marie, aged 14, married Philippe II d'Orléans, Duke of Chartres (1674–1723), whose father, Philippe I of France, Duke of Orléans (1640–1701), was the younger brother of King Louis XIV. Therefore, in marrying the Duke of Chartres who was the future Regent of France until Louis XV reached maturity at the age of 13, Françoise-Marie married her first cousin.

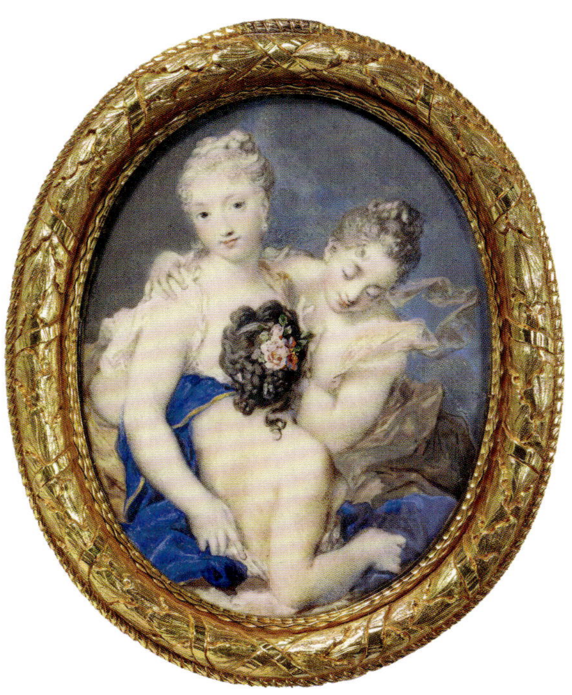

17 Rosalba Carriera, *Françoise-Marie, Duchesse d'Orléans, as Amphitrite*, 1697–1757, watercolour on ivory, 8.5 × 6.5 cm (3 ¼ × 2 ⅝ in), Royal Collection Trust

To depict the Duchess as Amphitrite meant to insert her within the traditional representations of marine thiasos that had been a popular theme within the European courts since the Renaissance. Versailles is a telling example of the extent of the popularity of marine iconography in France under the reign of Louis XIV. Numerous paintings and sculptures representing Neptune, Galatea, Amphitrite, the tritons or the nymphs were part of the Sun King's self-fashioning and propagandistic iconography. It is known that Carriera was inspired by a painting entitled *Galatea Triumphant* in Versailles which is an allegorical portrait of Mademoiselle de Blois by Pierre Gobert (1662–1744), probably painted in 1692 to celebrate her marriage to Philippe d'Orléans.[29]

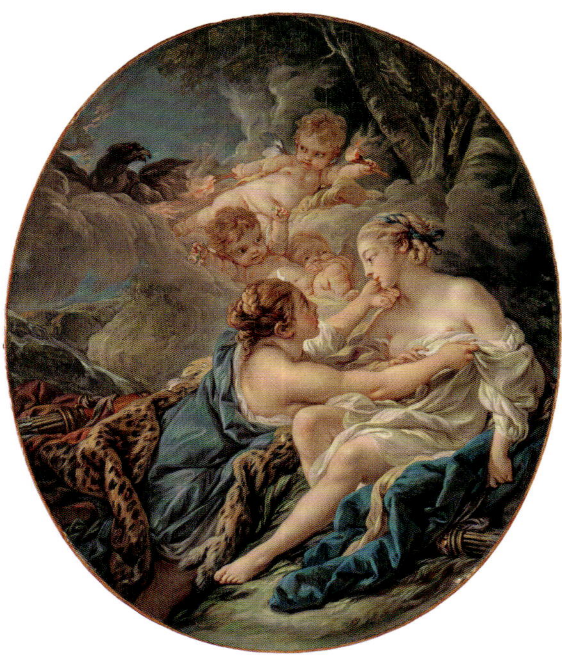

18 François Boucher, *Jupiter in the Guise of Diana, and Callisto*, 1763, oil on canvas, 64.8 × 54.9 cm (25½ × 21⅝ in), The Jack and Belle Linsky Collection, The Metropolitan Museum of Art, New York

However, in her miniature, Carriera concentrated on only Amphitrite and two nymphs in a titillating close-up of three half-figures intertwined in an erotic embrace.

While the eighteenth century produced a vast array of erotic images and literature that was consumed by men and women, the depiction of Sapphic love remained a somewhat vague theme. During the Middle Ages and until the Renaissance, the debate about homosexuality regarded primarily male relationships. In Florence, for example, where thousands of men were killed for acts of sodomy during the fifteenth century, there is no surviving evidence of the prosecution of sexual encounters between women. Female homosexuality was 'less threatening to the patrimony since reproduction, paternity, and legitimacy were not at issue. The acts were also less visible because they often went unnamed in the statutes and condemnations.'[30] Sexual practices among women were considered a form of inadequate, preliminary sex without penetration and reproduction and thus not of much concern, whereas the use of 'instruments' during an erotic encounter between females incited the most fear. The appropriation and counterfeiting of the phallus made those women particularly masculine and threatening. Overall, silence and ignorance predominated the legal, moral and ecclesiastic writings regarding sexual acts between women, a form of invisibility that slowly changed during the Renaissance when 'images of women bathing together and touching each other appeared'.[31]

The most typical way of suggesting or directly showing physical attraction and eroticism between women in art was through mythological figures like Diana and her nymphs. The setting in which the goddess of chastity bathes and cavorts with her companions in an enclosed and paradisal space offered the perfect excuse to depict naked women in close bodily contact. In a kind of a twist that mingles power dynamic and cross-identification, these depictions included the exploitation of the myth of Callisto. Ovid's *Metamorphoses* (Book 2, 417–40) recounts how the nymph Callisto was seduced and raped by Jupiter in the shape and disguise of Diana, rendering a sexual encounter between a male and a female part of the process of the cultural negotiation of same-gender female love.[32] Paintings focusing on the moment of Callisto's seduction simultaneously highlight the pastoral sensuality and the overt erotic attraction between two females, as the scene is often devoid of any iconographic encoding of Jupiter, as in this example by François Boucher (1703–70) (fig.18).

In Carriera's miniature, the onlooker cannot find the traditional mythological justification. The artist offers no clear hints that would identify or define the broader context of this all-female gathering. It is only the clothes that create some kind of timely distance;

instead of wearing eighteenth-century dresses, the figures are attired in the pseudo-ancient garments that Carriera used in mythological or allegorical scenes. Françoise-Marie, who was known as Duchesse de Chartres after her marriage, is looking straight into the eyes of the beholder, who is drawn into a 'gazing-game',[33] where glances oscillate between the protagonist, the viewer, and the other two women. At the same time, Françoise-Marie seems to invite the onlooker to participate, a suggestion that seems to be indirectly repeated by the composition of the miniature. While the Duchess is flirting with the beholder, the woman on the right is embracing her with her right arm while the left arm is bent. It is not possible to see where her left hand is placed – it is left to the onlooker's fantasy to decide. The same woman is looking down to the third figure who is depicted on a lower level and differentiated by her dark tresses. She has turned her back to the viewer and her face is close to Françoise-Marie's breast, leaving little to the imagination as to what she is doing. It would be hard to find another example in pre-eighteenth-century European art in which three women without mythological disguise are depicted in such a startling and overt visualisation of all-female eroticism. And it would be even more difficult to find another woman artist before the twentieth century who pushed the boundaries in a similar manner.

Another interesting aspect is the circular configuration, in which two females face the onlooker and the one in the middle turns her back to the viewer, with the artist suggesting a reference to the ancient theme of the *Three Graces* (fig.19). The incorporation of this well-known subject matter is yet more proof of Carriera's erudition as well as her artistic and intellectual finesse.

It is equally important in this context, however, to analyse how Carriera managed to blend the subject-object realities. The position of the black-haired woman in the centre of the miniature corresponds to the position of the person who is holding it close to the eye. If one imagines the viewer not only visually enjoying the small-scale painting but also kissing it – a practice recorded regularly in the history of miniatures[34] – Carriera's composition proves to be much more than the result of refined aesthetic and artistic choices. The holding and potentially kissing of the miniature are not visualised but implied in the composition of the figures. The artist deftly mingles the internal and external realities of the artwork. Subject and object are intrinsically intertwined.

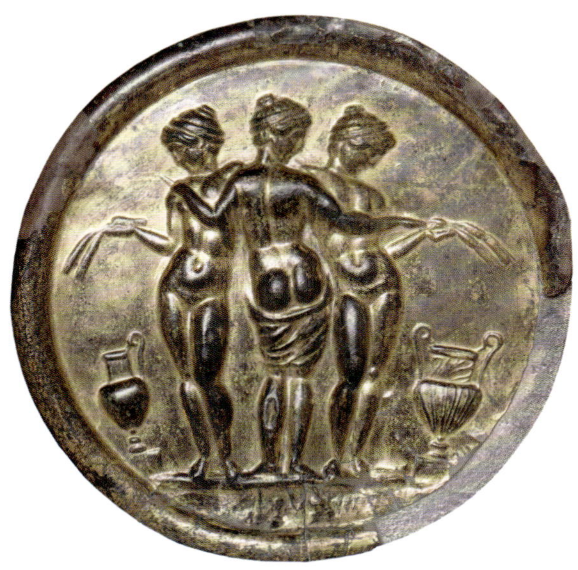

19 Gilded bronze mirror with the Three Graces, mid-second century CE, bronze, silver, gold, diameter 12.1 cm (4 ¾ in), The Metropolitan Museum of Art, New York

This overlap of realities becomes even more intense due to the aspect of touch, which is an inevitable element in the handling of miniatures. The three women in Carriera's miniature are touching each other; at least one hand is on somebody else's body. They are entangled in such a tight embrace that all three bodies are touching simultaneously. The pronounced emphasis of skin-to-skin contact implies the depiction could be read as an allegorical rendering of touch as one of the five senses.[35] Considering the haptic and sensual aspects of holding, touching or even kissing the miniature, there is a similar fusion of realities as described above in the discussion regarding the composition of the scene: the haptic experience creates closeness, inclusion. When taking the small painting in hand, holding and turning it, and stroking its surface, the onlooker is placed in the position of the three women in the painting and, to a certain extent, repeats their actions.

INITIAL INTERNATIONAL RECOGNITION: MEMBERSHIP AT THE ACCADEMIA DI SAN LUCA IN ROME

With a lack of rivals and her artistic and intellectual excellence, Carriera likely achieved an enviable level of skill in the production of miniatures by the end of the seventeenth century, at the very latest. Based on her correspondence, she had already received, by 1700, various commissions for these precious artworks from England, France, Germany and Denmark. Forgeries of her works were already in circulation at the beginning of the eighteenth century, testifying to the popularity of these paintings during this initial stage of her career. It is also the period in Carriera's life when the artist received the first official recognition of her artistic capabilities: her nomination and acceptance as a member of the Roman Accademia di San Luca.

Particularly advantageous in this matter was Carriera's friendship with Christian Cole (1673–1734), a British diplomat who worked from 1707 to 1708 as secretary to Charles Edward Montagu, Lord Manchester (1662–1722), the British Ambassador in Venice. Lord Manchester would later become a major commissioner of Venetian artists like Luca Carlevarijs (1663–1730), Giovanni Antonio Pellegrini (1675–1741), Marco Ricci (1676–1730) and Carriera herself. Christian Cole became himself Secondary Resident of Great Britain in Venice, a position he held from 1708 to 1714.

Carriera and Cole probably met around 1701, and over the years, he continually made gestures of kindness to the artist. It is also thanks to Cole that Carriera learned English, which enabled her to appreciate Judith Drake's *Essay in Defence of the Female Sex*, one of the most influential English feminist texts of the era.[36] It is unclear whether or not Carriera's knowledge of Drake's essay served to fuel her own sense of emancipation, but the fact that she translated some parts of the book into Italian reveals that she at least had some interest in the theme as well as a willingness to improve her English, a language she seems to have liked. The author and historian Joseph Spence (1699–1768) reported that she had asked him to speak in English to her because she enjoyed the language, adding: 'I pray in English because that language is so short and expressive.'[37]

By January 1705 at the latest, Cole joined what was likely a premeditated campaign orchestrated by Sebastiano Ricci, Antonio Balestra (1666–1740) and Felice Ramelli (1666–1740) designed to gain Carriera's admission as an official member of the Accademia di San Luca in Rome. Carriera herself, however, made the process more complicated than it already was. For months and months, she hesitated, procrastinated, and avoided, as it appears, answering Cole's letters. Carriera was probably apprehensive considering the prestige of the institution, the impending expectations of the director Carlo Maratta (1625–1713), other members, and even her friend Cole. But she finally sent her reception piece to Rome, a miniature depicting a *Girl with a Dove* (fig.20). In mid-September 1705, a meeting was held at the Accademia, and Carriera was proposed as a candidate for membership.

The painting shows a young girl, a *donzella*, as referenced in the records of the Accademia, in white clothes against a simple background. She looks at the observer directly with vibrant eyes, a smile playing on her slightly open mouth while she holds her skirt with both hands, sheltering a fluttering dove inside. The miniature most likely represents an 'Allegory of Innocence', as it was titled in the Accademia's early guidebooks;[38] and, as such, it follows an eighteenth-century tradition of depicting innocent children in literature and painting as metaphors for physical and moral purity.[39] Christopher Johns claims convincingly that Carriera intended to depict the innocence of the soul rather than of the body, while simultaneously conveying to the male audience and male judges her self-awareness as an unmarried woman.[40]

Carriera's general artistic interest in allegories is noteworthy, for she was the first eighteenth-century artist to explore allegorical themes extensively in miniature paintings. In presenting this type of allegory in this particular situation (and not one of her portraits or genre scenes), Carriera managed to 'transcend the decorative "feminine" medium',[41] thereby cleverly positioning herself on the traditional, more highly esteemed level of a history painter. Alongside mythological and biblical scenes, allegories were associated with the highest genre of art, that of history painting. Unlike the less significant genres, history paintings 'were made to teach, to lead, to instil virtue, and to capture *gloire*'.[42] In this, Carriera justified her position as a female painter in front of one of Europe's most highly regarded institutions, whose membership roster included those judges viewed as the most competent in recognising and rewarding excellent art. Until that point in history, only very few women, including Lavinia Fontana (1552–1614) and Elisabetta Sirani (1638–65), had worked as history painters. Not until many decades later did Elisabeth Vigée-Lebrun (1755–1842) use the same strategy, when in 1780 she submitted an allegory of *Peace Bringing Back Abundance* to the Académie royale de peinture et de sculpture as her *morceau de reception* (reception piece).[43]

On top of delivering a reception piece, Carriera was, like her colleagues, expected to present the Accademia with a self-portrait, as Cole had mentioned in various letters. However, Carriera failed to produce the work, and it was finally Sebastiano Bombelli (1635–1719) who painted her portrait, which still hangs in the Accademia as proof of Carriera's first authoritative recognition.

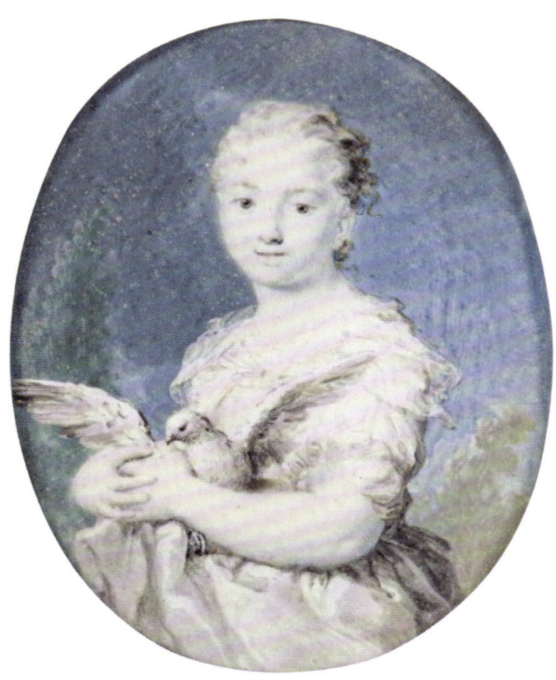

20 Rosalba Carriera, *Girl with a Dove*, *c.*1705, watercolour, gouache on ivory, 15 × 10 cm (5 7⁄8 × 3 7⁄8 in), Accademia Nazionale di San Luca, Rome

Carriera was made a member of the Accademia di San Luca on 27 September 1705, and in an extraordinary turn of events, the institution admitted her as an *academica di merito*, a title and rank superior to that of *academica d'onore*, which was reserved for collectors, connoisseurs or patrons of the arts.[44] The decision to award Carriera the highest possible title was made by three distinguished men: the Director of the Accademia at the time, Carlo Maratta; the painting professor Benedetto Luti (1666–1724); and the Accademia's life secretary Giuseppe Ghezzi (1634–1721). A cultural celebrity, which the successful Venetian miniaturist had become, was a commodity in which art academies were increasingly willing to invest. It is possible that Maratta's decision to support Carriera as an *academica di merito* might have been influenced by his daughter and only child, Faustina Maratta Zappi (1679?–1745), who was also a miniature painter.[45]

The minutes taken of the Accademia meeting of 27 September read:

> Having Signora Rosalba Carriera, Venetian painter and miniaturist, formally requested admission by proof of academic merit and having, to this effect, exhibited a portrait in half figure of a young woman, painted by her hand [...] intending that it should remain in her memory in our Academy: whereupon it was immediately and with jubilation and applause received, admired and approved and [she] of being worthy of being an Academic.[46]

She was recorded as a *pittrice e miniatrice* (painter and miniaturist). No mention whatsoever was made of pastel, the technique for which she would become famous in subsequent years. The special designation chosen for Carriera at this renowned institution was a testament to her professional status as an artist, and elevated her to a position far above her female predecessors. It was, indeed, an unprecedented situation, given that the rules of the Accademia did not make provision for such a nomination. The minutes, mentioned above, continue: 'Thus by common consent and with no reservation, she was declared worthy of our academy even though not instated by secret ballot in conformity with the decrees as this was preferred for this foreign maiden who draws applause everywhere and is truly virtuous in reputation and in her virtues.'[47]

By this time, Carriera was 32 years old. Had she not decided to dedicate her life to her career, she would most likely have been a married woman by that time. But she was not married, and never would she be.

2

An Independent Single Female Painter

Carriera was one of the few women of her age who chose never to marry. She opted for independence not only professionally but also in her private life. This preference meant swimming against established conventions, and it compelled her to promote a role and an identity for a social group that was not officially acknowledged to exist. It also entailed renouncing the predefined role of the wife who receives financial and social support as well as protection from her husband. It was a decision accompanied by potential intimidation. Community morality could be stained, societal expectations exerted pressure, family honour could be compromised, and estate succession was at stake.[1] Not surprisingly, therefore, Carriera was part of a tiny minority of the society in which she lived. Fewer than 10 per cent of eighteenth-century women remained spinsters.[2] Nevertheless, she was relatively representative among seventeenth- and eighteenth-century female artists, a striking number of whom also remained unmarried, including, to name just a few, Giovanna Garzoni (1600–1670), Chiara Varotari (1584–1663), Maria van Oosterwijck (1630–93), Elisabetta Sirani and Giulia Lama.[3]

Carriera's decision to remain unwed posed something of a dilemma for her male contemporaries, some of whom sought to accredit her unusual lifestyle to her physical appearance. Dézallier d'Argenville, for example, opened his 1762 biography of Carriera as follows: 'Beauty, which is usually the lot of women, was not at all that of *Signora Rosa Alba Carriera*.'[4] Later in the text, he became even more explicit: 'Moreover, love couldn't divert her from her intended purpose; a woman, under the aegis of ugliness, is saved from lovers.'[5] On 4 July 1764, the author and historian Edward Gibbon (1737–94) noted: 'One must admit that she is not worshipped as are her companions, as far as beauty goes.'[6]

At a meeting at the Accademia di Belle Arti in Padua on 6 December 1781, Girolamo Zanetti (1713–82) read out a eulogy in honour of Carriera, and while he focused primarily on her talent and her success as an artist, he also added the following:

> Nature is mother to us all, but she is not prodigal with all her gifts, and precisely for this she does not usually give everything to everybody. She gave Carriera sublime talent, beauty however she did not bestow upon her, indeed it seems that in exchange for her liberal gift of that, she deprived her altogether of this last. Thus did the Emperor Charles VI turn to his court painter, whose last name was Bertoli […] who was presenting her to him, She may be worthy, Bertoli mine, he said, this painter of yours, but she is very plain. Carriera, who knew her own physiognomy only too well, heard him, and discreetly smiled, because she

knew equally well the plainness of others and among these those of this august monarch, with whom in this matter of beauty Nature had been no less stingy, as everyone knows.[7]

Carriera's case is not isolated. Her colleague Giulia Lama was described by the scientist and intellectual Abate Antonio Schinella Conti (1677–1749) with the same stereotypical and misogynistic approach. In one of his letters to Marthe-Marguerite Le Valois de Villette de Mursay, Marquise de Caylus (1673–1729), dated 1 May 1728, Schinella Conti described Lama as being as ugly as she was witty: 'I have just discovered a woman here who paints better than Rosalba, as far as large compositions go. […] her name is Giulia Lama […]. While true that her ugliness matches her wit, still she speaks with grace and refinement, so that her face is easily forgiven her.'[8] The same fate of an 'unforgiving face' befell Carriera's younger colleague Katherine Read (1723–78), whom the author Fanny Burney (1752–1840) described as follows: 'Miss Reid is shrewd and clever when she has any opportunity given her to make it known; […] She is most exceedingly ugly, and of a very melancholy, or rather discontented, humour.'[9]

Taken altogether, these comments suggest an intellectual difficulty dealing with an exceptionally talented social anomaly such as Carriera, who continued to shake up the world view of her male observers.[10] They reflect a helplessness that goes beyond basic misogynistic tendencies. The focus on the artist's lack of beauty was evidently a tool to offset Carriera's outstanding abilities and talent and to deflate her success, making her more comprehensible and acceptable to a male audience.

Along with the dilemma of trying to explain her talent, Carriera's male critics played on her physical appearance to compare her to a man. De-sexing gifted women to separate them from the grace, delicacy and sweetness of more 'typical' women[11] was a strategy and trope that had been used concerning female painters since the Renaissance. As Katherine Rogers has pointed out in 1982 in her study of eighteenth-century feminism in England: 'Women could be strong and rational, therefore equal to men, only through rising above their sexual nature.'[12]

Artistic excellence and being a woman created a paradox as far as gendered expectations were concerned and, therefore, 'Cross-gender appraisals were employed to prove that certain women were "marvels", outstripping expectations for their sex. […] Significantly, such remarks both maintain the status quo and create a special space for those women who are seen to transcend gender norms and display some of the male-associated virtues.'[13] Contemporaries of Carriera returned on several occasions to the same trope. Francesco Algarotti (1712–64), for example, wrote a report on the Dresden court's purchase of her paintings on behalf of August III (1696–1763), saying: '[Her] works showed that in a female person there sometimes lies virile spirit.'[14] Charles-Nicolas Cochin noted in his *Voyage d'Italie* in 1773: 'Mademoiselle Rosalba having chosen to work in pastels and miniatures, has raised these to such a high degree of merit that not even the most celebrated men have surpassed her in these genres, but moreover that very few can even be compared to her.'[15]

Noteworthy in this regard is a caricature by the collector, antique dealer, copperplate engraver and close friend of Carriera, Anton Maria Zanetti (1680–1767) (fig.21), which shows the artist with clear stubble around her mouth. It surely was made with a sense of irony and not intended to seriously hurt the artist. At the same time, though, the drawing points to a more general tendency that went far beyond comparing talented and successful women with men, and suggested that they were more 'manly' than a woman should be. Female artists in the eighteenth century moved in a sort of social limbo that had a negative effect on the way in which others perceived them.

Carriera sought to overcome these prejudices and difficulties and to continue to work independently in her own workshop without excessively pushing the boundaries of societal expectations. To do so as

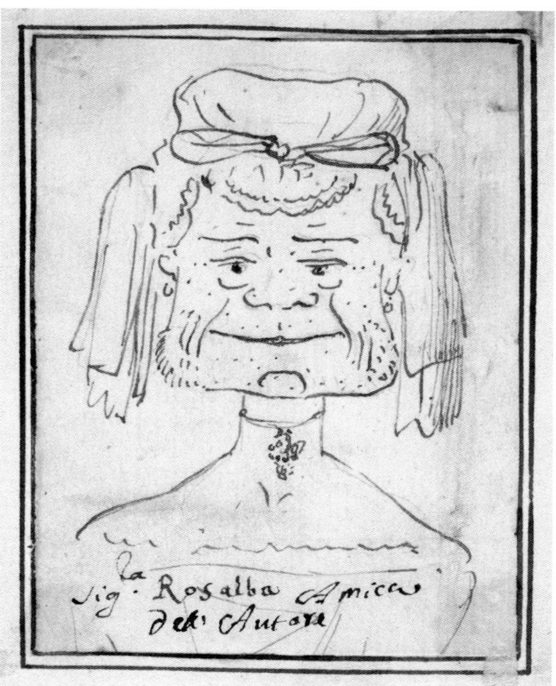

21 Anton Maria Zanetti, *Caricature of Rosalba Carriera*, 1720–30, brown ink on paper, 9 × 6.9 cm (3 ½ × 2 ¾ in), Fondazione Giorgio Cini, Gabinetto dei Disegni e delle Stampe, Venice

a single woman, Carriera recognised that she would have to behave impeccably and employ some clever tactics. One of her strategies was to fashion a niche and an image for herself, both of which offered her various advantages and opportunities that would not have been open to her had she married. Playing on the gender stereotypes of her time, she consciously propagated an unattractive picture of herself as a busy, inflexible and cold woman, the conventional image of an old spinster.[16]

This carefully constructed masquerade offered her both liberty and a potent shield, with one consequence of her efforts being the presumption by others that she was a virginal celibate woman who lived the exemplary life of a 'holy' painter.[17] Consequently, Carriera was commonly linked with sainthood, and the extent to which others used religious vocabulary and ideas in relation to the artist is rather noteworthy. Dézallier d'Argenville talked of a higher calling, from God's reign: 'but Heaven had destined her for more elevated things'.[18] Given that divine inspiration and genius were mostly gendered notions, it was unusual that a contemporary biographer of a female artist would use these terms in connection with her gifts and talent.[19] The nun Suor Maria Beatrice Davia wrote from Modena to Carriera on 3 March 1731: 'Blessed be the hand that has handled the brush so well in outlining so well the Holy Image of the Divine Saviour, for he is so beautiful as to seem alive and with an air of Paradise; tell me, have You seen our Lord in some rapture of the spirit?'[20] Carriera's supporter and friend Pierre-Jean Mariette (1694–1774) raised her above the level of an angel when he wrote: 'You appear a heavenly woman or an earthly goddess.'[21]

Surviving private documents further support the idea that Carriera deliberately leveraged her status as an unwed woman by cultivating her image as a fragile and modest holy spinster. Apparently, even her contemporaries became incredulous at times when her actions were occasionally too ostentatious. In a dispatch to Carriera from Rome on 18 August 1731, Don Bartolomeo Sampellegrini, a priest from Piacenza, accused the artist of exploiting the fact that she was a woman. Writing that he had been glad to hear of her intention to come to the 'Eternal City' – an intention, however, that unfortunately turned out to be a false rumour – he complained:

> but it is surely true that you do not have that great desire which you say you have to see it for if you did, the mere fact of being a woman would not prevent you from undertaking the trip which is not even the trip to Vienna: I do not wish to proceed further into this matter, limiting myself solely to protesting toward you all my sincerest affection.[22]

Knowing that she had stayed in Vienna the year before, the priest refuted her bogus argument that she could not travel because of her sex.

Apart from propagating a carefully constructed image of herself, Carriera used another clever strategy, namely, downplaying or veiling the success of her professional life. Fame and glory or ambition and success were dubious goals or qualities for a woman at the time,[23] and accordingly, Carriera made sure that she acted in line with society's expectations of her being a modest and humble lady. This somewhat curious pretence becomes evident from an analysis of her correspondence: her business letters do not contain personal details, and interestingly, they rarely refer directly to financial matters. She presented herself to the world as a woman who was taking care of her family, and focusing on her idealised, purified work, untouched by dishonourable motives. It seems she consciously and deftly downplayed any interest that she, as an independent artist, would have had in earning a living. Crude, common monetary concerns did not fit in with her image, so they were ignored.

Even though Carriera's commissioners regularly asked in their letters to let them know how much they owed the artist, hardly any of her answers has survived. It would appear that the artist did not make, or have made, any copies of the letters in which she must have given more precise details regarding commercial transactions. As there was a stigma attached to the notion of a woman earning money from art,[24] the idea of remaining 'pure' was far more important for a female artist than for her male colleagues. Talking of money did not suit any woman, including Carriera herself. The only references in her correspondence regarding her fees inform the commissioner that she would indicate the requested amount on the paper in which she wrapped the artwork.[25] That this was a well-considered strategy becomes evident when one looks at Carriera's diaries, where financial affairs play a far larger role, and where there are often minute details regarding money issues.

Furthermore, considering her status as an independent female painter, Carriera could not afford to become the target of gossip and scandal. Only too easily did women artists of her day become victims of slander, especially the ones who specialised in portraiture. Paradoxically, female painters were often associated with the genre of portraiture, yet, the activity of a female portraitist entailed an encounter with her sitter; who, if a man, could end up implying an intersubjective exchange of glances that went against societal conventions and expectations. Angela Rosenthal notes that a decent woman, according to the European ideal of femininity, was constrained by notions of domestic, private virtues, and was culturally regulated through books of etiquette, literature and other media.[26] In one of the famous conduct books published in England in the eighteenth century, *The Whole Duty of a Woman* (1737),[27] the anonymous author dedicated Chapter 7 to the subject, 'Of the Manner of Behaviour towards Men', making the significance and power of a glance unmistakably clear: 'It must engage them to have a perpetual watch upon their eyes, and to remember that one careless glance gives more advantages than a hundred words not enough considered; the language of the eyes being very much the most significant and the most observed.'[28]

The relationship between artist and sitter, as well as the studio or space where the meeting takes place, become important factors to understand if one not only regards a portrait as a finished product but also analyses the process of its creation. In Carriera's case, one of the morally questionable locations most likely would have been her home. As long as she painted at the court of the King of France or the imperial court in Vienna, the presence of the royal entourage or other guests would have turned the intersubjective encounter into a less risky affair. The practice of art in public was palatable in general and presumably slightly less awkward for the sitters. But could her home or studio be considered a 'controlled environment'[29] when the male sitter was more intimately exposed to the female gaze? Did the unconventional situation create tensions between her and her male models in a culture where social mores and conduct books such as *The Whole Duty of a Woman* reflected a morally loaded idea of female glances?

Unfortunately, to date there are no records of any risks of ocular intersubjectivity or threatening dynamics that Carriera may have encountered when creating likenesses of her male clients – Joseph Spence only left evidence of what he and the artist were talking about while Carriera was creating his portrait. The anecdotes that Spence wrote down include, for example, Carriera's emphasis on the importance of the eyes in portraits or her habit to 'study features and the expression of the mind [...] I know people's tempers from their faces'.[30] If Carriera, depending on her sexual orientation, could have been more or less easily seduced, or at least distracted, by her male clients and their glances, the men who came to her studio might have deemed that as a disorienting ambiguity. It seems reasonable to believe that the artist's mother and/or her sister Giovanna were present during the sittings, which most likely sanctioned the space of encounter as it did, for example, in the case of Elisabeth Vigée-Lebrun.[31]

Another critical aspect of Carriera's role as a female painter was that her contemporaries were often under the delusion that such women consorted in male circles with uncommon regularity and might even, as artists, be tempted to follow the lead of their male colleagues and paint nudes of men. It was therefore vital she avoided becoming the target of harmful rumour, malicious tongues and scandal, and that she strictly attended to the appearance of propriety, leading an exemplary life and showing impeccable behaviour, especially since she did not have support from a brother or a husband. Felice Ramelli, a good friend and colleague who maintained regular, close contact with her, was well aware of the perils to which his friend was exposed. In a letter dated 28 June 1703, he wrote to the artist that he intended in the future to address her as 'M. Jean Carriera' presumably so as not to compromise her by the large number of letters she, as an unmarried woman, received from a gentleman.[32]

Carriera's carefully constructed persona, which is patently evident in her letters and some of her self-portraits discussed later in this book, her caution, tactics and the control of her behaviour, worked out remarkably well if one takes into account that there is no evidence to date of any specific public criticism of her private life, her reputation or her morals. Her biographers never mention anything of this type. For an artist of international renown, someone whom people talked about at the various European courts, who received a manifold clientele from an impressive number of different countries, and who worked in a city where she could have easily become the target of envious, local painters, it is noteworthy that she managed to live a relatively undisturbed life.

The delicate nature of a famous woman's reputation, and the ease with which it could be ruined, can be gauged by the rumours of Angelica Kauffman (1741–1807) having an alleged affair with Sir Joshua Reynolds (1723–92); or the mistreatment of Giulia Lama by her male colleagues in Venice.[33] And it is easy to imagine that Vigée-Lebrun was embroiled in the talk surrounding Queen Marie Antoinette (1755–93) and her intimate circle of female friends even though no writer seems to have named the artist directly as a sexual partner of the Queen.[34] Such examples make clear the extent to which Carriera was vulnerable.[35] She must have been acutely aware of the risks she and her sisters Angela and Giovanna were taking. It was in the face of this reality that Carriera cleverly built her image of a cold, saintly spinster who also painted.

Carriera's decision not to marry was met in the court of public opinion with surprise and perplexity by some, and admiration and interest by others. Worthy of note in this respect is a letter of 5 June 1739, in which Rosana Pozzola wrote to Carriera from Vicenza, reporting that she had begun working for

Giovanni Antonio De Pieri (1671–1751) as an artist:

> as my demerits and bad fate, have not allowed me to come under Yr. Most Illustrious Ladyship, I have made every possible effort to submit myself to this Gentleman. Believe me that there has been no other motive, than that I have been persevering in drawing, that I have determined that I do not wish to marry, besides, having, up to now, such little fortune that I don't know how I have stayed with this opinion, but considering my state, possessing but little fortune, I have devoted myself with every possible energy, if I can do so much as obtain some merit [...]. I think you will take pleasure in this resolution of mine and will judge it excellent [...].[36]

Pozzola clearly saw Carriera as a role model, not only in her artistic career, but also in her decision not to marry. She apparently hoped for at least moral support in this respect. Something which met with spiritual opposition on the one hand was on the other able to serve as a guiding light and role model for emancipated women.

While it is impossible to ascertain, Carriera's decision not to marry may have been the result of her aspiration to be an independent woman, or because of her sexual orientation. Either conjecture would distract attention from one highly significant fact: marriage was never a real alternative for Carriera. For female artists of her time, marriage as a means of climbing the social ladder was only conditionally possible. Generally speaking, the professional career of the woman artist was hampered rather than helped by marriage, and, as a consequence, as Adelina Modesti notes in her book on the Bolognese painter Elisabetta Sirani, 'many women artists, once married, more often than not, abandoned their professions'.[37] Carriera's career would have been obstructed quite considerably by marriage. Additionally, had she married, it would have been her husband, not she, who would have benefited from her fame, her success and her fortune.[38] By renouncing marriage, on the other hand, she was able to safeguard her intellectual and artistic autonomy, which compensated for the loss of social advancement.[39] Simply put, as Chambers-Schiller's book title suggests: *Liberty, a Better Husband*.[40]

Her decision to remain single led Carriera to build and rely on a functioning network of prominent and influential men and women in her hometown and abroad. Representatives from all spheres of influence substituted a husband for social leverage, a system that worked exceptionally well, especially since her friends and acquaintances included ambassadors, intellectuals, aristocrats, businessmen and artists of both sexes. Carriera managed to interact with them at various levels, whether in person at her home, during social events or evenings at the theatre or opera, or through her fervent correspondence.

Looking at her relationships in Venice, it is interesting to note that Carriera executed more portraits of Venetian women than Venetian men, as Piero Del Negro has shown. About ten to twelve portraits of patrician ladies can be found through to about the end of the 1720s. In old age, she added at least another seven to this list to reach a total of roughly 20. The likenesses of male patricians were limited to roughly ten. The discrepancy is more pronounced if one looks at the number of females with whom she shared a social life. Indeed, Carriera's life and success in Venice seem to have been more generally determined and influenced by her contacts with women than with men. However, with regard to her portraits of foreigners, the ratio is reversed, with about five times more men depicted than women.[41] Carriera was not the only female to apply this strategy in reference to her private and professional links: 'One aspect of women's increasing participation in art practices of all kinds from the end of the Renaissance onwards seems to be the creation of [female] networks. Women who in many cases were denied formal training and professional opportunities shared resources [...] and exchanged the products of their artistic labors.'[42]

Three particularly important cases of female bonding in Carriera's life are represented by the friendships between the artist, her pupil Felicita Sartori (*c.*1714–60), the author Luisa Bergalli (1703–79) as well as Rosalba's sister Giovanna. Each of these links exemplifies specific complex aspects pertaining to eighteenth-century same-sex relationships. They represent noteworthy contributions to 'women shaping culture in eighteenth-century Venice'.[43] The cultural situation in the lagoon gave numerous Venetian women the opportunity to distinguish themselves in various fields.[44] This environment could only prove beneficial to the career of people such as Bergalli, who made her mark as a poet, playwright, director of theatre performances and translator of classic and French literature. In 1726, she published her anthology of Italian authoresses, entitled *Componimenti poetici delle più illustre rimatrici d'ogni secolo* (*Poetic Compositions by the Most Illustrious Poetesses of Every Century*), which at the time was the most comprehensive anthology of Italian female writers – as well as the first to be published by a woman. The volume comprises various works of 253 female poets, together with their biographies, including also Rosalba's sister, Giovanna Carriera.[45]

The ties between the painter, her sister, her student and the author also represent examples of female cooperation that these four women strategically leveraged to achieve, by means other than marriage, professional success in a public arena otherwise dominated by men.[46] They highlight how niches of mutual female support and intimate emotional bonds successfully created a 'powerful resource in the struggle for autonomy and authority'.[47]

3

Carriera, the First Female Trendsetter in Medium and Style

The beginning of the eighteenth century represented not only the first professional triumph in Carriera's life as an independent artist, with her recognition by the Accademia di San Luca in Rome, but it was also the period when she increasingly concentrated on a new technique: pastel painting, a fascinating and singular medium that proved to be the next milestone in her career. Over time, she showed a clear preference for this medium, becoming its foremost ambassador.

The English word pastel probably derives from the Italian *pastello*, a diminutive of the Latin word *pasta* or paste, and it refers to a form of dry painting.[1] It involves applying pigments to a working surface, usually grainy blue-grey paper, which was originally associated with Venice, where it was called 'Turkish paper' (*carta turchina*). Card, canvas and parchment were other forms of support. The artists used either pure pigments or, as was customary, pastel crayons or sticks. The latter were fabricated from coloured pigments and a white mineral or pigment, the so-called filler or base, to add physical substance. Generally, the additive was white chalk of various types, or gypsum, starch, plaster of Paris or tobacco-pipe clay, and a binder, usually gum arabic.[2] Before applying the pigments to the rough surface, the paper was dampened and glued to a fine canvas. Artists, including Carriera, often used blue Turkish paper, which was commonly available in smaller dimensions, 37.5 × 46.5 cm (14¾ × 18¼ in) or 42 × 52 cm (16½ × 20⅜ in).[3] With the pigments applied in layers of innumerable hues – it has been estimated that more than 1,650 different shades can be created with pastels – each pastel artist has to have a multitude of crayons ready before beginning the painting process. The various pastels are blended on the surface, either by the artist's finger or with the use of special brushes, 'making the pigments luminous or velvety, or given a soft and silky matness of grain'.[4] With their subtle distinctions and delicate shades, their friable, powdery nature, and soft and loosely layered pigments, pastel paintings remain susceptible to damage even when an artist uses a fixative. For this reason, most are kept behind protective glass. To keep dust out, paper strips are used to seal the glazing fully to the frame.[5]

Carriera probably discovered this delicate medium at the end of the seventeenth century, and we know that by 1704 (at the latest), the artist was in touch with English customers who were interested not only in her miniatures but, more and more, also in what they called her 'crayon paintings'.[6] Her unprecedented success in promoting pastel painting was an extraordinary achievement considering that, when she started using it, the medium was not particularly esteemed in the art world.

Similar to the production of miniatures, the technique of pastel painting offered significant advantages for women artists. Compared to oil painting, the use of crayons was considered simpler. The sticks could be used without any further preparation, and their quality and characteristics did not change during the painting process. No drying phase was required, the work could be interrupted at any given moment, and the paintings could be executed with relative speed, which resulted in briefer sittings; this spared the models hours of boredom, kept the costs lower, and allowed the painter to increase her output. Moreover, pastel did not stain clothes like oil paint, nor did it dirty the hands. In addition, there was no need for varnish or chemicals with strong and unpleasant odours. Further, contrary to widespread opinion, the pastel colour intensity tops that of oil paintings. As Jeffares has noted, 'With pastels, a "pigment volume concentration" of up to 90% can be achieved, while oil painting typically produces less than half this level'.[7] The portability of the medium represented another advantage, especially in a city like Venice, which was attracting an immense number of travellers from all over the world. Travellers passing through Venice were thus able to commission a portrait on the spur of the moment and then depart with an easily transportable work of art. Carriera's work could even be obtained by mail order. Historical documentation points to the impressive monetary values of her pastels and the often rapid payments she received, sometimes within only a week, probably depending on her visitors' itineraries, and sometimes even before she actually finished a portrait.[8]

The increasing admiration of pastel painting, together with Carriera's mastery of the technique, resulted in an unprecedented success for the Venetian artist, who went on to make it a popular fashion. She not only led the way in the use of ivory for miniatures, but she also became a trendsetter of an entire genre throughout Europe; two groundbreaking achievements for a woman artist.

One of Carriera's first documented works in pastel is a portrait of Anton Maria Zanetti, with whom she established an important, intimate and long-lasting friendship in her late twenties (fig.22). It might have been Zanetti who triggered her interest in pastel paintings.[9] Carriera invited him to her home, and he was one of the male friends who regularly accompanied her to Venetian salons and public events. Zanetti himself was trained as an artist, and was associated with the most illustrious artists and intellectuals of his day. He also distinguished himself as a refined conversationalist, prolific art collector and sophisticated connoisseur, and became particularly famous for his caricatures of well-known figures in the city's cultural life.[10] All of Europe turned to Zanetti when it came to acquisitions, opinions, appraisals or research regarding drawings, prints, cameos or gems.[11] His role as an intermediary between the young and ambitious Carriera and his wide-ranging cultural network was enormously important. He opened an extensive artistic horizon for this determined woman at the beginning of her spectacular career, and she undoubtedly profited from Zanetti's position.

Carriera's pastel is a bust portrait of the young Zanetti, who was around 20 years old at the time. He is turned to the right, wearing a curly, powdered white wig, and his angelic face shows a subtle smile while he looks the observer directly in the eye. From the texture of the brown and blue fabric or the white of his shirt, it is obvious that Carriera had just started using the new medium. Her treatment of the textiles seems tentative, although the quality of satin, silk or cotton becomes more tangible in her later paintings. In addition, her rendering of Zanetti's face suggests a certain insecurity in achieving the perfect skin colour and hiding the movements of the pastel sticks on the paper surface. Even so, it is considered a valuable document of a precious friendship.

Among the earlier works by Carriera is a remarkable pastel depicting a beautiful Venetian lady (fig.23). In the past, it was identified as the

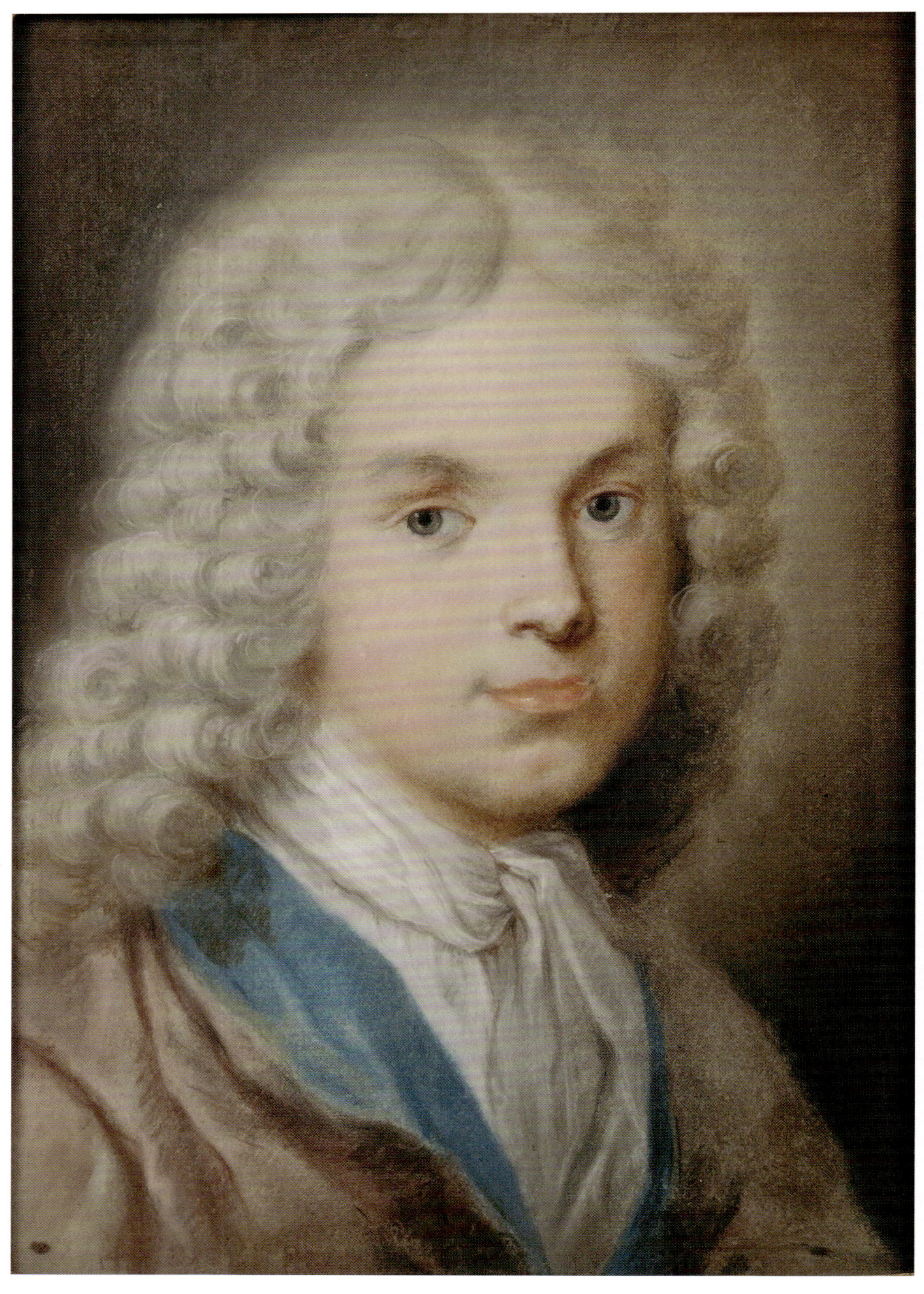

22 Rosalba Carriera, *Portrait of Anton Maria Zanetti*, *c.*1700, pastel on paper, 45 × 31.5 cm (17 ¾ × 12 ⅜ in), National Museum, Stockholm

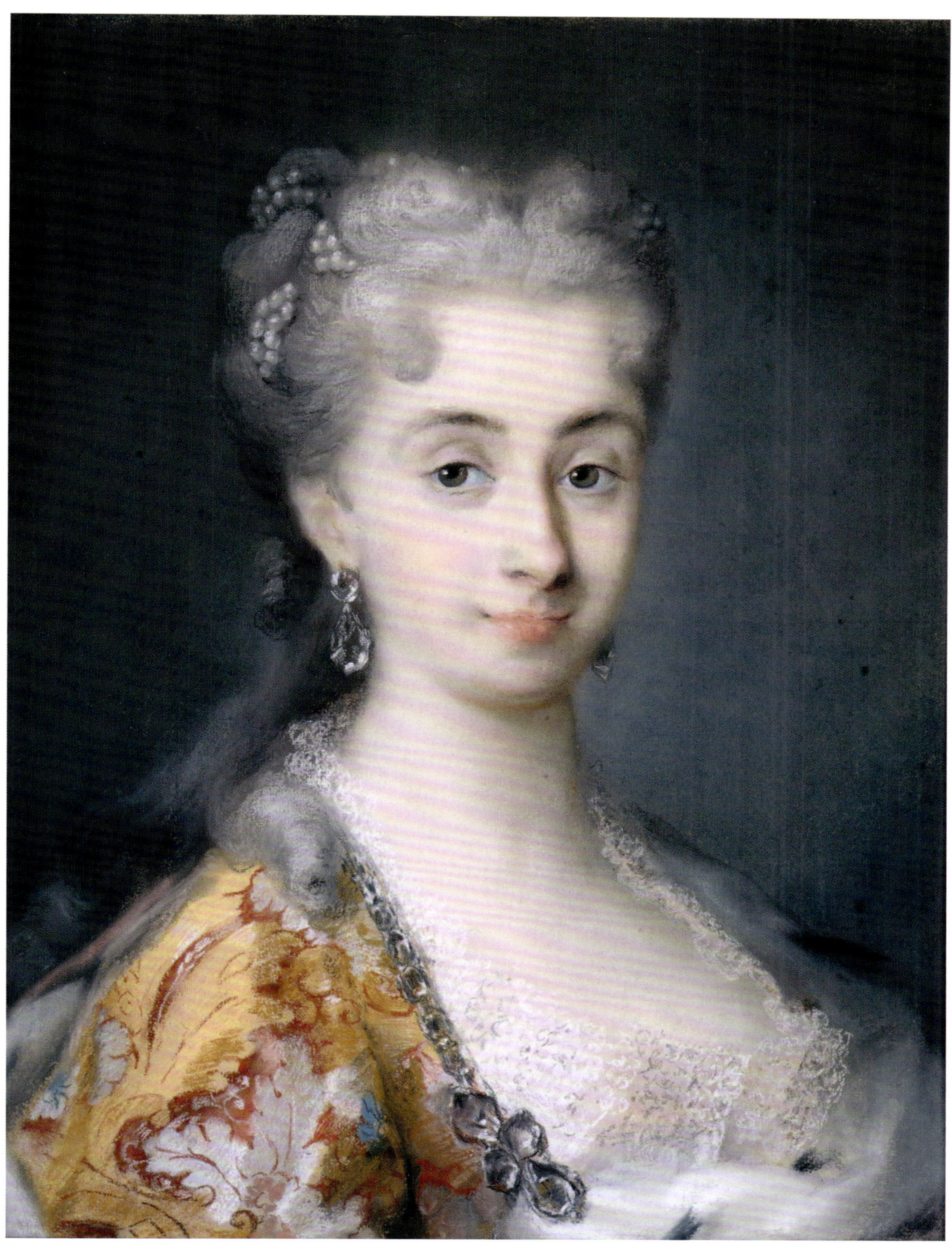

23 Rosalba Carriera, *Portrait of Pisana (Corner) Mocenigo*, undated, pastel on paper, 52 × 41 cm (20 ½ × 16 ⅛ in), Staatliche Kunstsammlungen, Gemäldegalerie Alte Meister, Dresden

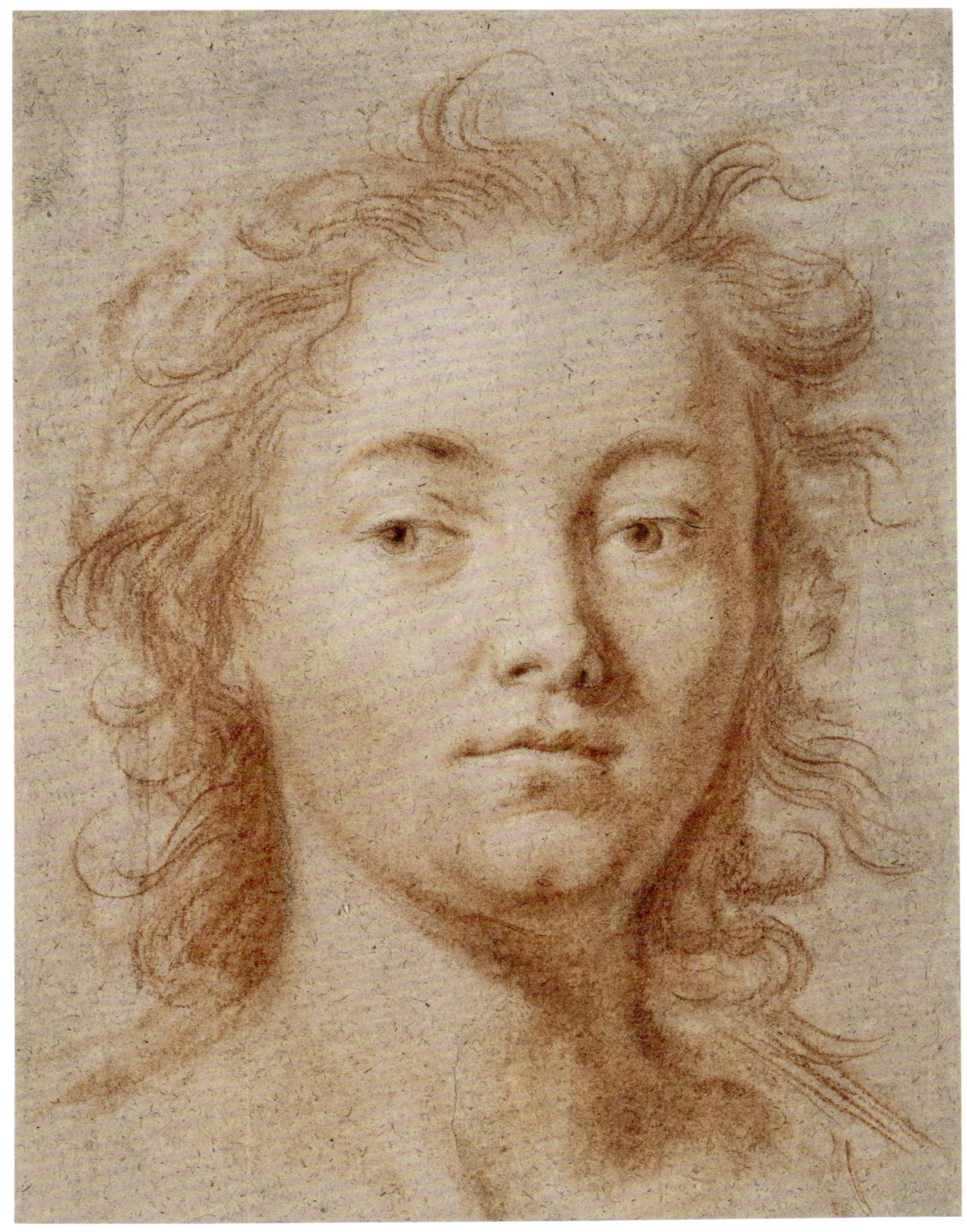

24 Rosalba Carriera, *Self-portrait*, *c.*1708, red chalk on paper, 35 × 26.6 cm (13 ¾ × 10 ⅜ in), Staatliche Museen, Preußischer Kulturbesitz, Kupferstichkabinett, Berlin

portrait of Lucrezia Mocenigo, but a mention of the work in the Dresden collection's 1765 catalogue and a reference to it in a letter written in 1740 by August III, King of Poland, are compelling arguments that it most likely depicts Pisana Mocenigo, born Corner (Cornaro).[12] She had married the patrician Alvise IV Antonio Mocenigo (1685–1759) in 1703, and she was known in Venice as one of the more famous *salonnières* of her time. Dressed in a lavish gold dress with a pattern of leaves and decorated with the customary white lace around the cleavage, she looks at the spectator with a friendly captivating glance in her big round eyes. A faint smile rests on her glowing lips. Her light grey hair is combed back while one long curl falls over her right shoulder. Large, dangling crystal earrings, a glittering brooch with a chain at the level of her right breast, and pearls in her hair are trappings to emphasise this Venetian lady's exclusive position. The ermine cloak playfully hanging over her left shoulder serves the same purpose.

A particularly interesting example of Carriera's early artistic production is a sketch that has been identified as a self-portrait dating from around 1708 (fig.24).[13] Most likely, the painter created her own likeness directly in front of a mirror to show herself looking intensely and self-confidently at the observer from an angle to the right. She captured 'what [she] saw in a direct, non-idealised manner, almost like an uncensored visual diary entry'.[14] Her dishevelled hair underscores the private nature of the moment. She has not set herself in a scene, nor does this sketch show the slightest hint of Carriera trying to conform to the ideal of beauty in the eighteenth century. It is the only example in Carriera's oeuvre that presents an authentic version of the painter herself. It was most likely a personal study, a private record, produced for self-exploration rather than for a commissioned painting. It represents an image of spontaneous realism without artifice, pretence or a specific message to transmit. At the same time, her wild, uncombed hair and her eyebrows bring to mind Cesare Ripa's description of 'Painting' (*Pittura*) and of the fact that the quality of hair often symbolised that of intellect:

> Beautiful woman, with black, thick hair, spread out and ringleted in various ways [...]. The hair on her head is depicted black and thick because as the good painter is always thinking about the imitation of nature and about art as far as it creates perspective and is the object of the eye, and for this reason he needs to almost continuously have in his fantasy all the visible effects of nature.[15]

Carriera possibly played with the idea of representing herself as the personification of Painting for practice, experimentation, or the purpose of self-reflection.

A significantly different pastel self-portrait, held at the Uffizi in Florence (fig.25), was executed around the same time. Documents show that it has been hanging in the Uffizi collection of self-portraits in Florence since 17 July 1714. However, it was most probably executed in conjunction with a commission that the artist received at a considerably earlier date, believed to be from Prince Ferdinando de' Medici (1663–1713).[16]

Carriera appears as a relatively plain woman of about 30 years old, half-length against a neutral beige background. Her gaze appears to touch only lightly on the observer, while she holds a portrait of her younger sister Giovanna in her left hand. She wears no jewellery, gold or pearls – only a little lace adorns the simple clothing of the woman who has a flower pinned in her hair. It is not a sign of vanity but a key to her identity: a white rose, a *rosa alba.* Carriera deliberately shows herself as a pastel artist standing in front of a sheet of blue paper placed against a drawing board while holding her professional tool – a porte-crayon for pastel sticks – which she is using to complete a portrait. More crayons are lying on a table in front of her. The neutral beige wall in the background alludes to her studio.

Carriera's decision to include a smaller picture in her self-portrait is most likely due to the input of Grand Duke Cosimo III de' Medici (1642–1723), who continued the collection of self-portraits that his uncle Cardinal Leopoldo de' Medici (1617–75) had initiated, and who aimed at unifying the formats of the paintings.[17] She would have known that Cosimo III not only specified the dimensions of the paintings for his collection, but he also expressed his wishes concerning certain details in the portraits, such as that the artist should depict a person either painting an artwork or holding a small 'drawn figure'.[18]

If the second woman in the painting, the 'picture in the picture', can be identified as Carriera's sister Giovanna, it begs the question as to how the portrait should be interpreted. Why did Carriera choose to include her sister Giovanna herself in her self-portrait? A comparison between Carriera's painting and other self-portraits by female artists from the fifteenth century onwards reveals the existence of only a limited number of examples in which family members are included as ancillary figures next to the artist. For this reason alone, Carriera's painting in the Uffizi plays a special role among women artists' self-portraits. Furthermore, not only does she portray a close relative, but she includes her sister as her most important assistant. Nonetheless, Giovanna's role remains subordinate, as reflected in the difference in size between the two women. At a different level of interpretation, the artist is also the author portrayed as standing at her work, while the assistant appears as a picture within a picture.

Remembering that Rosalba had taught her younger sisters and that Giovanna's role in the Carriera studio was to complete or copy her elder sister's work, this portrait in the Uffizi acquires an even deeper significance: Carriera depicts herself not only as painting Giovanna but as quite literally 'creating' her. It is also interesting to note that this work is Carriera's only self-portrait to include both hands. This detail seems rather ironic when considering that it was Giovanna who generally completed the hands in Rosalba's portraits. The younger sister was also the one who frequently executed the lace often seen adorning the garments of her clients. With Giovanna also responsible for protecting the fragile pastel paintings behind protective glass, it may well have been Giovanna herself who finished the details in this particular painting before covering it with glass.

Comparing this pastel for the grand dukes with the drawing discussed above, it becomes obvious that Carriera restrained the image of her persona in the official portrait.[19] But what were the other aspects of the artist's persona that became visible at other times in her career? Her eyes do not appear radiant or self-confident. With a touch of melancholy and restraint, she appears to look straight through the observer, beyond the mundane world of everyday life. The absence of jewellery on the artist herself is also noteworthy. This painting in the Uffizi and her last self-portrait in Venice, which will be discussed later in the book, are Carriera's only works eschewing any allusion to luxury or financial well-being, as if she wanted to downplay these aspects of her success. These curiously austere choices do, however, go hand in hand with how she avoided discussing money issues in her letters. Carriera presented herself unadorned and in comparatively simple clothes only at the very beginning and at the very end of her career: in doing so, she defied the expectations of her contemporaries and clients to see her attired respectably and elegantly. One can gather, therefore, that this was part of Carriera's wisely applied artistic rhetoric. Her intention, it would appear, was to promote her artistic self as one who privileges art over decorum.[20] And this specific emphasis on the superiority of her refined artistic activity over societal expectations dovetails with another interesting peculiarity about this artist.

When looking again at the Uffizi self-portrait, one realises that the artist did nothing to embellish her physical appearance; she copies, almost brutally, a rather non-feminine, unattractive face. Thus, this self-portrait conforms precisely to the image which Carriera so carefully presented of herself to her

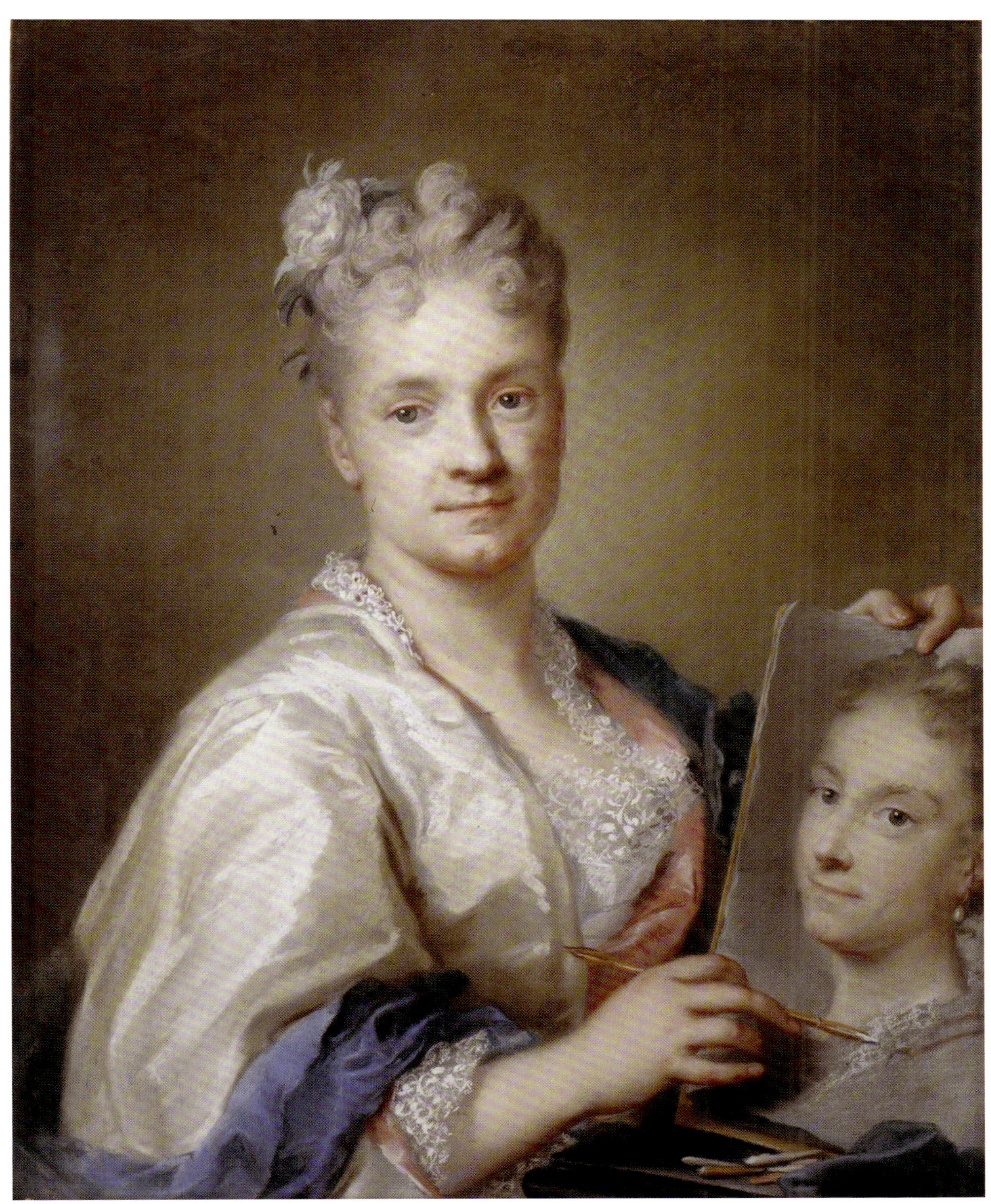

25 Rosalba Carriera, *Self-portrait*, 1708–9, pastel on paper, 71 × 57 cm (27 7/8 × 22 3/8 in), Galleria degli Uffizi, Florence

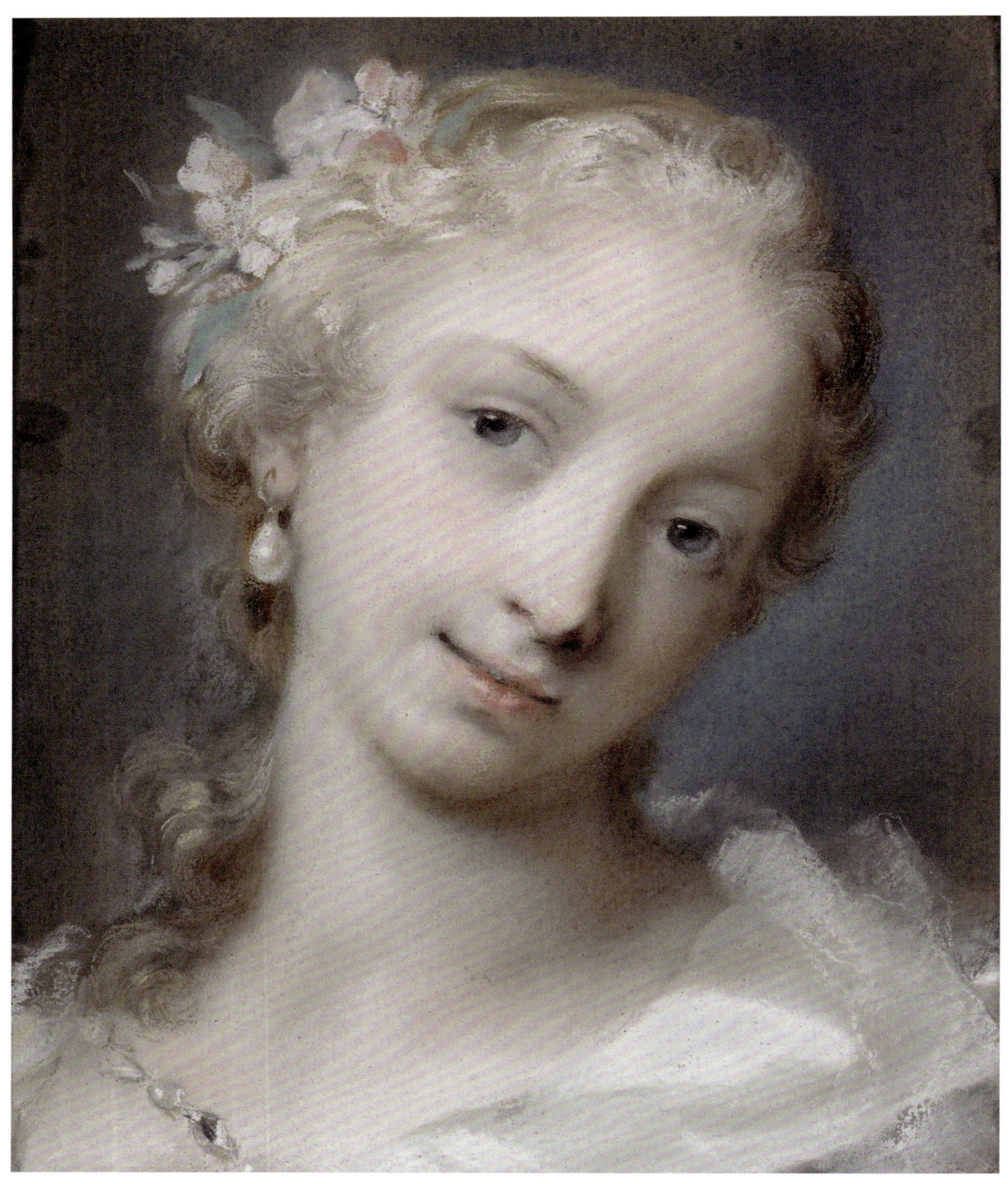

26 Rosalba Carriera, *Girl in a White Dress*, undated, pastel on paper, 32 × 26.5 cm (12 ⅝ × 10 ⅜ in), Staatliche Kunstsammlungen, Gemäldegalerie Alte Meister, Dresden

contemporaries: that of a modest, reserved spinster, uninterested in worldly matters.[21] The way Carriera decided to depict herself for the world to see was intentional. It was a premediated tactic, an elaborate and subtle strategy, and the outcome of an original and efficient self-enactment.[22] Carriera never emphatically rebelled against the social conventions and ideas of her day, but she was able to instrumentalise both by using these very conventions to her own advantage in ways that conceivably may have been too subtle for her contemporaries to recognise.

The Uffizi work represents the last time that Carriera highlighted her professional role by presenting herself at work with her clearly visible tools. Apart from the requirements given by the Grand Duke, Carriera apparently still considered it necessary to define herself in this manner. She thus draws attention to the paradox of women artists who were closed in an ideal of female passivity and private virtue while they were confronted with an art market that required their visibility and public representation.[23] In later self-portraits, she seems to have grown beyond this urge to focus on her professionalism, concentrating on other aspects of herself.

Turning to Carriera's portraits of other women, it is clear that she developed early in her career a formula that was extraordinarily popular. While art critics and historians over the centuries have disparaged many of her paintings as monotonously uniform and excessively embellished, there must have been a different agenda at work for the eighteenth-century public; to date, no contemporary document has surfaced containing criticism of women 'who all look the same'.[24] Carriera's *Girl in a White Dress* in Dresden (fig.26), for example, shows a woman typical of the idealised beauty that can be found in numerous other depictions of women: attractive young females with a mask-like white make-up, a tender smile on red lips, some rouge, elegant clothes, and no distinct personal identity.

It is known that Carriera's visual rendering of the requested theme, whether a portrait, an allegory or a mythological subject, met the expectations of her clients: her artistic interpretations resonated with them and the world in which they lived. Carriera seems to have been able to encapsulate an image her supporters identified with. According to Thea Burns, Carriera's understanding of artistic idealisation needs to be considered in the context of the eighteenth century's 'social norms relating to individual appearance'.[25] Burns writes that elaborate conformity to the fashion of the moment, the attempt to look like everybody else but slightly different, and artificiality in the creation of a self or a second self, adhered to an elitist notion of decent representation and longed-for recognition. They were standards to follow and proof of one's capacity to find ornamentation within the system. One result of this attitude, Burns continues, was a widely accepted manipulation and control of one's face, aided by clearly visible cosmetics. This fabricated, forced appearance was not restricted to women; during much of the seventeenth and the first half of the eighteenth century, men wore make-up as well, reflecting the idea of an artifice necessary to civilised social intercourse: 'cosmetics were less a matter of gender than of class'.[26] And it is precisely in these 'works of art', so to speak, that Carriera depicted representatives of idealised, uniform beauty in a fair number of her pastel portraits, including for example this work in Stockholm (fig.27).

Burns also points out the similarity between the dry powdery pastel pigments and dry powdery cosmetics, by virtue of which 'seductive play with illusion was heightened because identical materials were used to paint (make up) faces and to paint pastels'.[27] The matte appearance and the haptic qualities of both materials intensified the enthusiasm for the pastel portraits on the part of the audience.[28] As only aristocratic or refined women used cosmetics, the production of a pastel portrait or being depicted with this technique served to reinforce the social status of these privileged individuals.

Unfortunately, Carriera left no personal written record of her views about the aim and nature of portraiture. However, it is not too far-fetched to assert that many of her female clients would have fancied a charming and flattering portrait of themselves. Her clients' personal preferences in conjunction with societal expectations regarding the appearance of women and the making-up of an identity partly explain why and how Carriera embellished and idealised a great number of the female subjects in her oeuvre.

Moving beyond analogies between the powdery substances of cosmetics and pastels or a general ideal of beauty, another level of meaning to Carriera's method can be tied to a phenomenon in seventeenth- and eighteenth-century England, namely, Sir Godfrey Kneller's (1646–1723) codification of another specific canon. At the beginning of the eighteenth century, Kneller was commissioned to produce a series of 48 likenesses of members of London's Kit-Cat Club, and in doing so, he created his own portrait formula. Along with the specific size he chose for each of them, the leading politicians and men of letters of the club were depicted each time in the same fashion, that is, as less than half-length figures presenting one or two hands. The portraits showed a certain poverty of poses, gazes and facial features. The term 'Kneller mask' was coined from the clearly recognisable pattern which dominated English male portraiture for half a century. Instead of complaining about the similarity of their portraits, his clients identified with this pictorial system that guaranteed a public display of good breeding. Also, it bestowed the gentlemen on the canvases with character and politeness.[29]

For this reason, I have suggested that Carriera, whose images were distinctly different from the more realistic renderings of her sitters, developed a similar formula.[30] Her female clients finally had their own stage in being depicted independently of their husbands in pendant portraits; the ladies were eager to be shown as belonging to a certain social class, and as representing a certain ideal of beauty that was more important than a true likeness. Timothy H. Breen has argued that appearance was codified in 'a visual déjà-vu'[31] that included recognisability, fashionable clothes and expensive jewellery, which replaced the need to be identified through truly individual facial features, as evidenced previously.

It is worthwhile to go back to another aspect I have pointed out, 'the importance of owning a Carriera'.[32] Once the artist managed to attain one international success after another, many of her clients no longer specified the subject or theme of their commission; it was enough to own a painting from her hands. Significantly, it had become 'a must' to put a Carriera pastel on display in an upper-class household, and anyone represented in such an artwork would be ennobled automatically.

Appearing on a pastel by Carriera, these women became part of a unified group of equals which accordingly earned them a special status, a status that was correspondent to an ideal of beauty, but that was created by 'being a Carriera'. Her paintings had increasingly gained a status of their own, and so too did the women depicted in them. Being portrayed by the Venetian artist in a recognisable 'Carriera fashion' created a sense of collective identity, with the voluntary acceptance of what I call the 'Carriera mask'. Being 'a Carriera' meant instinctively being part of an exclusive group of women, of a 'visual community'.[33] It implied an elevated social and cultural status, refined manners, exclusive taste as well as outstanding beauty. A stunning physical appearance representative of the ideal of beauty at the time further signified femininity and virtuousness, and more importantly the public prominence of these women. The Carriera mask thus blurred boundaries of class. Any woman of any social standing could easily turn into a Carriera woman. And, considering the artist's success across Europe, also of any nationality. It allowed for the permeability of social classes without causing a clash or any form of rebellion, and it shaped an identity whereby individual features or national roots were deliberately and freely neglected.

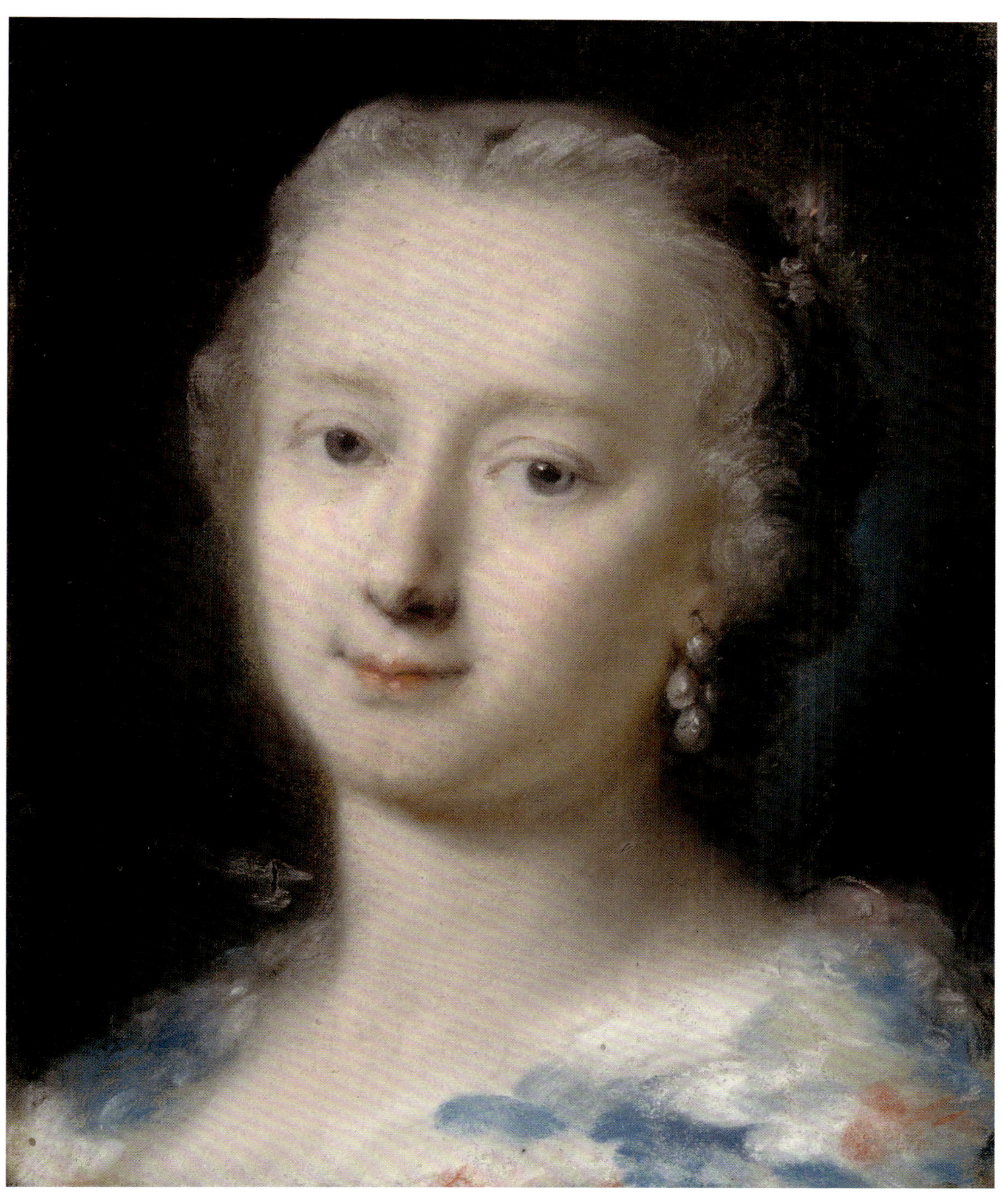

27 Rosalba Carriera, *Young Woman with Flowers in her Hair*, *c.*1735, pastel on paper, 32 × 26 cm (12 ⅝ × 10 ¼ in), National Museum, Stockholm

It seems to be no coincidence that this sense of unity within a recognisable group is a quality that we find primarily among Carriera's female portraits.

A fair number of her female clients apparently longed to be associated with the delicacy of Carriera's women. Nevertheless, the sense of group identity offered by the Carriera mask was an element that could be negotiated. Interestingly, strong female characters whose role in society was exceptional for one reason or another, like Caterina Sagredo, Faustina Bordoni, Empress Amalia Wilhelmine or especially Carriera herself, chose different ways to be depicted, as will be explored later in the book.

4

Invitations Abroad and Carriera's International Network

To preclude the risk of becoming financially dependent or losing her artistic independence, which could easily have been the painter's fate at any European court, Carriera never relied on the support of a fixed patron in Venice or abroad. Unlike Pietro Bellotti (1625–1700), her brother-in-law Giovanni Antonio Pellegrini (who between 1703 and 1704 had married her sister Angela) or Giovanni Battista Tiepolo, for example, she stayed in her home city, refusing to take up any lucrative offers from foreign rulers. The miniature and pastel market that she had conquered gave her a great deal of autonomy, both at home and abroad.[1] Eventually, she arrived at the enviable position of not having to look for clients. Her customers found her on the free market; indeed, they competed amongst themselves for her favour, which was indeed a privilege she was reluctant to surrender. And her contemporaries were well aware of it: on 6 March 1706, Felice Ramelli wrote a letter to the artist informing her that she would soon receive an invitation from Düsseldorf to work for the local court, but it would entail abandoning a city where she was celebrated as if she were a queen.[2]

Carriera declined the flattering invitation from Germany while also renouncing any affiliation with the multifaceted group of artists, musicians and authors at the Düsseldorf court. Elector Palatine Johann Wilhelm (1658–1716), whose second wife was Anna Maria Luisa de' Medici (1667–1743), had called together this international party of talents. The impressive list of foreigners working for him included Carriera's countrymen, such as the artists Giovanni Battista Foggini (1652–1725), Antonio Bellucci (1654–1726) and her brother-in-law, as well as the castrato singer Valeriano Pellegrini (*c.*1663–1746). The composer Carlo Luigi Grua (*c.*1700–1773) and the opera librettist Stefano Benedetto Pallavicini (1672–1742) worked there as well. Had she accepted the offer, Carriera would have also had the chance to meet the celebrated Dutch flower painter Rachel Ruysch (1664–1750), who worked in Düsseldorf from 1708 to 1716. The negotiations between the German ruler and the Italians were left to his secretary Giorgio Maria Rapparini (1660–1726), who would become a regular correspondent of Carriera's. In courteously turning down the offer to move to Germany, Carriera managed to sustain her relationship with the glamorous court, as shown by the commissions she continued to receive from Düsseldorf.

By the end of the seventeenth century, Carriera was also in contact with the court in Dresden. Frederick Augustus, Augustus II, called 'the Strong' (1670–1733) – whose role as art patron coincided with his dominance in international and internal politics – initiated Dresden's extensive and world-famous collection of the Venetian artist's pastel paintings.

While French painting and fashion initially had the greatest influence on artistic taste in Dresden, the city's royal collections at the beginning of the eighteenth century shifted their emphasis towards the Italian market. This change in the politics of art acquisitions was an unavoidable consequence of Dresden's far-reaching geopolitical and dynastic efforts to fortify the position of Augustus and his court within the whole of Europe. The King had decided to Catholicise Dresden: he himself had already converted in 1697, and he was preparing his only legitimate son, Frederick Augustus II (1696–1763) – the young Elector of Saxony and later the King of Poland as Augustus III as well as Grand Duke of Lithuania – to convert as well. Hoping to gain papal support for his plan to link his family through marriage to the imperial Habsburg court in Vienna, Augustus the Strong sent the Elector of Saxony on an obligatory Grand Tour, which included conversion to Catholicism in Bologna in 1712. By August 1719, his father's dynastic ambitions, paired with his diplomatic and political skills, had translated into success: the 'transconfessional apotheosis of his dynasty'[3] was crowned by the marriage between Frederick Augustus and the Archduchess of Austria, Maria Josepha (1699–1757), the first daughter of the Habsburg Emperor Joseph I (1678–1711) and Amalia Wilhelmine von Braunschweig-Lüneburg (see fig.44, p.87).

Presumably on the occasion of his Grand Tour, the then Crown Prince Frederick Augustus was in contact with Carriera. Apart from his first trip to Venice where he arrived on 2 February 1712, he visited her repeatedly during the seven years thereafter, having not only his own portrait painted by her hand but also likenesses of various court and family members, including his wife. He increasingly became a genuine enthusiast of Carriera's art, adding to his father's collection of her works with acquisitions of her pastels that were the nucleus of the Dresden gallery's Carriera collection. Together with the paintings that arrived in Dresden through agents such as Andreas Philipp Kindermann, Count Francesco Algarotti and Giovan Pietro Minelli (d.1772), and those taken to Germany by friends and courtiers, as well as the works donated as diplomatic gifts, more than 150 of her pastel paintings eventually adorned the walls of the so-called Kabinett der Rosalba (Rosalba Gallery). The Kabinett was first located in the former stable yard building, called 'Johanneum', which was converted into a museum and opened in 1746. Today, the Dresden collections still boast the largest number of Carriera's works.

Augustus III's hunger for Italian art seemed endless, as did his means to invest: in the course of one single year, 1742, he acquired 715 paintings and numerous graphic works for the royal collection.[4] His son, Prince Frederick Christian of Saxony (1722–63), continued the family tradition of being interested in Italy and especially Venice. Travelling from 1738 to 1740 under the pseudonym Comte de Lusace, Frederick Christian decided on a long sojourn in Venice on his way back from a trip to Naples, where his sister Maria Amalia (1724–60) had married Charles VII of Bourbon, King of Naples and Sicily, later Charles III of Spain (1716–88). The Prince arrived in the Republic on 21 December 1739 and stayed for the next six months, keeping a diary where he meticulously recorded his activities. These included Lenten devotions and private tutoring, but also elaborate Venetian events such as the regatta, and a bull chase organised in his honour, concerts, carnival celebrations, sightseeing, visits to the government-owned gambling house, the Ridotto, and numerous encounters or '*conversazioni*' at the Ca' Foscari, which he had leased.[5]

One of his guests was Carriera. On 5 April 1740, he noted that the famous Rosalba had come to meet him for the first time, to start a portrait of him which she completed in June, only a few days before his departure.[6] Carriera created an official, representative court portrait of the prince who, at that point, was 16 years old (fig.28).[7] He is shown with his natural hair, bound together with a ribbon with a tress cascading

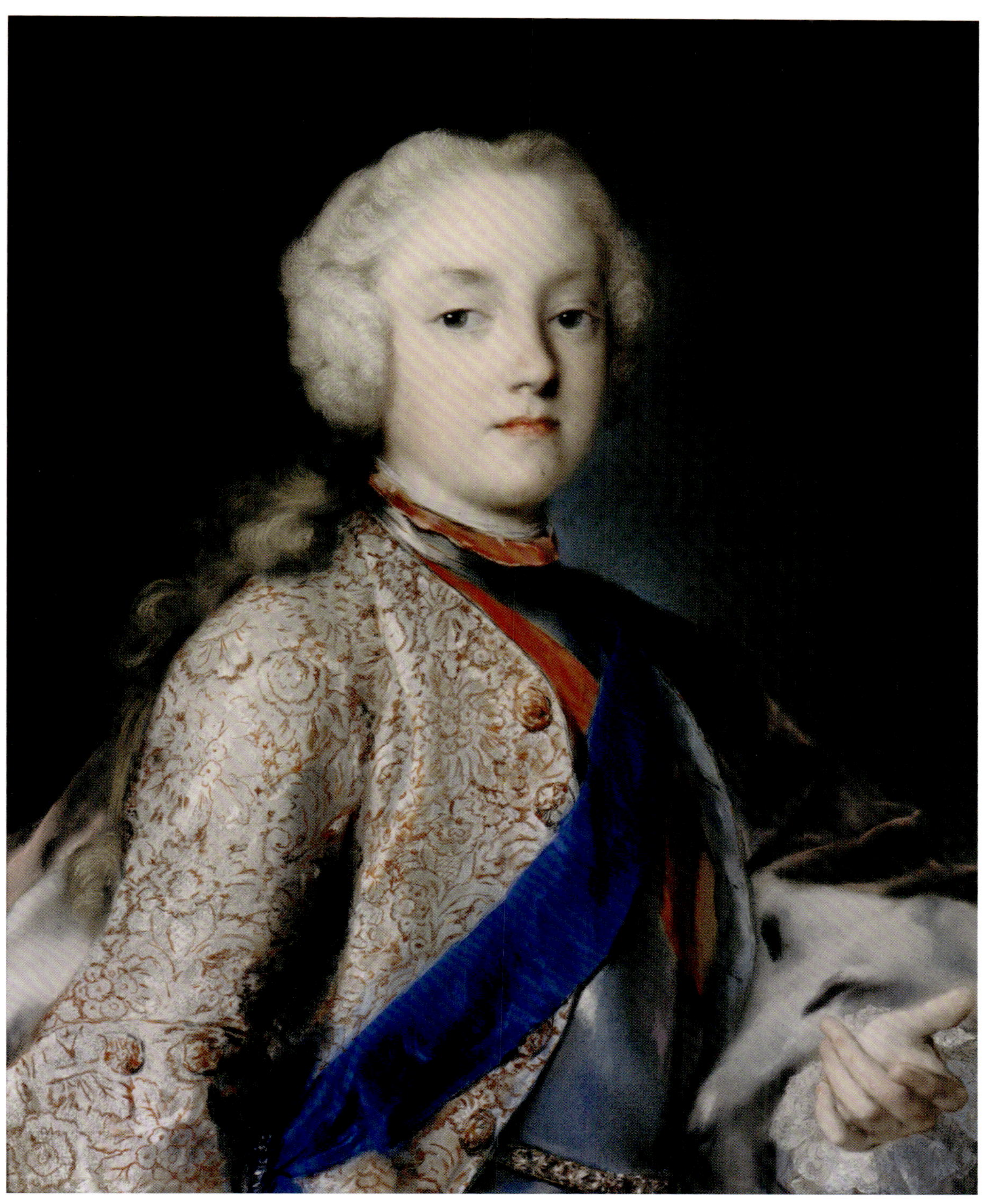

28 Rosalba Carriera, *Portrait of Frederick Christian of Saxony*, 1740, pastel on paper, 63.5 × 31.5 cm (25 × 12 3/8 in), Staatliche Kunstsammlungen, Gemäldegalerie Alte Meister, Dresden

down his back – the full-bottomed periwig had by then gone out of fashion. The Prince's family had convinced him to abandon the wig in Italy, alongside other advice such as savouring fresh seafood.[8] He is dressed in armour cloaked by an elegant brocade mantle and the obligatory ermine cape. The blue sash across his chest represents the Order of the White Eagle, which had been instituted by his grandfather Augustus the Strong in 1705. The red ribbon underneath indicates the Neapolitan Order of Saint Januarius, founded by Charles VII of Naples in honour of his marriage to Maria Amalia in 1738.

Considering Frederick Christian was born with what might have been a neurological disorder that made it difficult or impossible for him to stand, walk, and also dress or eat without help, one might more easily understand why Carriera depicted the Prince with a distanced, introverted look and a skin tone that is paler compared to other examples of her faces. With his right eye slightly more closed than his left and his mouth lacking the hint of a smile we see in many of her other pastels, Carriera has given further subtle but noticeable hints of the young aristocrat's precarious health. The gesture of his left hand, which seems to invite the onlooker to get closer or to participate in the scene, is, in its artificiality and awkwardness, not fully convincing, especially if assessed with the Prince's tangible weakness suggested in the pastel's upper section.[9] It is unlikely that he would have been able to stand freely with one arm lifted, which thus could explain the gesture Carriera added, following tradition, as Cassidy-Geiger has emphasised, to chronicle and portray the Prince as able-bodied.[10]

Another pastel that depicts a member of the Saxon court shows Ursula Katharina of Altenbockum or Teschen (1680–1743) (fig.29). Each change in her life brought about a change in her name. When Ursula Katharina was 15, she married the Polish Prince Jerzy Dominik Lubomirski (1654–1727), who was 26 years her senior. Her husband's prominent position as a member of one of the most famous Polish noble families was promising, but the marriage ended in divorce five years later,[11] with Augustus the Strong purportedly responsible for the break-up. The Saxon ruler was a voracious womaniser who courted the young lady without any reserve in front of her husband and the entire royal entourage, which caused embarrassment, humiliation and rage. Before the unpleasant situation turned into an open scandal, the Pope agreed not only to annul the marriage but, extraordinarily, allowed Ursula Katharina to marry again.[12]

When precisely the King had met the young girl for the first time and under what circumstances is not clearly documented. In 1700, Ursula Katharina became the King's official mistress, succeeding and replacing the Austrian Countess Maximiliane Hiserle of Chodau (d.1738), known as Countess Esterle. On 26 August 1704, only five days after having given birth to Augustus the Strong's son, Johann Georg (1704–74), also called Johann Georg of Saxony, Ursula was named Imperial Princess (*Reichsprinzessin*) of Teschen by the Holy Roman Emperor Leopold I (1640–1705). The following year, the King replaced Ursula with a new mistress, the Countess Anna Constantia of Hoym (1680–1765), later called Countess of Cosel. Humiliated and outlawed from the Dresden court, the Princess of Teschen eventually moved to her Silesian residence in Breslau. When Augustus the Strong also banished the Countess of Cosel in 1713, Ursula Katharina returned to Dresden where she led a respected life at court again.

Almost 20 years after his arrival in Saxony, in October 1722, the army commander Frederick Louis of Württemberg-Winnental (1690–1734) quietly married Ursula. The wedding ceremony was discreet due to the House of Württemberg's serious reservations about the nuptials. After her husband died in Italy in 1734, by the marriage agreement and despite the House of Württemberg's opposition, the Imperial Princess continued to use the name and coat of arms of her deceased husband until her own death at the age of 62.[13]

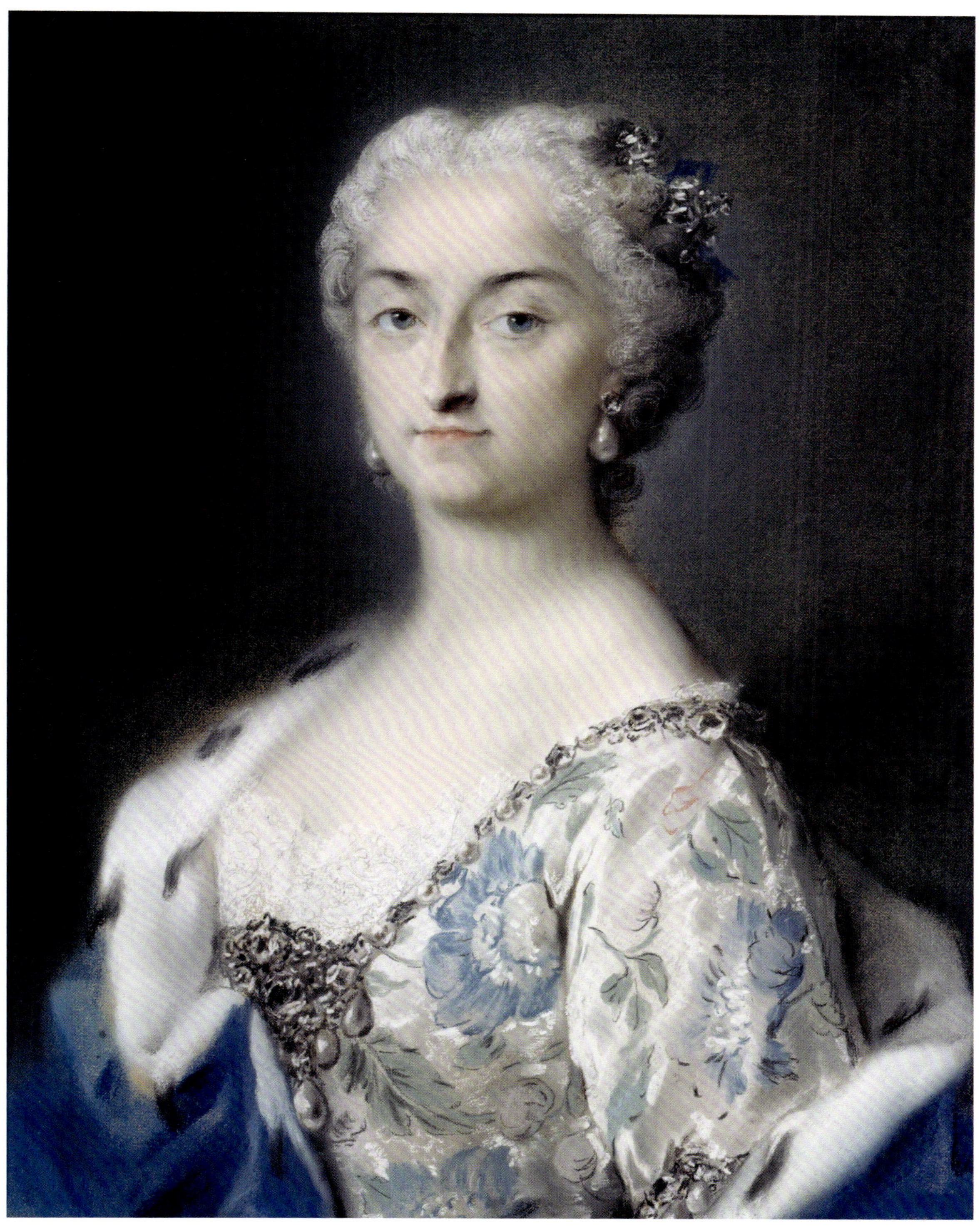

29 Rosalba Carriera, *Portrait of Ursula Katharina Lubomirska*, c.1730, pastel on paper, 57.5 × 46 cm (22 5/8 × 18 1/8 in), Staatliche Kunstsammlungen, Gemäldegalerie Alte Meister, Dresden

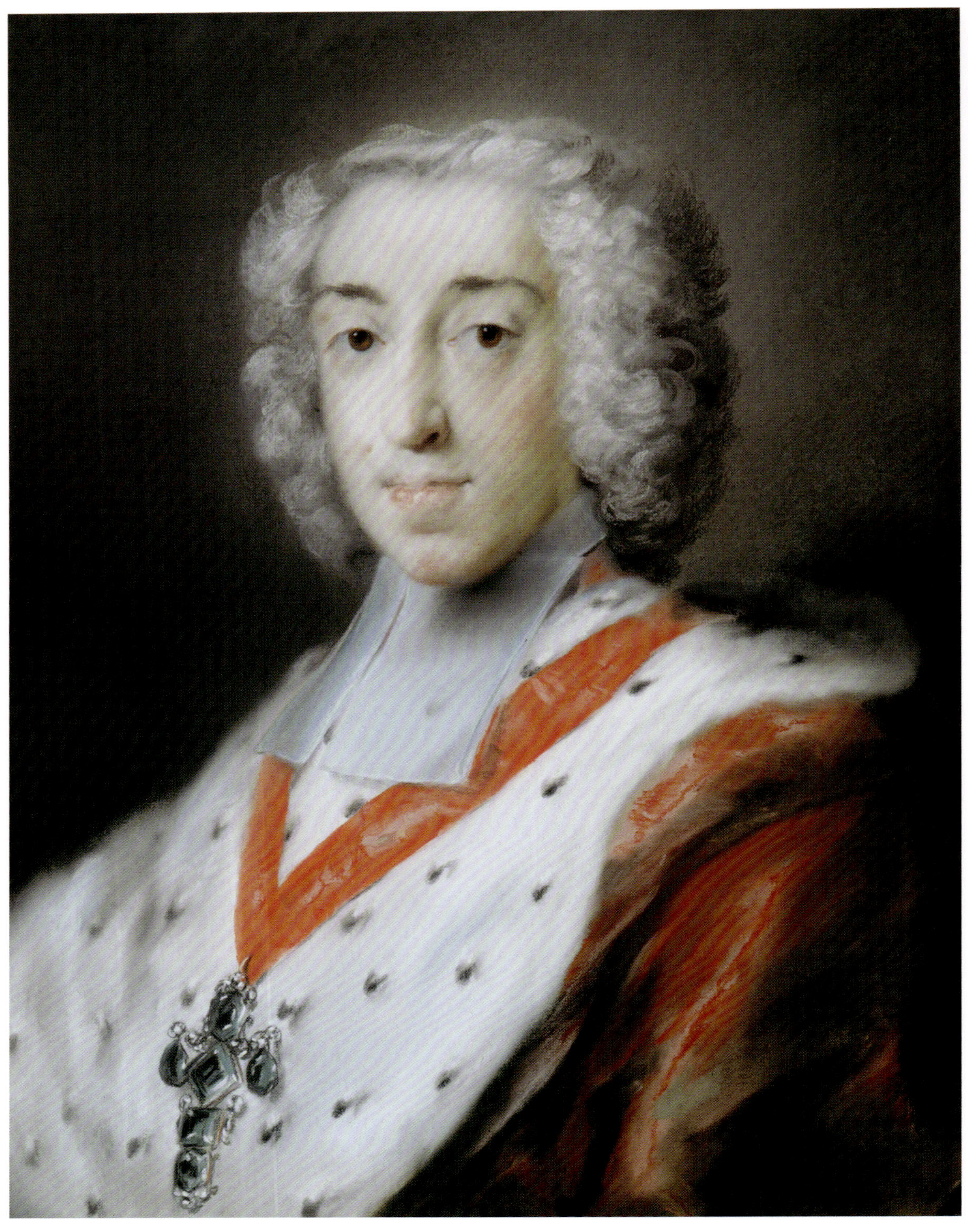

30 Rosalba Carriera, *Portrait of Clemens August of Bavaria*, 1727, pastel on paper, 57 × 45 cm (22 ⅜ × 17 ¾ in), Staatliche Kunstsammlungen, Gemäldegalerie Alte Meister, Dresden

Carriera's pastel of Ursula Katharina is dated about 1730, thus depicting the Princess of Teschen at the age of around 50. Although no clear documentation regarding the commission has emerged thus far, it is plausible to believe that she went to Venice to have her portrait done while living in Italy with Frederick Louis of Württemberg. It seems more likely to have been her idea than that of her husband, who was chiefly interested in his military life and career. But the Princess had spent several years of her life within the sphere of a ruler who had a sophisticated taste and whose impressive art collection was enjoying international esteem. When considering the value of owning a Carriera work and the prestige, especially for women, of being portrayed by the artist, Ursula Katharina probably commissioned her portrait with dual intent: to become one of the beautiful women the artist had painted so many times, and to show her respectable social standing to the world.

The Princess is depicted in a luxurious white silk dress with a delicate blue and green floral pattern, looking directly into the eyes of the beholder. The embroidered lace covering her cleavage and the ornate silver and pearled jewellery on her chest are placed alongside the ermine lining of a blue velvet mantle that seems to slide down from her left shoulder. Similar jewellery adorns the sleeve and the short white wig and is complemented by glittering earrings with huge pearls. The noblewoman's upright pose, her calm and self-assured glance, and her faint, amiable smile are all features suggestive of an individual whose primary aim seems to be to record visually, for posterity, an attractive, proud woman with exceptional artistic taste.

Notably, the painting contains no reference to her husband's family and origins, a conspicuous omission, considering that she aligned herself with the House of Württemberg until her death. Instead, she appears as an independent woman at the peak of her social career. The abandoned, humiliated and banished mistress presents herself as a gratified, respectable noblewoman honoured by the Emperor himself. She poses in front of the spectator celebrating her prestigious status. The ostentatious display of the bright blue velvet mantle with ermine lining is particularly compatible with the exclusive lifestyle of an imperial princess.

Another of Carriera's important contacts from beyond the Alps was Clemens August of the Bavarian House of Wittelsbach (1700–1761) (fig.30). He was son of Elector Maximilian II Emanuel of Bavaria (1662–1726) and Theresa Kunigunde Sobieska (1676–1730), brother of Emperor Charles VII (1697–1745), and he was Archbishop-Elector of Cologne. One of the most prominent clerical imperial princes of his day, he also proved to be a generous art patron.[14] Many artists found employment at his court, which was modelled on Versailles and was celebrated as one of the most magnificent in all of Germany. Apart from being a highly knowledgeable music lover, Clemens August developed a great taste for painting in general, but increasingly he focused his interest on miniatures, porcelain and other valuable *objets d'art*.[15] Under his orders, a number of palaces and castles were built in his territory, including Augustusburg and Falkenlust in Brühl and Herzogsfreude near Bonn. When the Imperial Prince travelled to Rome to be consecrated as Bishop of Viterbo by Pope Benedict XIII (1649–1730) in 1727, he stopped off in Venice, and, as his mother had done roughly ten years before, commissioned his portrait to be painted by Carriera.[16]

Clemens August is depicted with both worldly and ecclesiastic insignia. He wears a red archbishop's mantle trimmed with broad ermine, on top of which rests an ornate crystal cross, the *pectorale*. The intense red colour contrasts beautifully with the white fur and light grey wig, while his intelligent dark brown eyes look benevolently at the beholder. The contrasts of shades and colour counteract, but do not annul, the unique physique of the famed ruler with a long nose and slightly protruding chin. Carriera made a splendid official portrait where the Archbishop appears as a distinguished, elegant but also a kind, sympathetic man.

Carriera's ties to Sweden are evidenced by her pastel of Count Nils Bielke (1706–65), which is now part of the collection of the National Museum in Stockholm (fig.31).[17] The Count came to Venice in 1729, where he met the artist and commissioned his portrait. According to an inscription on the back of the painting, Bielke was 'in his twenty-fourth year' when he posed for Carriera. He is shown as a half figure, turned to his left while his bright blue eyes look over his right shoulder, directly at the beholder. He wears a lilac velvet jacket with a blue lining over a white shirt decorated with a lace collar. A blue velvet cap covering Bielke's head matches the colour of his jacket. He seems to be closing his jacket with his left hand, which bears a glittering gold and ruby ring. Bielke's glance and his facial expression are those of a self-assured young man, somewhat defiant, challenging, and with an attitude bordering on arrogance. Bielke seems to have challenged tradition in having himself painted without any other accessories, and especially without a wig, opting for a portrait that shows his short, natural, reddish-blond hair.

As Marcia Pointon has admirably shown, headgear and especially the wig were visible signs of order, and were clearly gendered items of fashionable male apparel; together they represented a symbolic system with multifaceted connotations:

> The wig possesses a life of its own as a patterning far beyond the bounds of questions of dress and manners. It is invested with a powerful symbolic significance and becomes widespread currency in ways that cannot be summed by the material object of the wig to which, however, this symbolic life always ultimately refers. […] In a discursive practice, the wig signifies across an entire field: the wearing of a wig by a particular individual at a particular time is implicated with the wig as depicted in portraits, just as the portraits are themselves implicated in the fashion for wearing wigs.[18]

Consequently, once it became an established convention to wear wigs, 'to appear without one was to expose oneself as eccentric, exceptional or deviant'.[19] It is reasonable to believe that Bielke knew the ramifications of his decision to be represented in this unconventional manner. Looking at his biography, his choice is not so surprising: his role as a rebel seemed confirmed by this point.

Bielke was born in 1706 in Stockholm into one of the most illustrious noble families in Sweden. As a firstborn, he would inherit the title, land and personal property of his father, Count Carl Gustaf Bielke (1683–1754), who was an officer and ambassador for the Swedish crown. When Carl Gustaf was sent on a diplomatic mission to Paris, his family came along. His son apparently relished his education and life in France so much that he decided to remain after his father went back to Sweden. It was in those years that Nils was attracted by Roman Catholicism, an attraction that would eventually alter his life permanently. When he returned to Sweden, his father learned about his son's interest in Catholicism, and attempted to curtail it by arranging a wedding in 1727 with Baroness Hedvig Elisabeth Sack (1708–60). Carl Gustaf's hope to reinforce his son's ties to Sweden and the Protestant faith proved to be in vain. By 1728, Nils and Hedvig travelled back to France where they stayed for about a year, leading what Stefano Fogelberg Rota called a 'glamorous' life spending a considerable amount of their patrimony.[20] With growing financial restrictions, the couple decided to sell their property in Sweden and settle in France. Hedvig left for Sweden to take care of the financial transactions while Nils waited in Germany for her return. But with the help of an official decree of the Swedish National Council, the Bielke family managed to block the sale and prohibited Hedvig from leaving the country. Finding himself on his own, Nils started to travel throughout Europe. His first stop was Venice, where he lived for some time under the alias of 'Cavaliere di Sant'Isidoro'. It would take another two years until he finally converted to

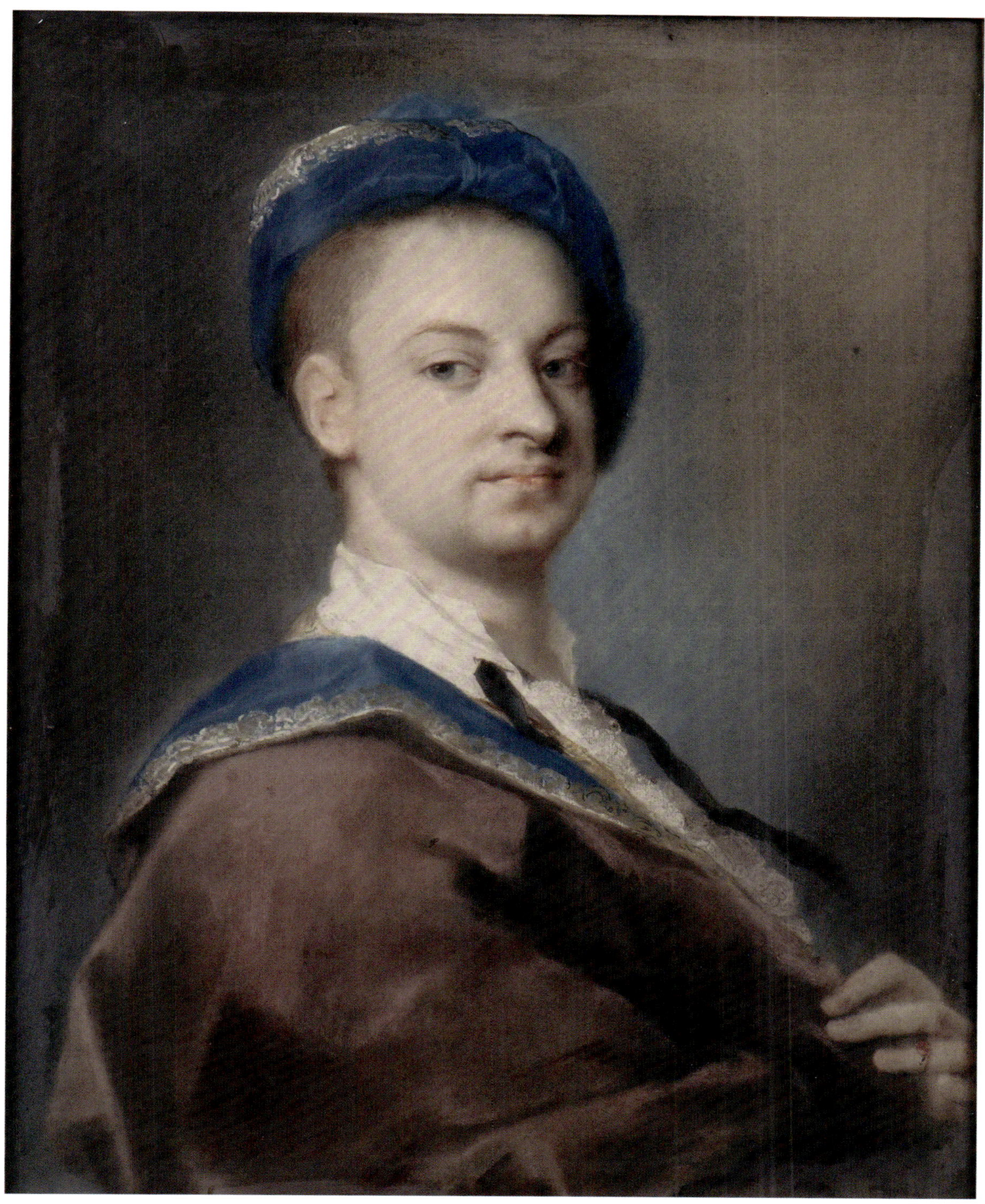

31 Rosalba Carriera, *Portrait of Count Nils Bielke*, 1729, pastel on paper, 58 × 46 cm (22 ¾ × 18 ⅛ in), National Museum, Stockholm

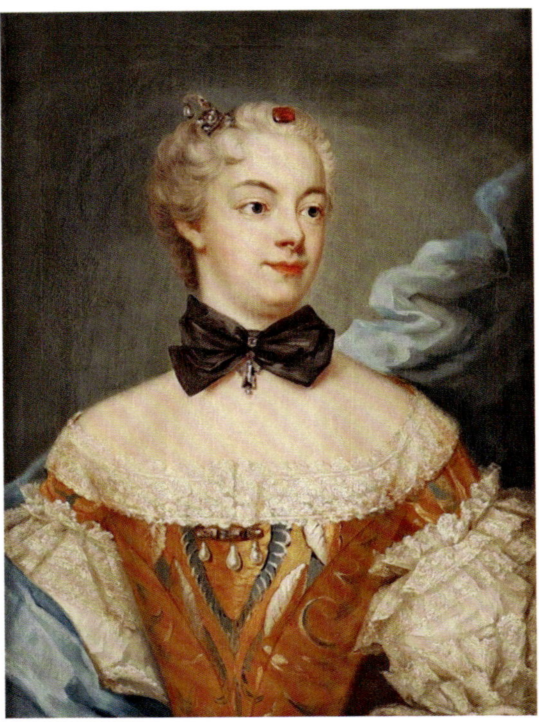

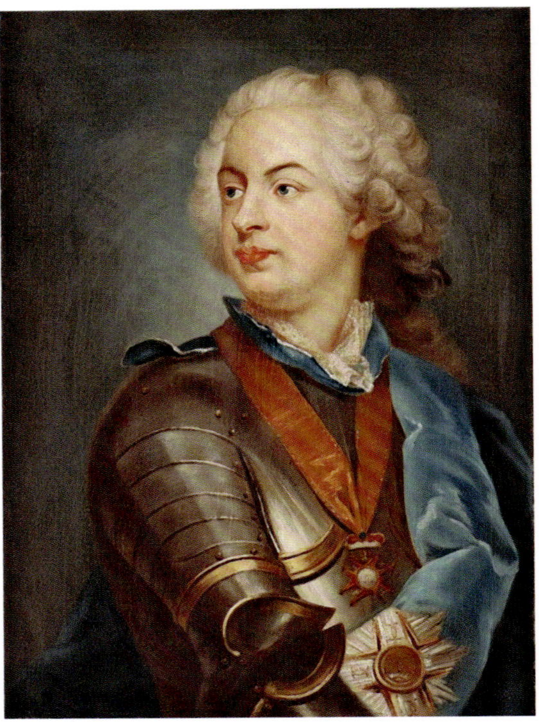

32 Johan Henrik Scheffel, *Portraits of Nils Bielke and Wife Hedvig née Sack*, 1727?, oil on canvas, each 69.5 × 51 cm (27¼ × 20⅛ in), private collection

Catholicism on 26 June 1731.[21] Bielke's conversion resulted in disinheritance under Swedish law, and increasing separation from his family. He was living in Rome then, and he was nominated '*Cameriere Segreto e Gentiluomo d'Onore*' (Secret Chamberlain and Gentleman of Honour) to Pope Clement XII (1652–1740). In 1737, the Pope even elevated him to the highly prestigious position of senator, which marked the peak of Bielke's Roman career.[22]

Eight years earlier, when he arrived in Venice in 1729, the break with his family was already manifest, and Bielke's religious convictions would eventually lead him to live a 'propagandistic mission for the sake of Swedish Catholicism'.[23] In light of these events, Bielke's decision not to wear a wig in Carriera's painting is fully understandable. When comparing Carriera's work with the double portrait of the Count and his wife Hedvig by the Swedish artist Johan Henrik Scheffel (1690–1781), the specific emphasis of the Venetian painting becomes blatantly obvious (fig.32).

In Scheffel's painting, Bielke is depicted in full armour, with the pendant of the Order of Fidelity of the Margraviate of Baden hanging prominently from a shiny orange sash. The same order is represented by a second, much bigger image at the edge of a blue velvet shawl loosely hanging over his left shoulder. Although the circumstances for the commission of Scheffel's painting are still unclear, the official tone of the double portrait suggests that it was done on the occasion of Bielke's wedding with Hedvig in 1727, as a typical official representative portrait of an illustrious noble couple. The same man appearing in Carriera's pastel shortly afterwards is radically different.

It seems plausible to argue that Bielke's personal situation was the underlying reason for his unconventional representation in Carriera's pastel. Aside from not wearing a wig, Bielke displays the long fingers of his left hand and a precious ring which signifies a departure from the majority of Carriera's male portraits, where there is no representation of the sitter's hands. Indeed, the position of the hand and the gesture are far from natural and look almost staged. Considering these aspects and the extraordinarily long fingers, I suspect that the work was painted upon a specific request and with a specific intention. While Bielke did not opt for a wig, powdered hair or shiny buttons to highlight his status, he did want to allude to his background, refinement, delicacy and grace with a hand featuring elegant long fingers and impeccable fingernails. The clearly visible ring on Bielke's fourth finger may have been a wedding band. The tradition of wearing a wedding ring precisely on that finger goes back to antiquity; the Egyptians believed there was a delicate nerve running from the fourth finger of the left hand directly to the heart. It is a thought also found in Henry Swinburne's *Treatise of Spousals*, published in 1686:

> By the received Opinion of Learned and Experienced in Ripping up, and anatomizing Mens Bodies, there is a Vein of Blood which passeth from thet Fourth Finger unto the Hearrt, called Vena amoris, loves Vein. And so the wearing of the Ring on that Finger signifieth, that the love should not be vain of fained, but that as they did give their Hand to each other, so likewise they should give their Hearts also, wherein that Vein is extended.[24]

It is interesting to observe that there are extremely few portraits in Italian art where a man who is not an ecclesiastic or a ruler ostentatiously presents a ring on his fourth finger. The existing examples, such as Raphael's (1483–1520) double portrait of Agnolo Doni and Maddalena Strozzi, were usually executed in the context of a wedding. If my assumption is correct, Bielke had himself depicted with his wedding ring as a visible symbol of the union with his wife, as if to counterbalance the fact that the couple had been forced to live apart from each other.

It is furthermore important to note that the portrait was commissioned for Nils's sister Eva (1707–78), as indicated by the inscription on the back: 'Painted in Venice by Mademoiselle Rosalba Anno 1729. This portrait of Monsieur Count Nils Bielke in his twenty-fourth year and given to his very dear sister Eva Bielke [...] from a brother who loved her tenderly until the last day of his life.'[25] This dedication unveils yet another layer of meaning to Carriera's pastel. Bielke's correspondence attests to his interest in ascertaining whether the news of his election to the prestigious position of senator in Rome would spread to Sweden, maybe even allowing him to re-establish ties with his own family, especially his father. Ultimately, he was hugely disappointed when none of his family members congratulated him and Stockholm society showed no noticeable reaction. In later years, Bielke attempted to be regularly updated regarding the situation in Sweden, and his continuous interest in his family seemed almost obsessive.[26] In light of the analysis above, Carriera's pastel, dedicated to Bielke's sister, encodes a fascinating message for his family. Even though they had managed to separate him from his closest relatives in Sweden and, what is more, from his wife, he, Count Bielke, would continue to live his rebellious, wigless life, openly in front of everybody. And the union between him and Hedvig, he stressed, would endure. Carriera thus created a captivating representation of religious and social rebellion mixed with passion and romantic love.

'ATTACKED' BY THE ENGLISH

Documented since the end of the seventeenth century, Carriera's relationship with her English clientele proved vital for her career. Young European noblemen were expected to travel to Italy which 'was at once the focus of the artistic, and more generally cultural, education and a peninsula of pleasure, whether the delights in question were, for example, those of opera or the more sensual joys for which Venice was noted'.[27] To stop in the lagoon city became a standard feature for the English aristocracy on the Grand Tour, and visiting the artist's studio on the Grand Canal soon became an obligatory part of their stays in Venice. Upper-class Englishmen either had their portraits painted directly by Carriera, or they ordered one of her paintings that they would later pick up or have sent from Venice. Carriera enjoyed much recognition in England, and her works were so highly admired that amateur pastellists began copying her portraits brought back from Italy. In deference to her fame, they came to be presented as the work of 'Roselby', often misspelling her name.[28] Considered overall, Carriera exercised a more direct influence on British contemporaries than any other Italian painter of the century.[29]

Her correspondence illustrates the extent of her fame in England. The first letter conserved in Carriera's correspondence written by a British client was penned on 1 November 1704 by the British diplomat Christian Cole, with whom the artist had built up a friendship over the preceding three years. On 14 July 1733, the antiquary and intellectual Martin Folkes (1690–1754), who had a wide circle of influential friends and who was one of Sir Isaac Newton's protégés, recorded in his travel journey:

> I went to Signa Rosalbas whose pictures in crayons have been with Justice esteemd the most excellent pieces of art of that sort. she is now better than 50, and was formerly as deservedly famous for her works in water colours; I was there extreamly well enter-taind with a great number of fine portraits some of my acquaintance very like.[30]

Other individuals who figured prominently among her English clients and acquaintances included Charles Sackville, 2nd Duke of Dorset and Earl of Middlesex (1711–69), and Owen McSwiney (1676–1754).[31] McSwiney was a failed impresario of the Queen's Theatre, who fled London in 1713 after having taken box office receipts and paper assets. He moved to Venice where he lived for 20 years, acting as a middleman between English art collectors and local artists such as Carriera and Canaletto.[32] With the help of Joseph Smith (*c.*1674–1770), whom Francis Haskell described as 'the most important link in Venice between the city and the outside world',[33] McSwiney managed to earn a decent living and gain some sort of acceptable reputation around town. Smith himself, who became British Consul in Venice in 1744, was another of Carriera's acquaintances.

Smith had arrived at the lagoon at the beginning of the eighteenth century, setting up office as a businessman and a merchant. During the 1720s, he began buying a large number of paintings, drawings and prints, which he then circulated in Europe, gaining him renown.[34] He was also interested in books, especially Greek and Latin manuscripts and various treatises on art, which he acquired for his legendary library. At the same time, he acted as the agent for Sebastiano Ricci and his nephew, Marco Ricci, Giovanni Battista Piazzetta and especially Canaletto. He collected not only paintings by outstanding artists of the sixteenth to the eighteenth centuries, but also coins, gems and medals, and was, generally speaking, Venice's most important facilitator of art acquisitions by British aristocrats visiting the city on their Grand Tour.[35] Carriera met Smith in 1721, and by 1723 she was working for him, making her one of the first painters he employed. Apart from acting as her agent in sending her pastels to clients in England, Smith also compiled a substantial collection of her paintings, 38 of which were eventually purchased by King George III (1738–1820). The list comprised the best-known group of her works that had remained in Venice.

Richard Boyle, the Earl of Burlington (1694–1753), who was known by the English as an 'Apollo of the Arts', bought 12 miniatures by Carriera. He also acquired a marble table and took these souvenirs and some porphyry vases back to England after his eight-day stay in Venice during his first Grand Tour in 1715.[36]

Sir Robert Walpole (1676–1745) and his sons Robert (1701–51), Edward (1706–84) and Horace (1717–97) were also in regular contact with Carriera about paintings they commissioned from her.[37] Carriera's portraits of the English politician and his sons were hung in the picture gallery in their salon in Downing Street, together with paintings by Peter Paul Rubens (1577–1640), Giovanni Francesco Romanelli (1610–62) and Jacob Jordaens (1593–1678).[38] Horace Walpole and Henry Fiennes Pelham-Clinton, the 9th Earl of Lincoln and the 2nd Duke of Newcastle under Lyne (1720–94), spent some time in Venice in 1741 with John Chute (1701–76), Francis Whithed (1719–51) and Joseph Spence, the author, scholar and travelling tutor to Lord Lincoln. Pelham-Clinton received his first influential positions at the courts of George II (1683–1760) and George III in his twenties and thirties before becoming Lord Lincoln in 1768, when he inherited the dukedom of Newcastle under Lyne. In 1744, he married his cousin Lady Catherine Pelham (1727–60). In the summer of 1741, he was on his Grand Tour in the company of his intimate friend Horace Walpole when they both sat for Carriera. The portraits in Nottingham University and Houghton Hall, Norfolk, show the two gentlemen turning towards each other while looking out at the beholder. Their position within the paintings, their similar clothes, and the fact that they chose to be depicted as pendant portraits serve as a sign of their friendship and a commemoration of their experience abroad. Carriera also made another portrait of Pelham-Clinton independently from Walpole (fig.33). Elegantly dressed in a blue cloak over a richly decorated vest with embroidered flowers and fancy buttons, he looks at the beholder with his blue eyes and a slightly melancholic expression on his face, his natural brown hair bound together at the back of his neck with a black ribbon.

Among her British clients was also Sir James Gray, 2nd Baronet (*c.*1708–73), who decided to travel to the Continent once he had achieved his MA in 1729 (fig.34). His first experiences abroad led him in the early 1730s to be a founder member of the Society of Dilettanti together with Spence, Gustavus Hamilton, 2nd Viscount Boyne (1710–46), Charles Sackville and others. The club members had all been to Italy on their Grand Tour and wanted to continue to build on their experiences. Their main idea was to encourage '*at home*, a taste for those objects which had contributed so much to their entertainment *abroad*'.[39] It was an attempt to exercise an influence in matters of public taste and fine arts in their country through studying antiquity. Eventually, the Society of Dilettanti turned out to be the prime mover in establishing the Royal Academy of Arts.

After his first trips abroad, Sir James came back to Italy where he started his diplomatic career in Venice in 1744 working as the secretary for Robert Darcy, 4th Earl of Holderness (1718–78). Darcy served as Minister Resident in Venice, and in 1746 Gray succeeded him, holding the position for six years. To date, we do not know when exactly Gray met Carriera for the first time, but he did eventually become one of her clients. The portrait she made for him shows a man in his mid-thirties wearing a powdered wig and dressed in elegant clothes in front of a neutral background, looking directly at the beholder with his brown eyes.

Carriera's clients also included members of the Stuart family and their supporters. Even Charles Edward Stuart (1720–88) himself was among her Jacobite clients. Known as the Young Pretender or as 'Bonnie Prince Charlie', Charles Edward had strong ties to Italy, having spent his childhood in Rome and

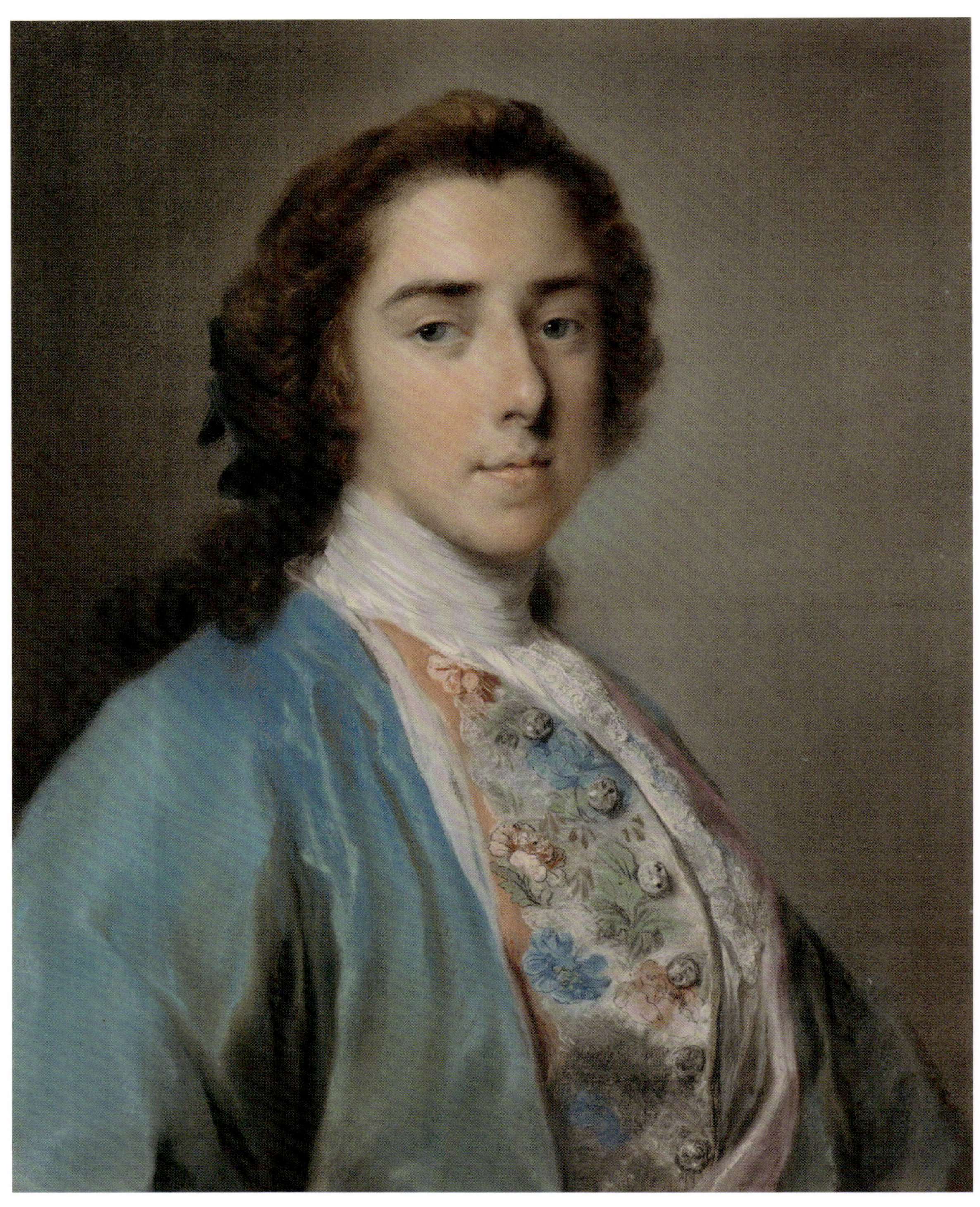

33 Rosalba Carriera, *Portrait of Henry Fiennes Pelham-Clinton, 9th Earl of Lincoln and 2nd Duke of Newcastle*, 1741, pastel on paper, 58.4 × 46.7 cm (23 × 18⅜ in), Yale Center for British Art, New Haven, CT

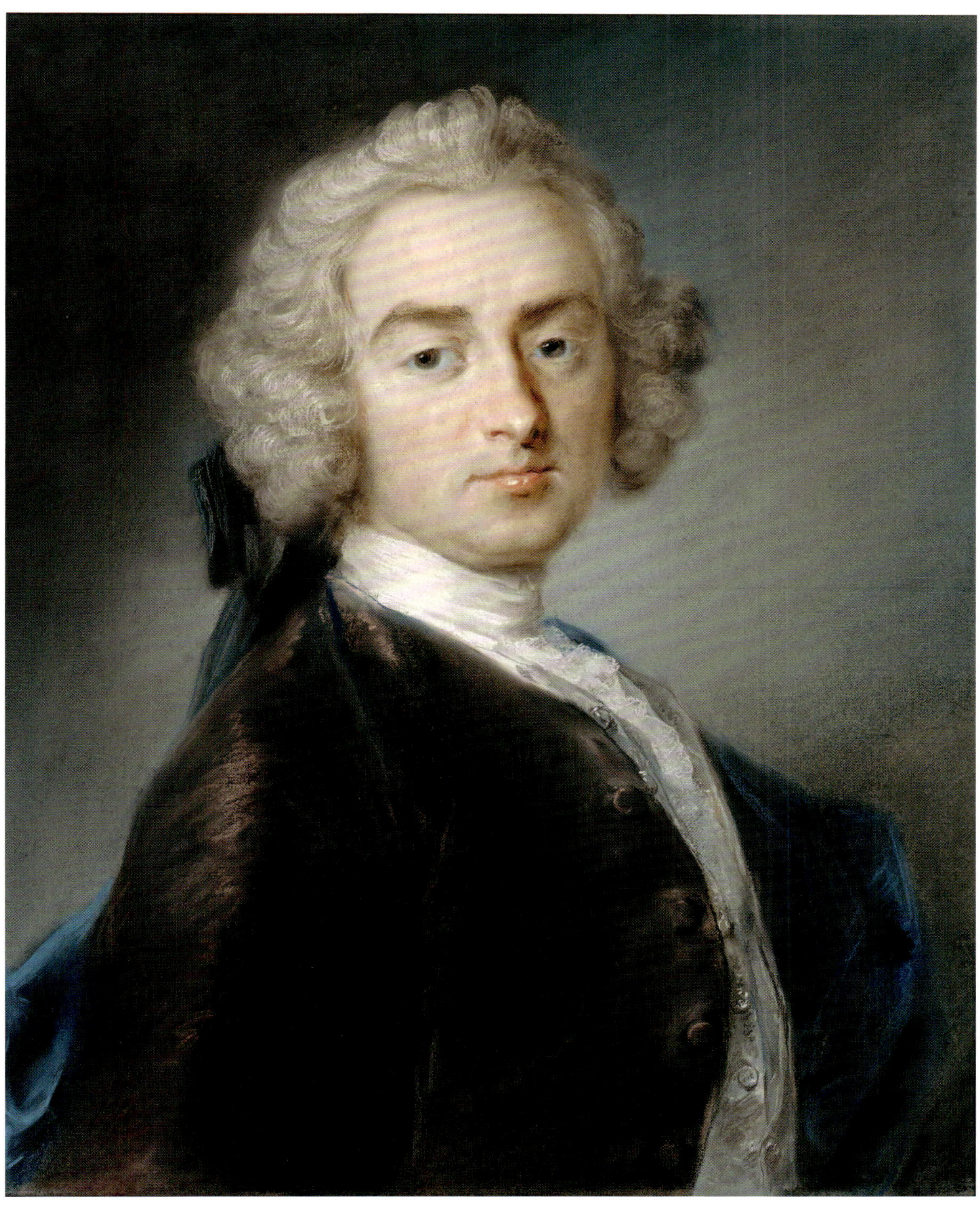

34 Rosalba Carriera, *Portrait of Sir James Gray*, 1744–5, pastel on paper, 56 × 45.8 cm (22 × 18 in), J. Paul Getty Museum, Los Angeles, CA

Bologna. In 1737, he travelled to Venice, a city that openly sustained the family's cause; it was on this occasion that he had his portrait done.[40]

Carriera's interest in music had led to her relationships with many Venetian musicians, while it also gave further impetus to her vivid cultural exchanges with the British aristocracy. Her portraits of her acquaintance Faustina Bordoni, for example, were often requested by British customers.[41] In addition, her clients Charles Lennox, 2nd Duke of Richmond (1701–50), and Lord Burlington were not only enthusiastic about her art but, as passionate patrons of music, they were also appreciative of Carriera's other capacities and interests.[42]

One of the last letters in the archive of the artist's correspondence was sent in May 1756 by a young peer who was one of the most famous female portrait painters in Britain in the eighteenth century: the Scotswoman Katherine Read. She had studied and copied Carriera's pastels which she had seen in Cardinal Alessandro Albani's (1692–1779) collection in Rome, and when travelling back from the Eternal City to London in 1753, she stopped in Venice to visit Carriera, who by that time had lost her sight.

With the continuing demand for the production of miniatures and pastels and her critical acclaim in England, Carriera eventually started using the English as an excuse for falling behind in her work. In 1721, she told her French colleague Nicolas Vleughels (1668–1737) that she had been 'attacked' by the English, leaving her hardly any time to finish other commissions.[43]

CARRIERA'S FIRST TRIP ABROAD: PARIS

Though Carriera managed to build a wide-ranging international network that included not only German rulers but also kings, aristocrats, artists and intellectuals in England, Denmark and Sweden, she opted to leave Venice only on a few occasions, and only for relatively short periods. Her trip to France proved to be the most important and influential one in her entire career, and it came together thanks to the French banker, art connoisseur and collector Pierre Crozat (1665–1740). Through his perseverance and regular letters, he ultimately convinced the artist to come to Paris and stay in his *hôtel*, or mansion, on rue de Richelieu, one of the city's most magnificent private residences where he regularly housed artists, friends and acquaintances. Travelling as a single woman at the time entailed not only the possibility of bodily harm, but also risks to one's reputation. Carriera was well aware of the hazards of touring without any protective male figure alongside her. She had no brother who could safeguard the trip and her father had recently died. The artist was surely encouraged when she learned that Crozat had resolved the issue, assuring her in a letter dated 22 December 1719 that their close friend Anton Maria Zanetti would accompany her to Paris.[44] In February 1720, after the Accademia Clementina in Bologna had voted to welcome the Venetian painter into its ranks,[45] the journey was confirmed, and in March 1720, Carriera departed, together with her mother and both of her sisters.

In the eighteenth century, Paris was Europe's second largest city, after London. The death of Louis XIV (1638–1715) in 1715 marked the beginning of the reign of Philippe II, Duke of Orléans, who served as regent of the French kingdom from 1715 to 1723. As he administered the state for the great-grandson of the deceased 'Sun King', Louis XV (1710–74), Philippe II transferred the court from Versailles back to Paris where he set up residence at the Palais Royal. Glittering opulence and pomp, amusements and entertainments were revived in Paris during his reign. The tone was set during this Regency period 'for an era of moral liberty – some might say debauchery – that was certainly urbane and sophisticated'.[46] The prosperity and relative stability of the period led to a gradual social change from a somewhat austere life under the autocratic Sun King to an easier, more comfortable existence. A resurgence of cultural activities, such as opera and theatre, became the hallmark of the Regency.

While staying at Crozat's mansion, the Carrieras regularly participated in their host's famous soirées of social, intellectual and cultural exchange. In his salon at his residence, Crozat entertained people who met for formal discussions of individual works of art, and who also enjoyed regularly scheduled concerts. After they arrived in April, Rosalba and her sisters were actively involved in these musical performances, playing for Crozat's guests. The painter herself played the harpsichord, and her violin performances drew enthusiastic applause from the audience.[47]

At the prestigious *hôtel* of her host, Carriera met most of the distinguished personalities of Paris, including the Regent himself and his wife Françoise-Marie de Bourbon, whose portrait as Amphitrite was discussed in Chapter 1, as well as other members of the court. Also frequently present was Madame Lavriellière, the Marchioness of Alincourt (1688–1742), a member of the reigning House of Bourbon who frequented the French court. During her stay in Paris, Carriera also met Antoine-Joseph Dézallier d'Argenville, who held the position of secretary and counsellor to King Louis XV and who studied art drawing and engraving. He would eventually become more interested in collecting than producing his own artworks,[48] and in the previously mentioned early biography of Carriera, *Abrégé de la vie des plus fameux peintres* (*Brief Lives of the Most Famous Painters*), he claimed to have met the artist at Crozat's mansion.

Carriera's clients and acquaintances in Paris included other famous collectors and critics, such as Pierre-Jean Mariette and Count Anne-Claude-Philippe de Caylus (1692–1765).[49] Mariette, who was also a friend of Caylus, was well known in Paris as a connoisseur, renowned art lover and publisher. In international circles he was considered an expert, serving as an art agent for Prince Eugene of Savoy (1663–1736) and organising the collections of both the Prince and Emperor Charles VI (1685–1740) from 1717 to 1718. It was, indeed, thanks to Mariette that the Habsburg court became increasingly involved with the Venetian art trade.[50] While he had compiled notes on collections, biographies and art criticism, and planned to write a dictionary of artists, he did not realise the project during his lifetime. It was not until 1851 that Charles Philippe de Chennevières-Pointel and Anatole de Montaiglon published his notes as a six-volume book, the *Abecedario*.[51]

Carriera's arrival in Paris coincided with a period of high enthusiasm for painting, which undoubtedly reflected the Duke of Orléans's personal tastes. An amateur artist himself, he was, in turn, copied by the nobility and bourgeoisie alike.[52] Carriera's work seems to have particularly suited the taste of the Regency court and appears to have filled a vacuum in French art during that period.[53] At the same time, the art collectors in the city who had started to concentrate on Italian sixteenth- and seventeenth-century paintings and drawings also discovered contemporary artists like Carriera.[54]

This period of her life is particularly well documented as a result of the diary she kept during her stay in Paris. Almost daily she briefly recorded events related to her business and her leisure activities, with her entries delineating how she occupied her time:[55] walks, invitations, dinners, visits to the theatre, opera or royal ballet, plus trips to the Louvre, Versailles or Montmorency, where Crozat had his country house, and visits to churches and scientific institutes were all part of her routine.[56] Each of these places increased her exposure to a variety of collections to admire and study, including the art of the Académie royale de peinture et de sculpture and the paintings owned by the Regent himself.[57] These expeditions also offered further opportunities for mingling with Parisian society.

In 1720, Regent Philip II commissioned Carriera to paint a portrait of King Louis XV, who was still a minor at the time. This commission undoubtedly marked the pinnacle of her experience in Paris and must have made her immediately even more interesting to the local high society. Carriera repeatedly wrote in her diary of her visits to the French court where she met with the ten-year-old

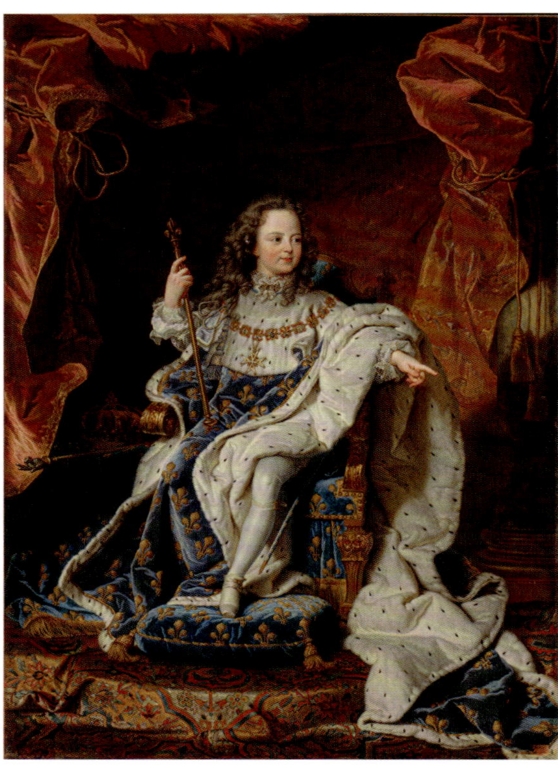

35 After Hyacinthe Rigaud, *Louis XV as a Child*, c.1716–24, oil on canvas, 195.6 × 141 cm (77 × 55½ in), The Metropolitan Museum of Art, New York

boy. More than a dozen diary entries record the various copies in different formats that Carriera was required to make of the King of France.[58]

Shortly after the death of Louis XIV, the court's foremost portrait painter Hyacinthe Rigaud (1659–1743) was commissioned to make a *portrait d'apparat* of Louis XV as a child in Versailles, here reproduced in an eighteenth-century replica (fig.35). Rigaud portrayed the young King of France in full size, seated on a throne with a brown full-bottomed wig on his head and clad in an exceedingly voluminous, shiny blue velvet mantle strewn with fleurs-de-lis and lined with ermine that seems to flow out of the painting towards the spectator. Next to the throne is the crown and the sceptre with the so-called 'Hand of Justice', while in his right hand he presents the royal sceptre terminating in a fleur-de-lis. A pendant exactly in the centre of the painting hangs from a heavy golden chain, on which shines the cross of the Order of the Saint Esprit. With a great majestic gesture, Louis turns and points towards his left. The impressive scene is set off by heavy, red drapery hanging behind the throne. It is not only the different technique (oil on canvas instead of pastel on paper) and the different size (195.6 × 141 cm or 77 × 55½ inches against 50.5 × 38.5 cm or 19⅞ × 15⅛ inches) that make this painting so different from Carriera's intimate close-up of the boy. It is Rigaud's monumentality and the stress on representation, status and courtly milieu that are emphasised by numerous attributes, also his regalia and all of the other prerequisites pertaining to the Baroque tradition.

Carriera's version of this king, which is to be seen today in Dresden, illustrates beautifully, as Angelo Walther has shown, the drastic change in the eighteenth century from the traditional Baroque ruler's portrait to the more restricted and intimate depictions in pastel by our female Venetian painter (fig.36).[59] In this version, the Dauphin is shown bust-length. He is turned towards his left but he looks straight at the spectator confidently, with a hint of a smile and a friendly countenance. The hair of his brown, full-bottomed wig falls loosely over his shoulders and his majestic jacket.[60] Carriera also included attributes of courtly representation, such as the Order of the Holy Ghost pinned resplendently to his jacket near the *cordon bleu* on his chest, identifying him as the sovereign of France.[61] The white royal ermine cloak appears like a footnote at the edge of the painting, in the bottom right corner. The emphasis is on the confident, calm expression of a self-assured and optimistic future ruler.

As Carriera moved in the most elite social and intellectual circles, her acquaintances visited her at Crozat's residence on the rue de Richelieu or invited her to their own homes. As the level of

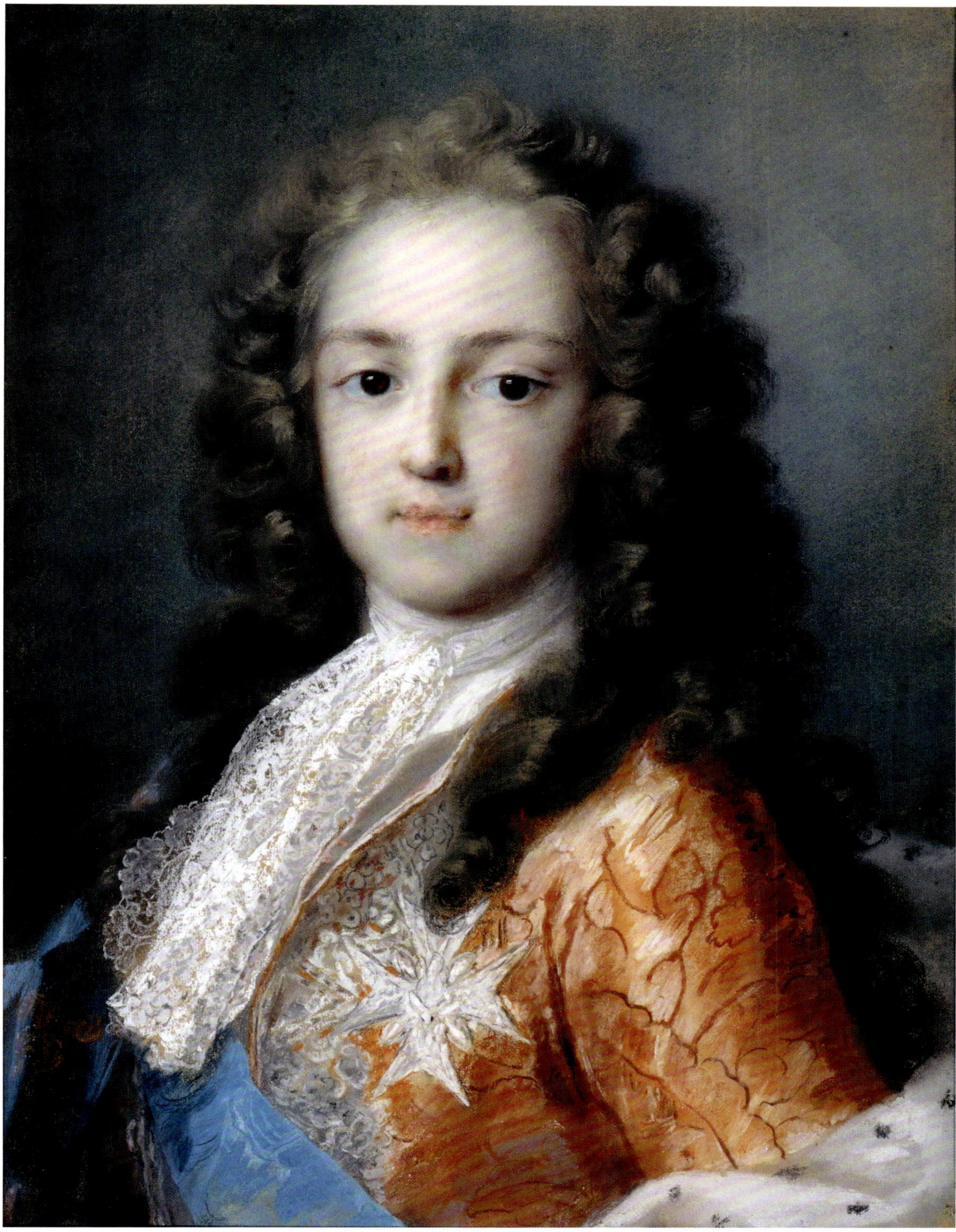

36 Rosalba Carriera, *Portrait of Louis XV*, 1720, pastel on paper, 50.5 × 38.5 cm (19 ⅞ × 15 ⅛ in), Staatliche Kunstsammlungen, Gemäldegalerie Alte Meister, Dresden

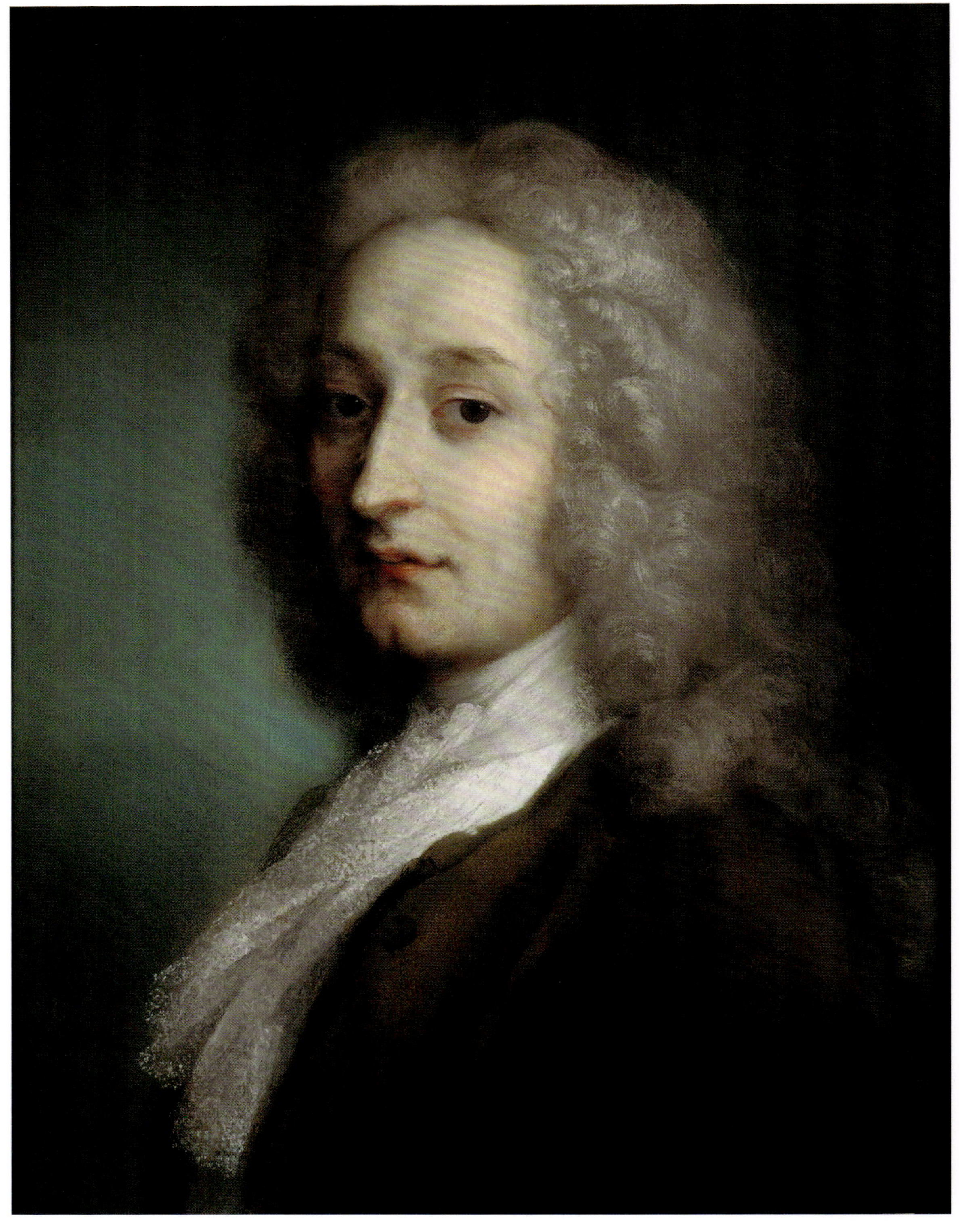

37 Rosalba Carriera, *Portrait of Antoine Watteau*, 1721, pastel on paper, 55 × 43 cm (21 ⅝ × 16 ⅞ in), Musei Civici di Treviso – Museo di Santa Caterina

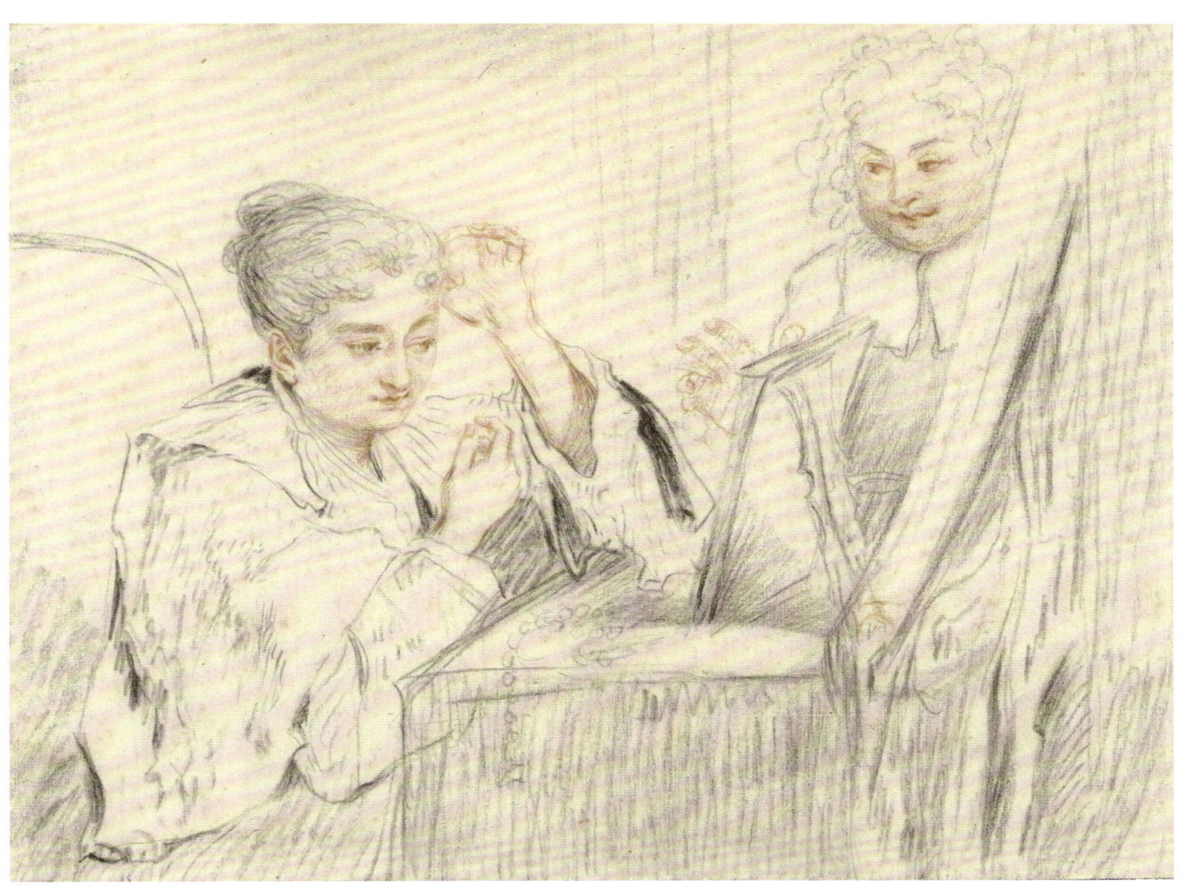

38 Jean-Antoine Watteau (?), *Rosalba Carriera doing Her Hair*, 1721, chalk on paper, 23.1 × 30.2 cm (9 ⅛ × 21 ⅜ in), Rijksprentenkabinet, Rijksmuseum, Amsterdam

interest in the exceptional painter and her art grew, new acquaintances showered her with commissions. Before long, she had become a luminary in the city; an entry in her diary on 21 February 1721 indicates that members of the aristocracy residing in Paris visited her as early as 6 am to pose for their portraits, for which they offered unusually high prices.[62] Specific examples will be offered later in the book. According to her personal notes, she executed approximately 50 of these likenesses during her stay in France.[63] Eventually, the rhythm accelerated to the point that she became overwhelmed. Her notes increasingly indicate that she had to postpone commissions, that she could not keep up with the schedule and that the workload was simply too much. Her sister, Angela, was not only worried but she ultimately labelled her a workaholic: 'You have resumed your usual practice of being constantly busy, even, at times, with things of no consequence, you know well that this has been your fate, which has at this point become a necessity.'[64]

The stay in the city on the Seine afforded Carriera the privileged circumstance of making acquaintance with various prominent artists who were of particular interest to her. Among these, she met Nicolas de Largillière (1656–1746), Jean-François de Troy (1679–1752) and Hyacinthe Rigaud,[65] and pastel artists such as Jean Baptiste Massé (1687–1767) and Joseph Vivien (1657–1734).[66] Nicolaus Vleughels was one of the French painters she already knew. In one of the letters he sent to Venice, dated 21 September 1719, he informed her that many of his acquaintances were quite envious of the fact that he had already seen her, had been introduced to her, and had even been invited to her home. One such acquaintance, he said, was a man of whom she had probably already heard, and who was anxious to meet her in person. As it was impossible for him to do so, this gentleman wished at least to have a miniature painted by Carriera to call his own.[67] The man in question was Jean-Antoine Watteau (1684–1721), a close friend of Vleughels (fig.37). Carriera actually did end up meeting him during a social engagement, and later she visited him many times. It seems the encounter with Watteau can be singled out as the most significant among her meetings with other artists, for she appears to have been captivated by him. On 11 February 1721, she began work on a portrait of this esteemed colleague and friend, but, shortly afterwards, at less than 37 years of age, he died of consumption.

The portrait of Watteau offers an eloquent example of Carriera's emphasis on intimate aspects, rather than official position or profession. The observer is immediately struck by the pure and genuine naturalness of Watteau's image.[68] Now housed in Treviso, this pastel is dominated by Watteau's expression, with Carriera skilfully evidencing his general state of health: the artist's illness is clearly apparent. Wearing a brown jacket and a white wig, he gazes at the observer with a sad look and tired, glassy eyes. Considering the commonplace clothes and wig, his face and his glance are the only defining characteristic of this work. In omitting the typical attributes of a painter and providing no indication as to the origin of his fame, Carriera highlighted his personal situation and the friendship they shared rather than the artistic interest and professional link that bound them together. A sketch, now in the Rijksprentenkabinet in Amsterdam, that has been attributed to Watteau (fig.38), represents a precious document of one of the encounters between the two artists.

Yet other prominent, cultivated Parisians must be mentioned: Antoine Coypel (1661–1722) and his son Charles-Antoine Coypel (1694–1752). Antoine Coypel was not only one of the most acclaimed artists at the French court with the official title *Premier peintre du Roy* (First Painter to the King), but he also served as the director of the Académie royale de peinture et de sculpture from 1714 and was a true admirer of Carriera's art. His own work shows that he was greatly influenced by her.[69]

THE ACADÉMIE ROYALE DE PEINTURE ET DE SCULPTURE MAKES AN EXCEPTION

In Coypel, the artist found a true admirer and untiring patron. The Parisian worked with Carriera's influential and esteemed friend Pierre-Jean Mariette to gain Carriera admittance to the internationally renowned French Académie royale de peinture et de sculpture. On 26 October 1720, Carriera was admitted, the first and only female foreign artist to ever receive this honour.[70] According to the *procès-verbaux* (minutes) of that day, Carriera brought the pastel portrait of Louis XV to the assembly as part of her official request for the admission procedure, and the Académie made her a member, justifying the decision as follows: '[...] recognizing in her obvious merit that is also known abroad and especially in Rome, Florence, and Bologna, where she had been admitted into the respective academies, [the Académie] has received the above-mentioned Demoiselle Carriera as an academician'.[71]

Her admission is even more astonishing considering the institution admitted more than 459 artists in its history (that is, between 1648 and 1793), of which only a mere 15 were women.[72] Except for Margareta Haverman (1693–after 1739), who was admitted in 1722 only to be expelled the year after, no other female artist followed Carriera to enter the ranks of the Académie for another 34 years, when Marie-Thérèse Reboul (1728–1805) was accepted in 1754.[73] Moreover, just 16 years earlier, on 25 September 1706, the official members had voted against accepting any women whatsoever, and whenever they broke this edict, as in Carriera's case, they were eager to emphasise that the acceptance of a particular woman was not meant to set a precedent. The crucial phrase concerning these women was also applied in the case of Carriera: '*sans néantmoins* [*sic*] *tirer à consequence*' ('however, without implying [future] consequences').[74] And once again, as in the case of Carriera's admittance to the Accademia di San Luca in Rome, the minutes of the first assembly session dated 9 November 1720 stressed that she had been received 'with the distinction due to her merit'.[75] The same day, according to normal practice, the artist agreed to present a reception piece.

The importance of this event and of Carriera's stay in Paris in general should not be underestimated as 'this visit marks the peak of Venetian influence abroad and the last time that contemporary Italian art was to make a serious impact on France'.[76] 'Not since Bernini had an Italian artist had such a reception as greeted Carriera in Paris.'[77] Despite the overwhelming success of the trip, Carriera, who was now called 'Queen of Pastel', and her family embarked on their homeward journey in March 1721.

Back in Venice, the artist once again had difficulties in finishing and sending the requested *morceau de réception* within a reasonable amount of time. In ordinary circumstances, these paintings both determined and embodied an artist's standing as an academician. They gained their authority to signify the artist's acceptance by and position within the Académie from the Académie itself. The obligation towards the institution that had bestowed Carriera with the highest honour possible for an artist at that time was therefore not to be neglected. Nevertheless, the painter took her time.

Again, she tried to explain the delay, asking for patience and comprehension. But unlike the earlier deferral in 1705, Carriera did not give the impression of someone who felt intimidated by the task or by the judgement of her colleagues; the wording and the excuses in her correspondence, instead, suggest that she was unsure about the subject matter or that she simply did not feel like thinking about it. A more logical explanation is that she may have wanted to continue accepting new commissions, putting her clients before her promise to the Académie; and once again she used the English and the pressure they exerted as an excuse. With it known that English visitors were regularly streaming into Venice, and Carriera's awareness of her valued reputation with numerous clients from that country, the artist apparently used the English more than once as a handy argument to 'explain' the delay.

It was not until October 1721, one year after she had become an official member of the Académie, that the artist wrote to Antoine Coypel in Paris to indicate she was sending the long-awaited pastel. The first part of the missive is what Kathleen Nicholson called 'an exercise in diplomacy and *politesse*'. Carriera knew that Coypel had lost his wife six months earlier. She had to find an elegant way to show him her empathy while trying to ensure his support even if her reception piece had failed to arrive nearly a year after she had been officially accepted. '"How could [the pastel] dare present itself without your patronage?" she asked, averring that it was Coypel who had persuaded his fellow academicians to accept her in the first place.'[78]

Carriera also included a description of the pastel she intended to send:

> I have attempted to make a young girl, knowing that one pardons the flaws of youth. She represents as well a nymph in Apollo's service who is about to present to the Academy of Painting, on his behalf, a laurel crown, judging it [the Academy] the only one worthy to wear it, and to preside over all others. She is moreover determined to stay in this city, preferring the lowest position in this very illustrious Academy to the heights of Parnassus. It is therefore up to you, I say again, to secure this advantage for her, so that I may enjoy your good graces and those of the illustrious Academicians, to whom you will be good enough to present my compliments.[79]

But the French still had to wait; the pastel was to arrive in Paris only in February of the following year.

Analysing the description of her pastel suggests another clever tactical move. At first sight, the letter with the canonical and rhetorical self-effacing hints towards the artist's modesty could be read as an attempt to make the academicians believe that her reception piece was finished, but her astute strategy of presenting a written description of her own work went way beyond trying to prevent the members of the Académie from becoming impatient. In giving a detailed *ekphrasis*, the artist inserted herself into the history of the numerous scholars, historians and art critics who have studied or used the dichotomy between the visual and the verbal. In her short piece of descriptive writing, Carriera demonstrated that she could paint with words just as well as with pastels, thereby becoming a participant in the age-old *paragone* debate that revolved around the question of which art form was superior: painting, sculpture, poetry or music? By writing that letter, the artist acted out what was a generally accepted idea: poetry/verbal description produces the usual formal justification for the idea of a painting.[80] On the other hand, Carriera deftly highlighted the reciprocal enrichment of the sister arts. More importantly, though, she simultaneously represented both positions in her own person – the 'poet' and the 'painter', the male power of an intellectual author and the capacities of a visual artist all in one – despite being a woman. It was a shrewd, well-calculated move to raise herself to the highest level of artistic production and the maximum of artistic self-governance.

Likewise, it almost seems as if she had planned first to describe the painting in textual form and later surprise the academicians with a colourful, witty pastel that would certainly surpass their mental images of it and far exceed their expectations. She would aptly demonstrate the superiority of painting. At the same time, by explaining the story of her pastel she emphasised once more – and even more effectively than she had done upon her admission to the Roman Accademia some 15 years earlier – that she was a worthy history painter with content based on stories drawn from canonical texts of mythology.[81]

The pastel that the artist eventually sent to Paris (fig.39) shows the nymph as one of her typical, idealised half-figures whose body turns towards one side and whose head is pivoting in the opposite direction. Unlike most of Carriera's figures, the nymph does not enter into direct eye contact with the observer, but instead looks directly towards

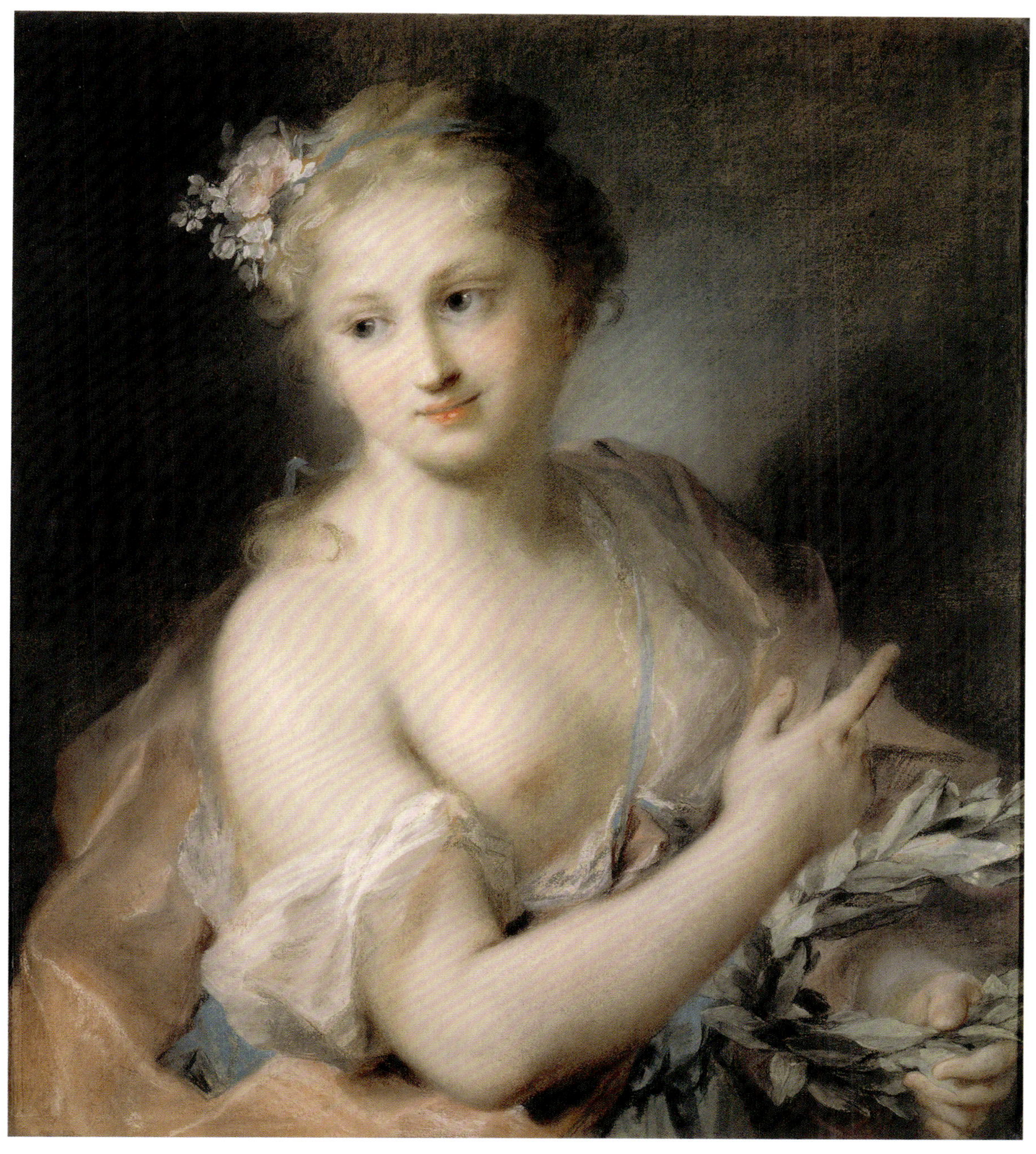

39 Rosalba Carriera, *Nymph from Apollo's Retinue*, 1721, pastel on paper, 61.5 × 54.5 cm (24 ¼ × 21 ½ in), Cabinet des dessins, Louvre, Paris

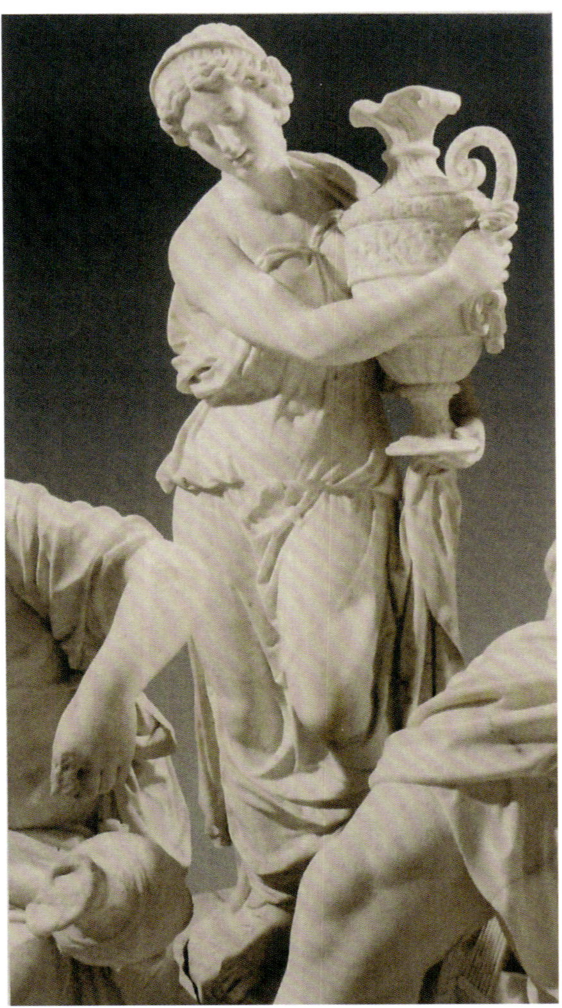

40 Detail of François Girardon and Thomas Regnaudin, *Apollo Served by the Nymphs*, 1666–74, marble, Apollo Grotto, Versailles

the lower left at someone or something. In her left hand, she holds the laurel crown that Carriera had mentioned in her letter as a gift from Apollo for the Académie, and with her right hand, she indicates a place somewhere further up, behind her. The young blonde nymph has her right breast unveiled, while her eyes and the slightly tilted head create a diagonal parallel to her right arm bent in front of her body.[82] Comparing the pastel with Carriera's letter, the nymph presumably points towards the peak of Mount Parnassus while she looks with a smile towards the Académie, the place that opens the road to the mountains that was sacred to Apollo. It is also the source of light that illuminates the scene, brightens the future and is beautifully reflected in her eyes. The typically simple background is divided into two parts. The back of the nymph is dark, almost completely black as if she has turned her back to a dull and difficult past. At the same time, the division creates a dramatic and high-contrast composition accentuating the contours of the nymph and emphasising her marble-like, smooth white flesh. The most highly illuminated spot in the pastel is next to her face on the other side, directly above her shoulder. The institution that the nymph is addressing with her glance and her smile is quite literally the place of illumination, not only for her but for the entire space in front of her that extends up to Mount Parnassus. Her allusion to the Académie is most likely the reason why Carriera departed from her usual pattern of having her figures looking directly at the spectator. One can well imagine that the academicians would have felt pleased and flattered by this celebratory painting once they saw and understood its meaning.

Starting in the 1690s, the majority of reception pieces to the Académie by Carriera's predecessors were based on mythological subject matters. The Venetian painter used the same source of inspiration, but what is striking about her pastel is the invention of a rather unusual iconography: a nymph of Apollo's retinue. What could have been her inspiration for this important work? The letter mentions Apollo, the sun god, even if he is not represented, who had been paramount to state iconography under the 'Sun King' Louis XIV. Extant documentation proves that wherever Carriera went, she tried to see as many paintings, as many artworks and as many collections as possible. Given the symbolic significance of the sun god during the reign of Louis XIV, Carriera would have had the opportunity to see a fair number of artworks featuring Apollo and his entourage. More specifically, while strolling through the gardens in Versailles, Carriera certainly saw the group of marbles by François Girardon (1628–1715), the official sculptor of Louis XIV, and Thomas Regnaudin (1622–1706) depicting *Apollo Served by the Nymphs* (1666–74). It was one of the prominent attractions of Versailles and the central realisation of the sun motif from an iconographic perspective. It seems reasonable to venture that Carriera found inspiration from this spectacular sculptural arrangement for her own invention. The standing nymph carrying a vase and looking over her right shoulder and identified as Drax may have been a creative stimulus. It shows striking similarities to Carriera's nymph, not only as far as the pose of her body is concerned, but especially regarding the position of both of her hands (fig.40).[83]

The pastel can be distinguished from most of Carriera's other works in that it includes both hands, one of which is extended in a conspicuous gesture. One of the best-known paintings to show a similar right-hand index finger crossing over the body and pointing to the left is Leonardo da Vinci's (1452–1519) *Saint John the Baptist* in the Louvre (fig.41). The pose, the slightly tilted head, the position of the arms, and the luminous face are all aspects that appear in Carriera's pastel. It does not seem far-fetched to assume that Carriera drew inspiration from Leonardo's work, especially as she must have seen it on her visits to the various galleries in Paris. More interestingly, it would appear that she reinterpreted the Renaissance artist's painting on a conceptual level as well: Leonardo showed the last of the prophets, standing on the threshold between the Old and the New Testament. With a smile on his face, the saint indicates Christ's earthly coming, and by extension, the way to salvation. Carriera translated the image into the figure of a smiling female prophetess, standing between the Académie and Mount Parnassus, indicating the Apollonian temple as the location for the apotheosis of the arts. John follows Christ and presents the cross on which the Son of God would sacrifice himself, thus offering Christians the possibility of gaining eternal life; Carriera's equivalent is the nymph who follows Apollo, symbolised by the laurel crown, who leads to Mount Parnassus where eternal fame is offered to those who reach its peak. If John's gesture can be interpreted as an allusion to Christ incarnate, human and divine, then the nymph's raised index finger signifies the human and divine status of the artist. Interestingly, neither Christ nor Apollo is physically present; they both appear only in symbolic form. By omitting the depiction of the sun god, Carriera turned her allegory into a purely feminine scene. The presence of the male god is only given through his symbol of the laurel crown. The prominent role of the traditional male protagonist, the god of the Muses, is called into question. His dominant position is left to a female guide, a 'prophetess' of the arts, which reflects Carriera's extraordinary admittance to the Académie – the only foreign female painter within the prestigious institution.

To conclude, by combining Leonardo with Girardon/Regnaudin, Carriera blended her Italian roots with what she could learn from her host country. She merged the undisputed brilliance of one of the most important Italian Renaissance artists with the highest expression of French Baroque art, and this fusion could easily be deciphered as a flattering gesture towards the excellence of the French royal collection that owned and exhibited both artworks. Drawing on a sculpture and not a French painting was a noteworthy decision and a deliberate statement within the ongoing *paragone* debate that surrounded this pastel from the very beginning. In this case, Carriera found a particularly compelling way to insert herself into the dispute. Writing about her pastel before sending it to the Académie

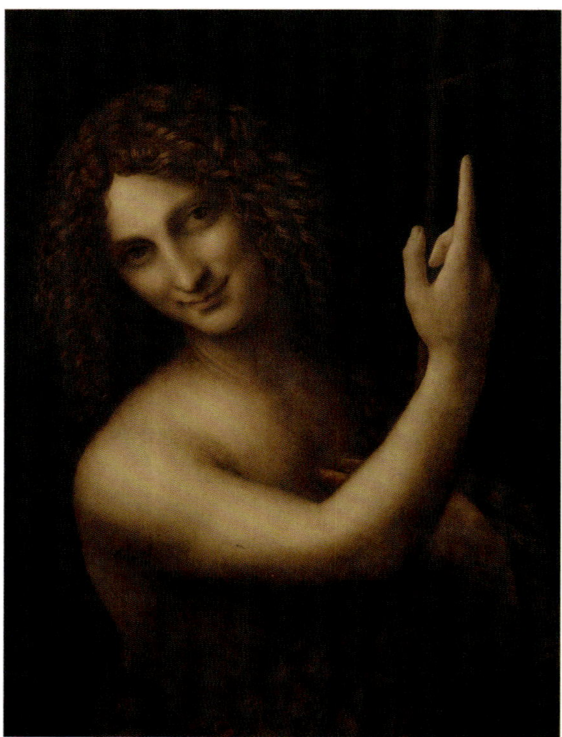

41 Leonardo da Vinci, *Saint John the Baptist*, 1508–19, oil on wood, 69 × 57 cm (27¼ × 22¾ in), Louvre, Paris

proved, as indicated, an astute approach to compare literature with painting. In addition, by almost brazenly copying Leonardo's figure while referencing Girardon/Regnaudin in a more subdued manner, Carriera literally emulated Leonardo's partiality for painting over sculpture, with the former thus being the supreme art form. Maybe with a winking eye, she issued a muted commentary on the status of French painting at the beginning of the eighteenth century. Was there anything worth being quoted among her contemporaries in Paris when she was the one who was copied and followed in France? It was Carriera who influenced French painters more than the other way round.[84]

With this intriguing reception piece, she finally managed to present herself officially as an intelligent, erudite and witty painter whose art is based on theoretical discourses, clever compositions, a reconsideration of precedents with reason, and the rationality which was gendered masculine, rather than on pure observation and emotion, gendered feminine.[85] At the same time, she flattered her hosts and publicised herself as an intellectual, professional and worthy member of the Académie. Much more than in her reception piece for Rome, Carriera was now well aware and proud of her personal and professional accomplishments and did not hesitate to show it.

And the city and its art lovers retained pleasant memories of her. As a result of the delivery of the reception piece, Carriera once again received official recognition in France: in 1722, the *Mercure de France* published an article titled 'Eloge de Rosalba Carriera' ('In Praise of Rosalba Carriera') in memory of her visit and her successes. The article, which highlighted her outstanding skills as a pastel painter, stated that her art and the preferred technique compared positively with oil painting, the biggest compliment she could have received:

> [The pastel] summarizes all the parts of painting, as much for the *coloris* as for the refinement of the details. [...] There is common agreement that this *demoiselle* has found a way to master this medium like no other before her. For this reason, even the most skilful declare that this type of pastel, with the power and veracity of the colours, boasts a certain freshness and light transparency which exceeds even that of oil paintings.[86]

CARRIERA AND THE ESTE PRINCESSES

Not long after her successful trip to France, near the end of June 1723, Carriera left Venice again to travel with her mother and Giovanna to Modena where, from July to November, she stayed at the court of

Rinaldo III d'Este (1655–1737), who had asked her to paint his daughters' portraits. The Duke had met the artist before: sometime between 1710 and 1720, Rinaldo d'Este himself had posed for Carriera. Two years before she arrived in Modena, while she was still in Paris, Giovanni Marquis Rangoni, the French Envoy Extraordinary and Resident Minister of the Modenese court, had advised the Duke to hire the singular female artist whose 'paintbrush would be able to raise the curiosity of the most distinguished people'.[87]

During her stay in Modena, Carriera remained at the court of the Este family to complete the requested pastel portraits of Benedetta Maria Ernestina (1697–1777), Anna Amalia Giuseppa (1699–1778) and Enrichetta Anna Sofia (1702–77). A nun, named Suor Maria Beatrice Davia, seems to have played the role of secretary and adviser to the Princesses, and functioned as an intermediary figure between the three young ladies and Carriera. Rinaldo's intention for these portraits was to send them to various European courts in the hope of finding suitable husbands for his daughters. One of the recipients was Duchess Louise Françoise de Bourbon (1673–1743), whose son Louis Henri de Bourbon (1692–1740) was expected to marry Enrichetta Anna Sofia, the youngest Princess.[88] Ultimately, these marriage plans proved unsuccessful and, in 1727, Enrichetta became the wife of the Duke of Parma, Antonio Farnese (1679–1731).

In this version of the official court portrait of Enrichetta (fig.42), the artist depicted her wearing a lavish white silk dress with light pink hues. One can also glimpse glittering crystals on a brooch or chain. An ermine cloak hangs loosely over her shoulders, leaving no doubt as to her noble origins. She looks directly at the observer with her warm brown eyes. A very slight hint of a smile plays on her lips, while her calm face discloses no specifics of her personality, thereby affirming the official nature of the painting.

Even though Giovanna and her mother kept Carriera company in Modena, the artist did not particularly enjoy her stay as she found the court offered little in terms of amusement. Completing copy after copy of the portraits, as demanded of her, was a process she found neither appealing nor varied; in addition, it appears that the princesses and the Duke became a burden to her, as can be gathered from a letter to her sister Angela in October in which she wrote that she would have left after two months had it been possible.[89] She was, however, able to find a sort of diversion in visits to the Duke's exquisite art collection.

Following this commission, Carriera remained almost exclusively in Venice for some years. One exception was a trip in the autumn of 1728, when her diary comes to an end: Carriera travelled to Gorizia in Friaul, where she attended the wedding festivities of Emperor Charles VI and his bride Elisabeth Christine von Braunschweig-Wolfenbüttel (1691–1750) and where she was introduced to the imperial couple.

CARRIERA AT THE COURT IN VIENNA

In May 1730, Carriera embarked on her last trip abroad, travelling to Vienna, where she visited and worked at the court of Charles VI. Life in Vienna at this time must have been fascinating and exhilarating for Carriera and her sisters. Under Charles VI, perhaps the most extravagant of the Habsburg princes, court life had reached an unprecedented level of elaborate luxury.[90] Although known for being withdrawn and reserved, the Emperor nonetheless showed a pronounced predilection for pomp and ceremony.[91] This preference is evident when comparing the number of attendants hired for Charles VI with those who worked in the court of Rudolf II (1552–1612). In Prague, Rudolf had an entourage of 531 courtiers, whereas, in Vienna, Charles VI employed an astounding 2,175 courtly personnel.[92] While assuring the majestic pageantry of the court, Charles VI exhibited a passion for the arts. His love for architecture resulted in a virtual building boom, with various eminent large-scale projects supervised by the court's architect, Johann Bernhard

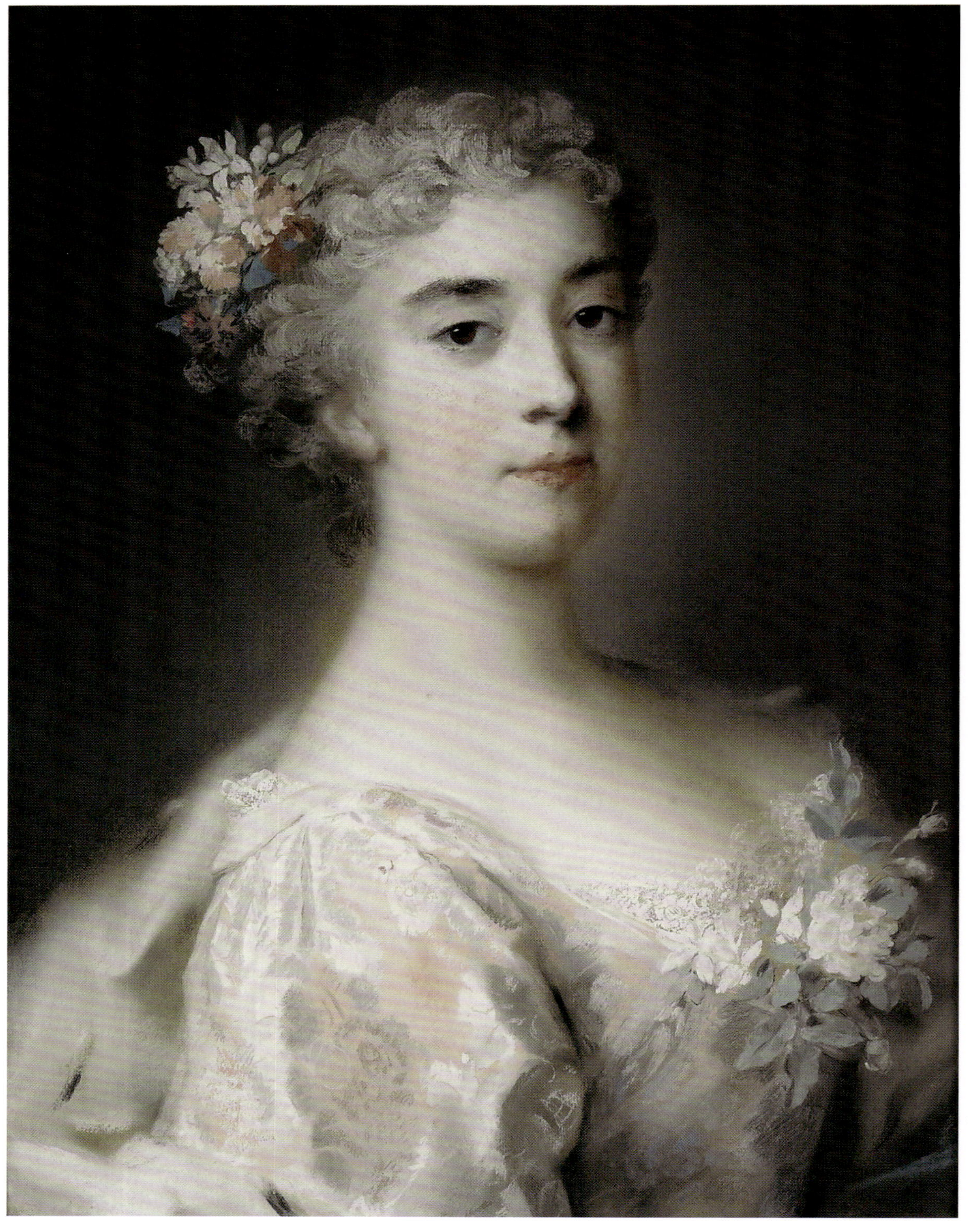

42 Rosalba Carriera, *Portrait of Enrichetta Anna Sofia d'Este*, 1723, pastel on paper, 55 × 42 cm (21 5/8 × 16 1/2 in), Gallerie degli Uffizi, Florence

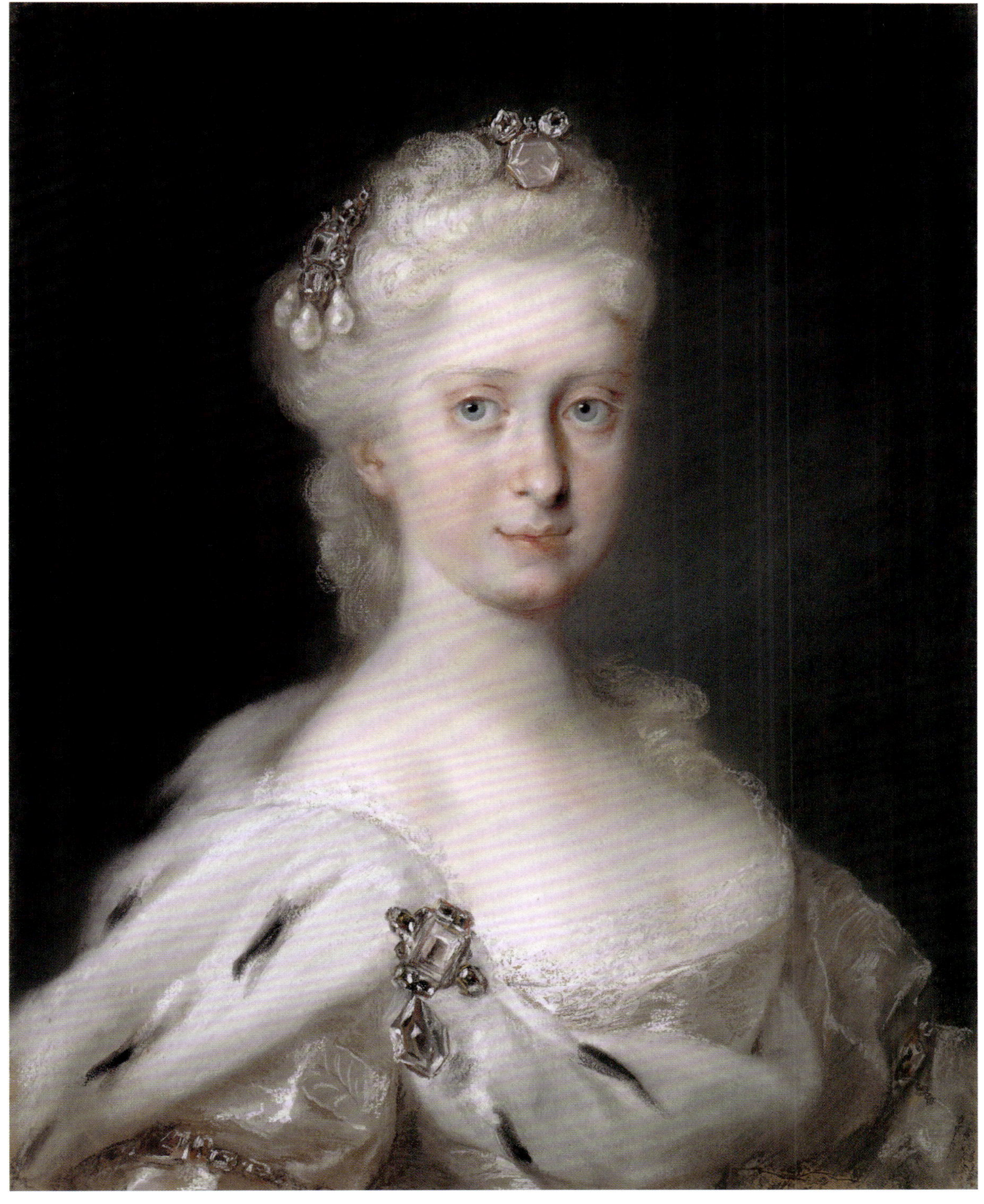

43 Rosalba Carriera, *Portrait of Maria Josepha, Wife of August III of Poland*, 1730?, pastel on paper, 53.5 × 42.5 cm (21 × 16 ¾ in), Staatliche Kunstsammlungen, Gemäldegalerie Alte Meister, Dresden

Fischer von Erlach (1656–1723), who had also worked for Charles's brother Joseph I. The Carriera sisters must have been dazzled by the ongoing construction of perhaps his most famous building, the Schönbrunn Palace, which became the imperial summer residence outside Vienna. The architect's son, Joseph Emanuel Fischer von Erlach (1693–1742), continued some of his father's building projects in the city, in particular the magnificent Karlskirche (St Charles Church). The Carriera sisters and especially Giovanna, who loved to read and write, must have also been thrilled by the brilliant court library, which had been finished just four years before their arrival. It was open to the public and had become a landmark in celebrating the Emperor's patronage of Vienna's intellectual life.

Charles VI was fluent in several languages and was a keen collector of *objets d'art*.[93] He also reorganised the imperial collections, moving the Habsburg dynasty's paintings from their various residences such as Prague and Innsbruck and bringing them together in Vienna. Nevertheless, his primary interest was music, a common passion of many Habsburg rulers and a feature of everyday life at court. He himself was a talented, ambitious musician who spent endless hours practising: under his aegis, the patronage and performance of music at the Viennese court was to reach an impressive standard, which the Carriera sisters would have undoubtedly appreciated. Huge sums were expended on concerts, ballets and opera. Like his brother, Joseph I, Charles VI was a composer of opera, oratorio, church and chamber music. In his function as imperial patron, Charles was also in the position to attract librettists such as Carriera's friend Apostolo Zeno (1668–1750), as well as Antonio Daniele Bertoli (1678–1743), who had been employed by Joseph I as court painter and who later supervised the gallery of Charles VI, and the court poet Pietro Antonio Domenico Bonaventura Trapassi, who went under the pseudonym of Metastasio (1698–1782).

As far as the visual arts are concerned, the traditional links between the Habsburg court and Venice dated back to Charles V (1500–1558) and Titian, and they had been reinstated by Joseph I by the end of the seventeenth century. The first Venetian-trained artist to arrive in Vienna was Sebastiano Ricci in 1702–3, who was joined by Antonio Bellucci in 1705; and Federico Bencovich (1667–1753) worked in the city from 1716 onwards.[94] Carriera's arrival marked a continuation of the trend.

Carriera went to Vienna accompanied only by her sister Giovanna, as travelling had become too arduous for their ageing mother Alba. Angela was already there, as her husband Giovanni Antonio Pellegrini had begun working in the city in 1725, commissioned by Amalia Wilhelmine von Braunschweig-Lüneburg (1673–1742), the widow of Joseph I, to paint the convent of the Order of the Salesian Sisters, which the Empress had founded. Presumably it was thanks to Pellegrini's influence that Carriera was invited to the court between May and October 1730 to paint the portraits of various members of the royal family and the nobility. Indeed, most of the commissions that Carriera received during her stay in Austria were directly linked to the Habsburg court. Her portrait of Amalia Wilhelmine, mother of Archduchess Maria Josepha (fig.43) and of Archduchess Maria Amalia (1701–56), is probably one of her most impressive works of this period.

After 12 years of an eventful marriage to Emperor Joseph I, Amalia Wilhelmine was widowed in 1711 at the age of 33. Her husband had been a notorious womaniser – with his continuous affairs drawing protest from both his wife and the Pope – and he passed along a venereal disease to his wife, which may have prevented her from having any other children after the birth of her two daughters.[95] Beginning in 1722, Amalia Wilhelmine took up residence in the aforementioned Salesian convent, where Carriera and her sister met her for the first time. It was during this period that the dowager Empress had a particularly significant impact on Viennese cultural life. Besides founding a boarding school and the city's first orphanage for girls, she was well known for her medical prescriptions.

44 Rosalba Carriera, *Portrait of Empress Wilhelmine Amalie*, 1730, pastel on paper, 65.5 × 51.5 cm (25 ¾ × 20 ¼ in), Staatliche Kunstsammlungen, Gemäldegalerie Alte Meister, Dresden

Carriera depicted Amalia Wilhelmine (fig.44) in her black mantua mourning dress with white trim and a black mourning cap. Heavy silver jewellery embedded with precious stones and huge pearls decorates her clothes, attesting to her position. Her royal status is even more clearly transmitted by the ermine scarf loosely draping her right shoulder. Her pose and her blue-grey eyes, which look attentively at the beholder, are suggestive of a woman who is proud and self-assured. The pastel is characteristic of Carriera's approach when producing a representational likeness: even though the artist respected the official nature of the painting, her rendering of the Empress widow emphasises the sitter's status and role, and the temporal power as sovereign, without excessive idealisation.

5

Pastel Painting: Carriera's Greatest Success

Around the time Carriera stayed in Vienna, she executed her famous self-portrait which is known as a representation of Winter and was dedicated to the Austrian court (fig.45). This time, the artist portrayed herself quite differently than she did in her staged self-portrait for the Grand Ducal collection in Florence (fig.25, p.49). Dressed in a flamboyant blue velvet coat with an ermine-trimmed cap covering her head, Carriera looks directly at the beholder. Two gorgeous pearl earrings glitter while her glance and a smile playing around her eyes and her lips accentuate her self-confidence or 'unaffected satisfaction'.[1] It is a captivating example of the artist's 'fantasy portraits that blurred the boundaries between reality and ideality through role-playing, in this case presenting herself as an allegorical figure of Winter and maybe, at the same time, alluding to the fact that she herself is approaching the "winter of her life"'.[2]

The work is one in a group of self-portraits the artist executed as an 'old woman' according to early modern standards, i.e., any woman past the age of 40. As a rule, portraits of aged women artists are particularly fascinating not only because these women call 'attention to the simultaneous weakness and magnification of vision', but also because they use these images to convey the essential significance of an artist's identity in general.[3] Carriera created an identity by exalting her social and, indirectly, professional, status as nobility. It reflects an important change in the history of self-portraits that started in the fifteenth century when artists sought to elevate themselves from purely manual workers to members of the world of liberal arts.[4] It was not until the end of the sixteenth century that the artistic and intellectual community succeeded in renegotiating the intellectual components of the creative process, and consequentially was able to elevate the standing of both its makers and their artefacts. For women painters, it was an accomplishment in itself to show themselves in the act of painting, that is, as practitioners of the visual arts. With her self-portrait as Winter, Carriera seems to have done the opposite, which makes the work even more fascinating. She completely suppressed any evidence of her artistic or professional life as if she had transcended those issues. Instead, she highlighted well-known ennobling signs of an elevated social rank such as lavish, even royal clothing, as well as an elegant noblewoman's self-assured pose. The self-portrait resembles the pastel of Amalia Wilhelmine in various ways. Both depict elderly women, both were born in the same year, which meant they were almost 60 years old in 1730/31, and both held the most powerful and successful positions in their respective spheres. It therefore seems reasonable that the reference to royal status in both pastels was not purely coincidental,

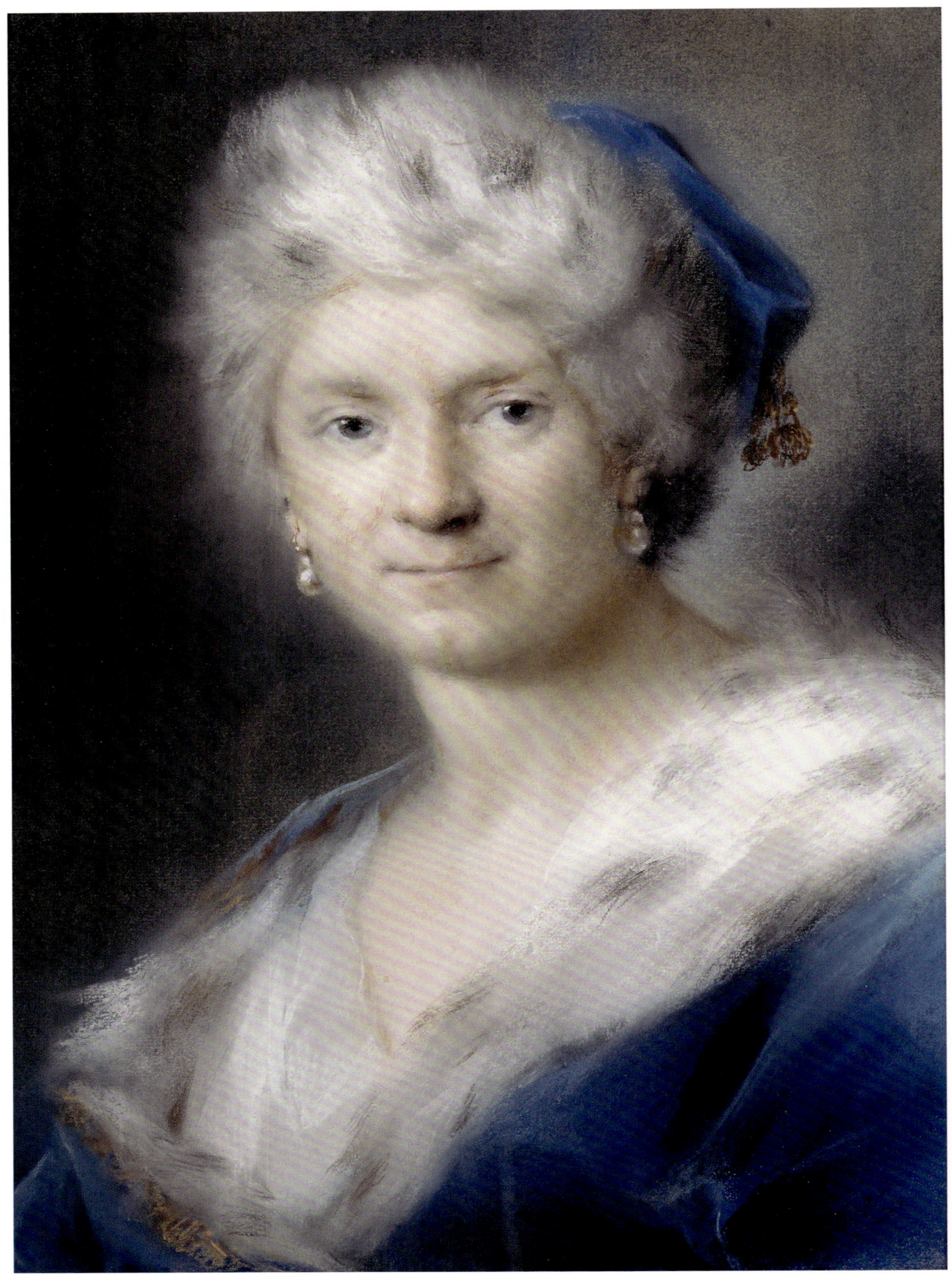

45 Rosalba Carriera, *Self-portrait as Winter*, 1730/31, pastel on paper, 46.5 × 34 cm (18 ¼ × 13 ⅜ in), Staatliche Kunstsammlungen, Gemäldegalerie Alte Meister, Dresden

especially as Carriera sent her self-portrait to the Empress dowager herself. Carriera was well aware of her unique status in Europe and she may have tried to post a shared identity with the Empress in the self-portrait by using the passive language of clothing to create her self-image. In excluding any hints of her profession while stressing her royal status in lavish, ennobling, allegorical disguise, she elevated herself to the rank of an ageing 'empress of painting' which paralleled the rank of her contemporary, the ageing Empress dowager of the Habsburg family. If this interpretation is correct, her self-portrait in Dresden fostered a rather grandiose, innovative, and probably provocative idea of the prominent role and social position of the artist herself and possibly of women artists in general. In doing so, she took the pastel portrait to a higher level. As a younger woman in Paris, she had managed to recast the genre into 'an expression of élite aspiration that appealed to those with recently acquired wealth who sought acceptance in aristocratic circles'.[5] In her older age, she transformed herself into an aristocrat.

Carriera mixed the genres of allegory and portrait with enormous pride, confidence and self-consciousness, intrinsically challenging how social identities were regarded; for female artists, such identities need to be further examined from another perspective. In depicting an elderly artist without alluding whatsoever to the burden of her age, the Dresden self-portrait can be deciphered as an interesting statement regarding elderly artists or elderly women in general. The culture of the eighteenth century had a widespread, negative attitude towards age, typecasting it as 'an abject and humiliated state, a fallen state of lost grace, beauty, and power'.[6] Women, including female artists, were particularly susceptible to gerontophobia. Some feared inevitable decline and infirmity would prevent them from working, others were terrified their beauty would wither, a concept conventionally associated with the female gender. Even worse, the old woman was often depicted as physically impaired, simple, unintelligent, and with a tendency towards emotional vulnerability, depression or melancholy. The description oscillated between parody, dignity and tragedy.[7] However, some early modern writings recount positive generalisations about the last phase of human life, alluding to exemplary or heroic reactions, intellectual competence and acuity, or emotional and spiritual strength that grow over the years.[8] Numerous examples in art challenge the generally negative outlook about ageing and, 'establish [instead] the visible signs of female old age as the visible signs of virtue'.[9] With the Dresden self-portrait, Carriera may have intended to overcome the hurdle of a denigrating stereotype by adding more positive aspects to her image as a liberating promotion of the female capacity for virtue in all ages, but especially in old age. Her self-portrait can be understood as being deliberately charged with the 'symbolic power of old women as moral exemplars'.[10] It shows the last phase in a woman's life 'in a positive and powerful new light [...], as a proud witness to the more lasting virtues of experience, wisdom, and penetrating intellectual vision'.[11]

In the very late seventeenth century and the early eighteenth century, Venice was a republic in decline, at a political, economic and social level. At the same time, in what seems a paradoxical development, cultural production flourished and the visual arts recovered from a century of stagnant conformity and indecisiveness before they 'flared up in a final, multifarious and brilliant blaze'.[12] It was also a period when painters like Carriera started finding solutions to what has been identified as an artistic dilemma and a 'neurosis of visual legacy'.[13] One of the apparently insurmountable difficulties for Venetian painters who had thrived since the seventeenth century was the question of whether they would continue to reinterpret the Renaissance tradition, which implied the stagnation of stylistic retrospection, or whether they would take the risk of brutally departing from their celebrated predecessors. Furthermore, there was the question of how they would react to the earlier personification of state identity. To what degree would artists decide to stick to the famous Venetian myth that had been carefully constructed over the last 300 years? On which grounds would painters continue to celebrate the city's divine image stemming from its mythological founding on Annunciation Day (25 March)? Could they still glorify its legendary wealth, infinite beauty, boundless fame, eternal peace and political stability, and if so, in what way? The inability of seventeenth-century painters to find adequate answers to these questions has been called the artists' 'neurosis'.[14]

This analysis in connection with Carriera and her work is particularly interesting since it highlights, from yet another point of view, the unique nature of her artistic choices. Perfectly aware of the 'Venetian myth', Carriera continued to allude to it or directly include it in her art when carefully catering to clients who were searching for exactly that: a legend. Travellers coming to Venice from Europe and elsewhere did not intend to participate in the city's sad final act of a spectacle that had been going on for hundreds of years; the grand tourists did not have any real interest in understanding Venice's decline, especially as the city 'may have appeared on the surface delightfully or deplorably hedonistic'.[15] Foreign visitors happily overlooked the social and political changes and the growing number of poor people on the streets. They indulged, instead, in whatever they thought was 'the Venetian experience': the extraordinary vitality and quality of theatre and opera, the splendour of the carnival and its air of freedom, and the city's glory and physical magnificence.[16] 'They wanted something they were already familiar with – the reliable, attractive, recognizable.'[17] And the carefully staged public events helped in this endeavour: displays of excessively luxurious apparel on the squares and streets, and the stimulating entertainment inside the gambling houses, during carnival, or at the opera house were all designed to camouflage the realities of descent and decay; the city was literally in disguise.[18]

The tendency of many of the foreigners to seek out this 'truly Venetian' experience and to return home with a painting to match it, a long-established, well-known canon, can be gauged in the number of Carriera's portraits whose sitters pose in carnival costumes and masks. These types of portraits were not only pictures of their elegant selves, but, more importantly, they were visual proof that the travellers had experienced and participated in the essence of Venice, according to their point of view. An example of this type of image is the likeness of Charles Sackville, Earl of Middlesex, or the very similar portrait of Gustavus Hamilton, 2nd Viscount Boyne (fig.46).

In January 1730, the Irish-born Lord Boyne arrived in Venice together with Edward Walpole, second son of the Whig Prime Minister, Sir Robert Walpole. Hamilton's portrait was executed when he came back to Venice the following winter. In the pastel 'of epicene beauty'[19] now housed in the Metropolitan Museum in New York, Carriera depicted the 21-year-old aristocrat in a bright blue fur-trimmed coat over a pink vest and a white shirt. His tricorn, the lace veil and the mask are part of one of the most famous carnival costumes in eighteenth-century Venice known as the *bautta*. When worn outdoors, it would have been completed with a full-length, circular black cloak. Jeffares has pointed out how Carriera cleverly placed the mask on her sitter's head with an erudite and playful reference to both the Greek god, Janus, and the allegorical figure of Prudence. Both see inwards and outwards, both have the wisdom of the past and the present: Janus thanks to his two heads, and Prudence thanks to a mirror she is holding up. Had Carriera actually included Boyne's coat of arms showing two mermaids holding a mirror, her portrait and the various allusions included would have been even more personalised, even more brilliant.[20]

The Venetians themselves enjoyed being seen as true citizens of a glorious and beautiful city, aspects of which can be found, for example, in the portrait of Caterina Sagredo (1715–72), who came from one of the city's most illustrious aristocratic families

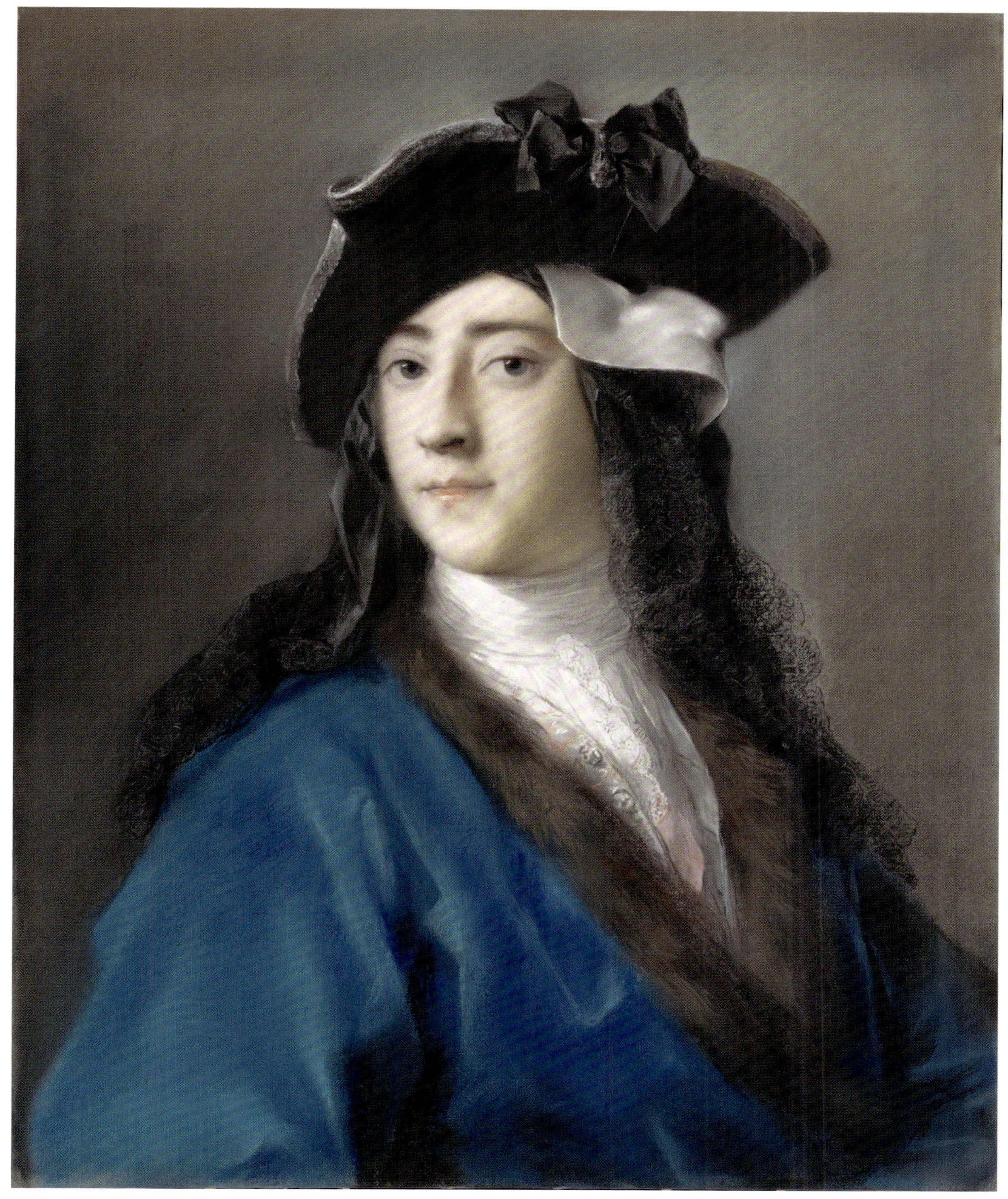

46 Rosalba Carriera, *Portrait of Gustavus Hamilton, 2nd Viscount Boyne*, 1730–31, pastel on paper, 56.5 × 42.9 cm (22 ¼ × 16 ⅞ in), The Metropolitan Museum, New York

with a long history of artistic patronage (fig.47). She was well known for the high level of education that her mother, Cecilia Grimani (d.1755), had assured her and her sister in their intellectual pursuits. Both sisters had an active cultural life, patronising, among other things, theatres and individual artists such as Giovanni Battista Tiepolo and Pietro Longhi; they read in several languages and managed the family patrimony.[21] Caterina was also praised for her outstanding beauty and was famed as a tireless traveller. For her first marriage to Antonio Pesaro di Leonardo in 1732, she received 48,000 ducts, the highest dowry ever recorded in Venice at the time. It was around the occasion of her second marriage, to Gregorio Barbarigo di Giovanni Francesco (1709–66) on 28 June 1739, that Caterina decided to have herself painted by Carriera.[22]

In moving away from the archetypical beauty that she had painted so many times in her earlier years and continued to paint, Carriera presented a highly original work. The portrait shows a self-confident woman tilting her head coquettishly to the right. Smiling, Sagredo Barbarigo looks directly at the spectator with a somewhat provocative glance. Her shoulders are draped with a blue mantle, as she wears her tricorn daringly askew over her right ear, likely a refence to her reputation as a skilled horse rider.[23] The exceptionally lavish jewellery consists of heavy pearl earrings with 66 diamonds, and alludes to the forthcoming wedding. Historical documentation indicates the earrings were worth 1,600 zecchini.[24] Her equally remarkable pearl necklace, highlighted by a bright red ribbon attached to her blouse, was not only a symbol of her noble status and financial well-being, but it was a reproduction of the same necklace that her mother had received as part of her dowry.[25]

To put wealth and social rank on display in a female portrait, especially if it was directly connected to a wedding, was normal practice, but the woman in this painting shows much more of herself. Carriera pulls the onlooker into a close-up view, stimulating engagement with Sagredo Barbarigo's bold glance. The portrait's dialogic and provocative nature, as well as the sitter's self-assured pose, reveal a coquettish, mischievous nature of one who is either challenging or flirting with the spectator, leaving no doubt about the woman's strength of character and alluring eccentricity. It is easy to imagine that her own *casino* close to the Procuratie Nuove, according to Mary Wortley Montagu (1689–1762), would attract as many as 300–400 people for its regular meetings.[26] These salon gatherings were among the most notable in Venice. This woman was a celebrity, and she became even more notorious when in 1747 the Inquisition closed the second *casino* she had rented on the Giudecca for its scandalous and unacceptable mixing of sexes.

Carriera transmitted a radically different personality, and yet again showed her dexterity in producing intimate character studies, in her portrayal of Suor Maria Caterina, which is kept in the Ca' Rezzonico in Venice and dated 1732 (fig.48). Clothed in the black and white habit of her order, the Dominican nun is depicted with a meditative gaze, downcast eyes and hands folded in prayer. The emaciated face alludes to a bony, skinny body, and the unkempt eyebrows and the wrinkled hands are expressions of deprivation consistent with a frugal, reclusive life. Both her entire posture and her detachment from the onlooker suggest that she has been caught in an act of meditation. She seems to be unaware of anybody looking at her, let alone painting her. The intense, honest and impressive rendering of this ageing, unpretentious nun might be seen as an exemplary image. As Erin J. Campbell has pointed out in her insightful article on portraits of older women in early modern Italy, these works often had a moral and spiritual function. Based on the study of conduct literature from the sixteenth century, Campbell notes that old age was seen as the final stage of virtue, as a phase of sanctity, 'a time when women were advised to set the cares of the world aside and devote themselves to God'.[27] Carriera's faithful version of Suor Maria Caterina exudes a

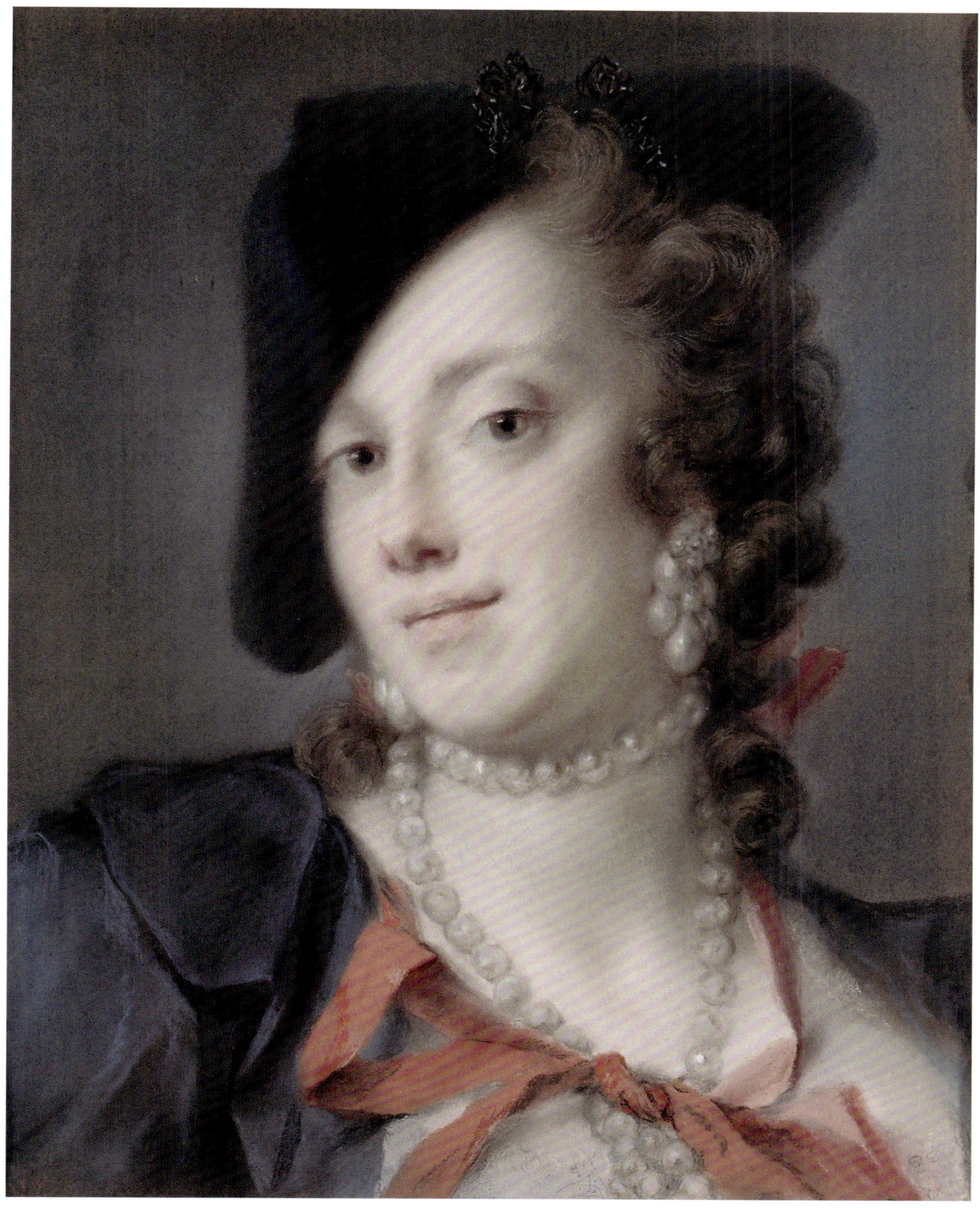

47 Rosalba Carriera, *Portrait of Caterina Sagredo Barbarigo*, 1735–40, pastel on paper, 42 × 33 cm (16 ½ × 13 in), Staatliche Kunstsammlungen, Gemäldegalerie Alte Meister, Dresden

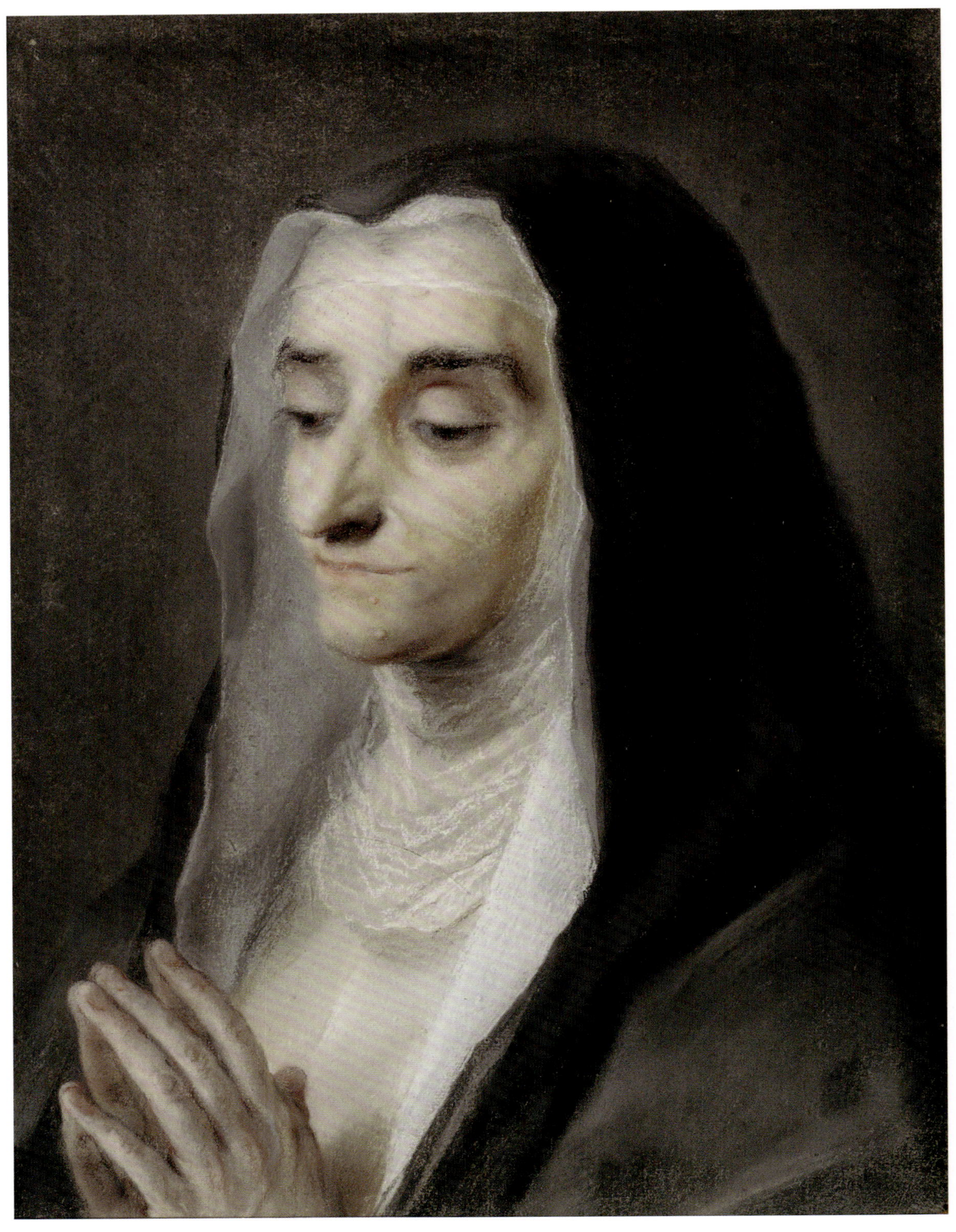

48 Rosalba Carriera, *Portrait of Suor Maria Caterina*, 1732, pastel on paper, 44 × 35 cm (17 ¼ × 13 ¾ in), Museo del Settecento, Ca' Rezzonico, Venice

sense of distance that was typically accorded to iconic images of saints. In this sense, the portrait of this woman, who died amid claims of sanctity, could easily also be read as an image of virtue. The exemplary nature of the pastel is even more convincing when considering that Carriera had already explored the position and potential significance of ageing women on other occasions and would do so until the end of her career – as will be discussed in Chapter 6.

CARRIERA AND THE ARTISTIC WORLD AROUND HER

Throughout her life, Rosalba Carriera was in contact with artists, musicians and intellectuals whom she met regularly or with whom she exchanged letters. She made portraits of some of these friends and acquaintances, including her ally and companion, the engraver Anton Maria Zanetti, and Jean-Antoine Watteau. In Vienna, she finished paintings of some of her Venetian painter colleagues, such as Marco Ricci, as well as the court poet Metastasio; the latter work hangs in the Gemäldegalerie in Dresden. Leaving Rome at the age of 32, Metastasio arrived in Vienna in 1730, the same year Carriera landed there. He stayed for over half a century, making a name for himself primarily with opera librettos such as *La Clemenza di Tito*, which Mozart (1756–91) later set to music. Interestingly, Carriera's depiction of the poet (fig.49) is consistent with a description of him written by the composer and music historian Charles Burney (1726–1814) in the third volume of his *Diaries of a Musical Journey* (1770–72), even though he met Metastasio many years after the portrait was executed: 'This poet and musician are the two halves of what [...] once constituted a whole; for they are possessed of the same qualities of true genius, taste and judgment; so richness, consistency, clarity and rigour are alike inseparable companions.'

With a personal interest in music, Carriera developed relationships with many Venetian musicians. Her oeuvre includes, for example, various portraits she made of the Venetian mezzo-soprano Faustina Bordoni (1697–1781), one of the Italian artists and musicians whom the Elector Palatine had invited to work for the Court of Düsseldorf. After a successful operatic debut in the San Giovanni Crisostomo Theatre in Venice in 1716, the Venetians dubbed her *La nuova sirena* (a modern-day siren).[28] Having become one of the internationally celebrated opera divas in Europe, she performed in Florence, Bologna, Rome, Munich, Naples and Vienna. In London, where George Frederic Handel (1685–1759) dominated the musical scene at the time, she became the legendary rival of Francesca Cuzzoni (1696–1778), whom she had previously met in Venice. During the last performance of Giovanni Bononcini's (1670–1747) opera *Astianatte* on 6 June 1727 at the King's Theatre in London, an unpleasant onstage scuffle broke out in the presence of members of the royal court. The incident inspired a series of lurid newspaper articles, a pamphlet entitled *The Devil to Pay St. James's: Or a full and true account of a most horrid and bloody battle between Madam Faustina and Madam Cuzzoni*, and nasty gossip all over Europe. Notably, in the aftermath, the two performers enjoyed a sudden boost in their fame in various countries, even though recent research has shown that it was the singers' supporters who behaved badly and not the opera stars themselves.[29] In 1730, Bordoni married the composer Johann Adolph Hasse (1699–1783), who was particularly revered in Venice for his contributions to the *opera seria*. The following year the couple moved to Dresden, where they became part of the illustrious court of Augustus the Strong. Hasse played an important part in establishing the tradition of Italian opera there and Bordoni, the *prima donna assoluta*, continued to work successfully in Saxony, interpreting, among other things, the works of her husband. For the next 20 years she performed at various European theatres.

Carriera's earlier portrait of her (fig.50), probably executed in 1724–5, shows the singer with dark brown hair, wearing a blue cloak over a thin white blouse

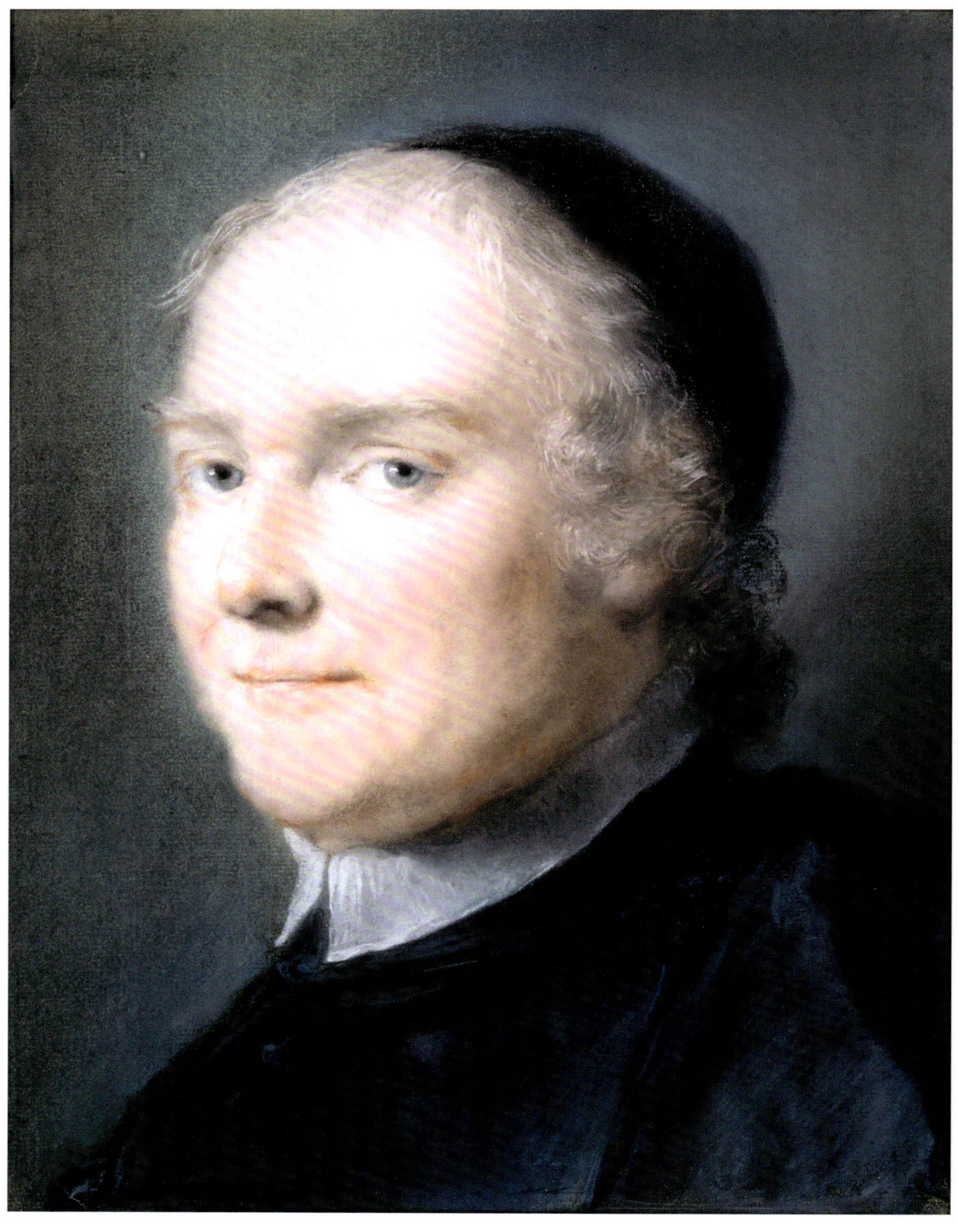

49 Rosalba Carriera, *Portrait of Abbé Pietro Antonio Metastasio*, 1730, pastel on paper, 32 × 25.5 cm (12 ⅝ × 10 in), Staatliche Kunstsammlungen, Gemäldegalerie Alte Meister, Dresden

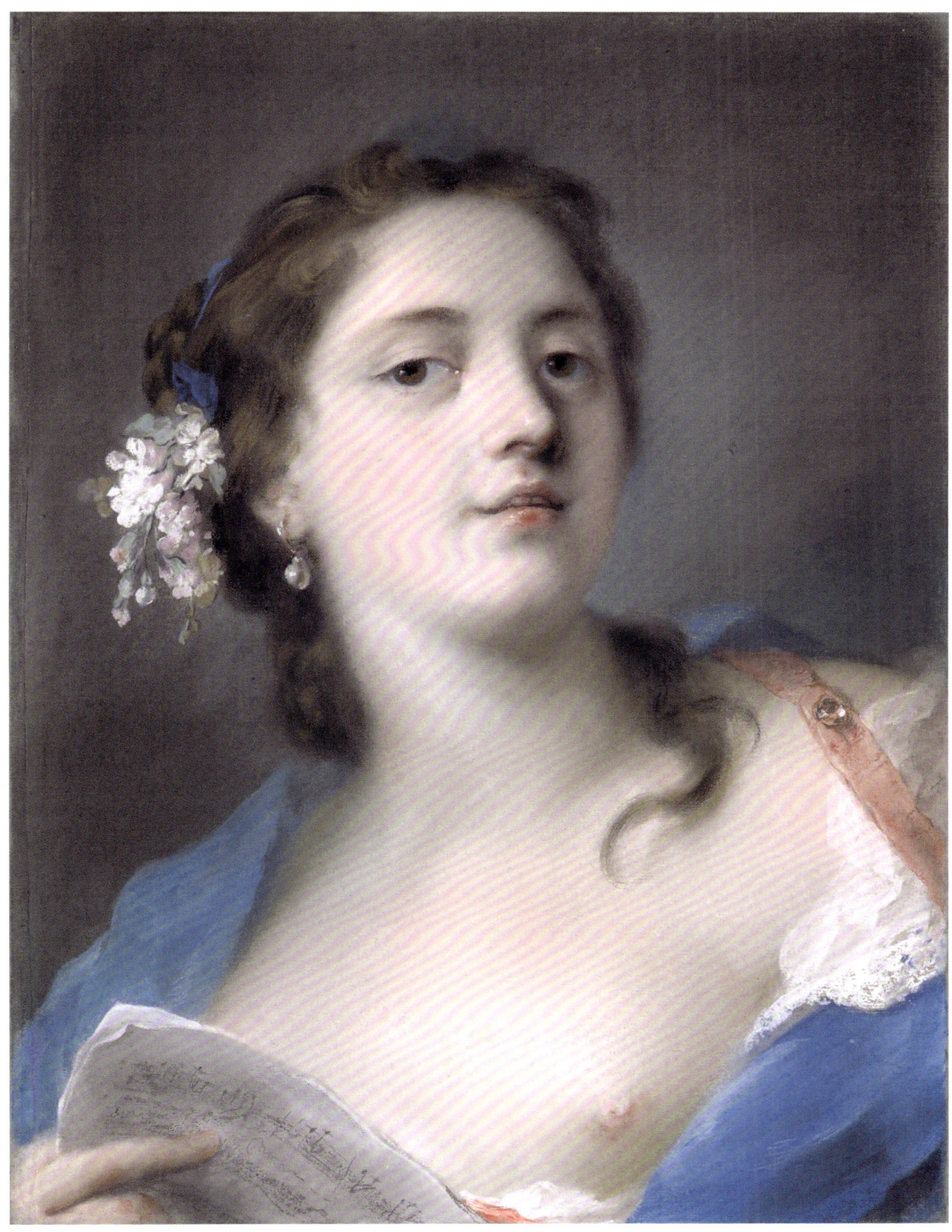

50 Rosalba Carriera, *Portrait of Faustina Bordoni*, 1724–5, pastel on paper, 44.5 × 33.5 cm (17½ × 13¼ in), Staatliche Kunstsammlungen, Gemäldegalerie Alte Meister, Dresden

that leaves her left breast exposed. The delicately depicted nipple picks up the hue of her lips and the red ribbon on the singer's left shoulder while the white blouse is visually balanced by the flowers in her hair and a luminous pearl earring. Her exposed bosom, her mouth slightly opened as if she were about to sing, and the sheet music she holds are all elements to suggest she should also be identified as a muse or an allegory about music or song. Thus, Bordoni not only champions music, but she is the embodiment of it; and her physical appearance seems to epitomise these allegorical expressions of success and social identity. In Florence, Giuseppe Broccetti (1684–1733) had employed a similar approach when, on behalf of Cosimo III, he cast a medal of Bordoni in 1723 to be given to adoring fans and would-be suitors. On the obverse of the medal, he presents the singer in profile elegantly dressed and adorned with precious jewellery. The reverse is captioned VNA AVIS IN TERRIS ('the only song-bird on earth') and shows an allegory of Music with a pile of musical instruments.[30] Carriera managed to combine in a single painting what Broccetti had depicted on two sides of a medal.

In a portrait of the singer at a later stage in her life, Carriera depicted her quite differently (fig.51). This artwork is a realistic portrait of a woman in her mid-forties. It was a period in Bordoni's life when she was reducing her engagements abroad and mostly staying with her husband in Dresden. In moving her sitter closer to the picture frame, Carriera concentrated on the stillness and serenity of the face. She also depicted Bordoni with her natural hair. The singer is shown with a bright blue mantle over a dress of which only the white lace collar is visible. Two large pearl pendant earrings are complemented by the pearls that decorate her hair. At this point in her career, or at least for this painting, the mezzo-soprano no longer needed to allude to her profession; yet she still promoted herself as a successful artist with the artificial laurel crown on her head. At the same time, this painting can be considered a character study of an accomplished and self-confident woman.

Carriera depicts another eighteenth-century celebrity in the pastel portrait of the dancer Barbara Campanini (1719–99), also known as 'la Barbarina' (fig.52). The ballerina appears at the age of around 24 in a bright blue corset dress with a row of white bows that narrows from the chest to the hips. With a gentle smile emanating from her light pink lips, she looks directly at the viewer with her dark, sparkling eyes. Flowers and pearls adorn her brown unpowdered hair. Her earrings and the choker style necklace are decorated with large pearls that seem to mirror the dancer's snow-white cleavage. She has raised her partly visible right arm to her shoulder, while her left arm rises only slightly above her hips, hinting at lively movement. In her hands, she gracefully holds an airy white veil which forms a U-shape at the lower edge of the picture. When the veil is viewed with the curvature of her shoulders, an oval emerges to round out the composition of the pastel.

Campanini was born in Parma on 27 September 1719.[31] Following in the footsteps of her mother, she studied dance along with her two sisters, and as early as 1736, Barbara and her older sister, Domitilla, began performing at Parma's Teatro Regio, which was then one of Italy's most renowned opera stages.[32] Her debut at the Académie royale de musique, i.e. the Paris Opera, was a huge success, and she soon danced for Louis XV. In October 1740, she performed at Covent Garden in London, becoming a favourite of England's high society. In a very short time, the young talent had become an internationally celebrated star. The most famous event of her life, though, is connected with an offer that arrived from Germany. In 1743, Barbarina and her sister accepted a position at the Great Court Theatre of Frederick II (1712–86), who had yearned to see her on stage in Berlin. Only one year earlier, the then 31-year-old King had inaugurated the local opera, Unter den Linden, which was at the time the largest theatre building in Europe. He intended to track down and engage the best

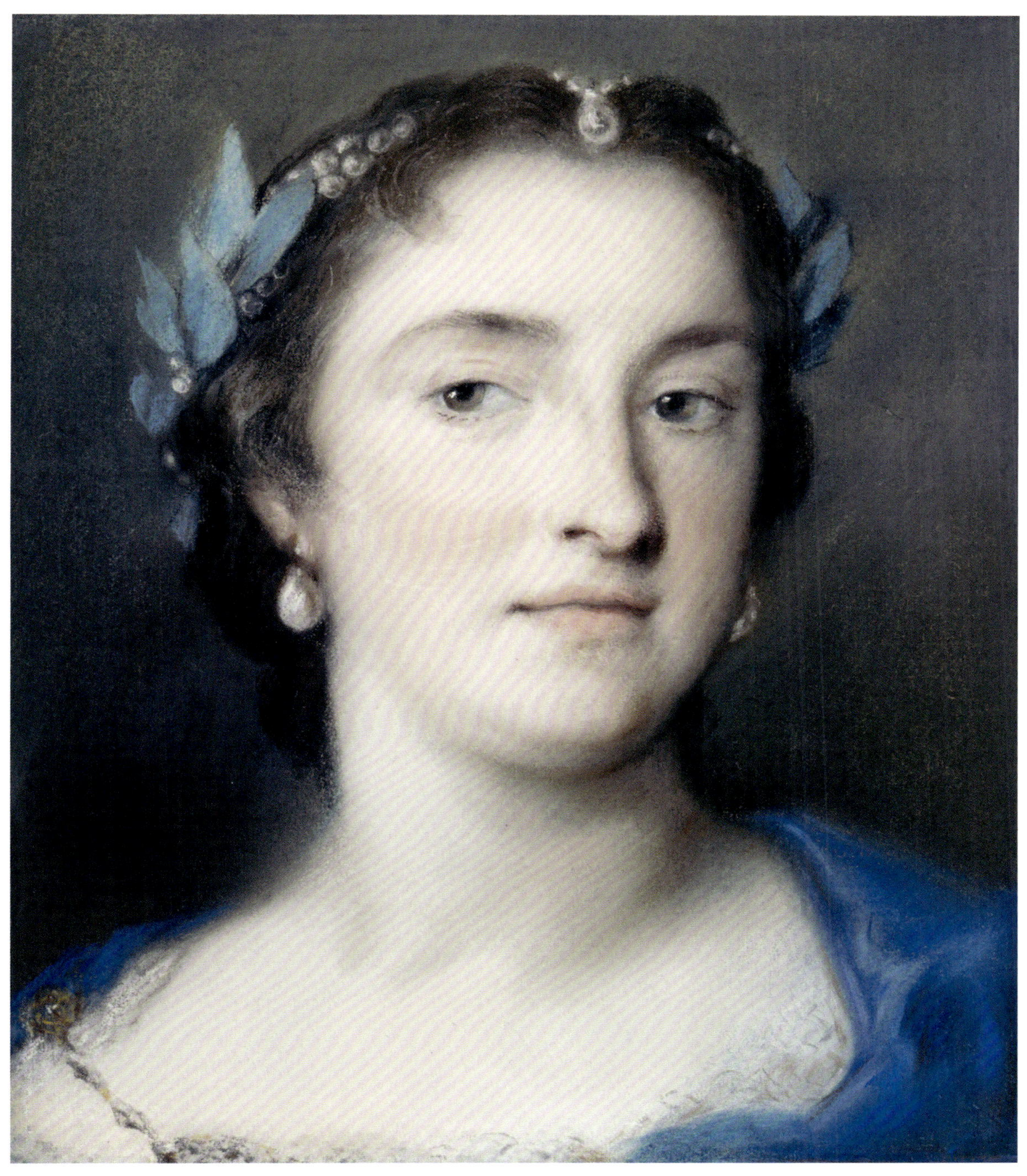

51 Rosalba Carriera, *Portrait of Faustina Bordoni*, *c.*1739, pastel on paper, 30 × 26.5 cm (11 ¾ × 10 ⅜ in), Staatliche Kunstsammlungen, Gemäldegalerie Alte Meister, Dresden

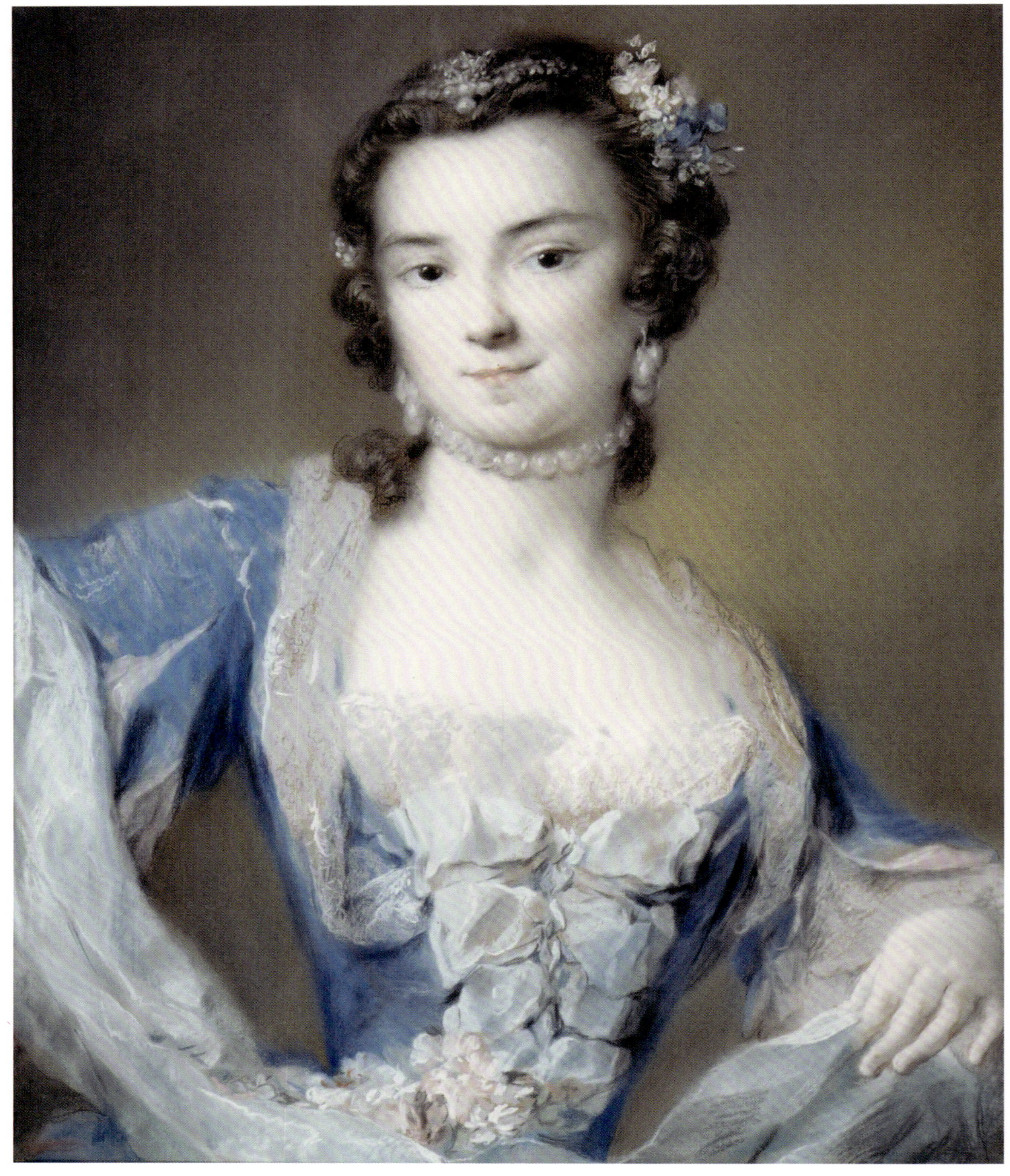

52 Rosalba Carriera, *Portrait of Barbara Campanini*, 1743–4, pastel on paper, 56.5 × 46.5 cm (22 ¼ × 18 ¼ in), Staatliche Kunstsammlungen, Gemäldegalerie Alte Meister, Dresden

musicians and dancers of his time, using his extensive European network of diplomats and military officials, who were encouraged to find new artists and establish the appropriate relationships.

After having received a verbal commitment from the ballerina, the impatient King waited in vain for a written contract and her arrival in Berlin; months later, the affair began to take on the form of a scandal. The dancer's missing signature resulted in an international political crisis that involved Prussia, Austria, France, Spain, England and Hungary. But the matter was far too delicate for any of the diplomatic officials to take a clear position, and the Republic of Venice had also been elegantly sidelined at first. Frederick II responded to the impasse by confiscating the passport of the Venetian ambassador in London who was travelling through Prussian territory on his way to England. It was only then, in mid-February 1744, that various magistrates of the Republic of Venice decided to arrest the dancer. 'La Barbarina' was under house arrest in Venice with her mother for over a month before it was decided how she should be brought to Berlin. Finally, on 8 May 1744, the ballerina and her mother arrived in the Prussian capital.

Just five days later, Campanini was on stage and the King was delighted. He had a contract drawn up, signed it as 'Frédéric', and surprisingly left the amount of the compensation to the dancer's discretion. The ruler had never shown such generosity towards any other artist, which led to malicious rumours and endless gossip – and not only at the Prussian court. Voltaire (1694–1778) was also amazed at the sums the King was willing to pay. In his biography of Frederick II, *La vie privée du roi du Prusse*, he not only penned the famous paragraph alluding to the King's assumed homosexuality by writing that he was probably in love with the dancer because she had male legs, but he also added that Campanini earned more than three ministers together.[33]

But 'la Barbarina' was successful not only as a dancer; the list of her admirers and of the scandalous articles grew longer and longer. In Paris at the beginning of her career, the local press was already spreading stories of at least 15 suitors, whose appointments were apparently coordinated with Campanini's mother.[34] Four years after her first performance in Berlin, another scandal erupted. Karl-Ludwig von Cocceji (1724–1808), the son of the Grand Chancellor of Prussia, Samuel von Cocceji (1679–1755), made a public confession of his love for the dancer. Both Karl-Ludwig's family and the King were enraged. Eventually, despite bitter resistance from the Cocceji family, Campanini managed to marry Karl-Ludwig in secret. The couple were exiled to Silesia and the marriage ended in divorce 40 years later. Four decades, as Campanini herself wrote, of unhappiness. But, even after the divorce, the ballerina bore the title of Baroness, albeit illegally. In the year of the official separation from her husband, 1788, Campanini was nearly 70 years old, but her ambitions had by no means diminished. She decided to found a home for poor girls; and she guaranteed Frederick II's successor, Frederick William II (1744–97), the considerable sum of 10,000 thalers in the form of a foundation in return for appointing her Countess.[35] On 6 November 1789, this extraordinary woman reached her ultimate goal. Barbara Campanini, the scandal-ridden ballerina from Parma, was allowed to call herself Countess. And she enjoyed the title for the remaining ten years of her life.[36]

Little of this fascinating biography would have been known to Rosalba Carriera when she executed this portrait of 'la Barbarina'. In the past, it has generally been assumed, albeit with reservations, that the pastel was acquired for Dresden in 1739 along with numerous other works by Carriera. While it is true that the dancer's biography indicated she was sufficiently ambitious and self-confident at the age of almost 20 to travel to Carriera around 1738–9 for the portrait, this trajectory is not entirely convincing as the dancer was working in Turin and France during that period. It is difficult to imagine that the ballerina would have made a detour to Venice at that point of her career without a professional engagement. Furthermore, there is no historical documentation to record that Campanini stayed in the lagoon city at that early point of her life. Therefore, it appears more plausible that the contract was awarded to Carriera in connection with Campanini's sojourn in Venice in 1743–4.

Turning again to the portrait, it is worth examining some of the more salient aspects of the work and what it represented within Carriera's oeuvre. In contrast to Carriera's otherwise typical representation of women, the work is a half-length portrait with both of the sitter's arms raised. The slight rotation of the upper body in combination with the arm and hand position suggests the dancer is moving. In Carriera's other figures, apart from the miniatures or pastels with allegorical content, the subjects' arms lie close to the body, often without any display of the hands. The pose of the raised arms was emphatic, and is similar to other depictions of ballerinas of the seventeenth and eighteenth centuries. With the ever-growing success of classical ballet and professional dance starting in the seventeenth century, various painters turned out a growing number of portraits of ballerinas and the scenes of their stage activities.[37] The increasing recognition of their skills and their growing popularity finally made these women worth portraying, in genre scenes or portraits. Almost without exception, since the Baroque, ballerinas had been shown as a full-figure, dancing, with their arms raised, as in Nicolas Lancret's (1690–1743) painting of Marie Anne de Cupis de Camargo (1710–70) in the State Hermitage Museum in St Petersburg. Even if the position of the legs or feet may not precisely indicate the activity of the painting's personage as in Henri Gissey's (*c.*1621–73) famous drawing of Louis XIV as Apollo in the *Ballet de la Nuit* (1653), it is the raised arms which identify the movement of dance.

Considered altogether, these aspects explain why the Dresden pastel is an exception in Carriera's oeuvre and, similarly, a novelty in the tradition of depicting dancers in European painting. I am unaware of any other example in which a ballerina is painted as a half-figure expressing the essence of her profession. Dancers appear either as full-length dancing figures, or as half portraits or busts without reference to their artistic undertakings. Carriera has immortalised an extraordinary person, an outstanding ballerina with a unique biography, in a portrayal that is just as exceptional in its own way.

Carriera's portrait of Felicita Sartori not only features another member of the artistic community associated with the artist, but, importantly, it is the image of her favourite student who was also one of her closest friends (fig.53). Sartori is depicted around the age of 25, half-length against a neutral dark background in a provocative, sensual stance, her head inclined slightly backwards and leaning to the side. She has a pensive, slightly melancholy look on her face, and her languid gaze is fixed on the observer. She is dressed as a Turk, possibly for a carnival party or as a representation of eighteenth-century *turquerie* fashion. Her head is adorned with a white turban decorated with jewels and a black feather, while her blue, floral print cloak hangs open, giving the observer a glimpse of the white satin and lace blouse underneath and the sitter's smooth, marble-white skin. In her left hand, she holds a black mask, called a *moretta*, which was traditionally worn for carnival. The black colour contrasts beautifully with the white blouse, Sartori's skin and her bright blue cloak.

Sartori moved into the Carriera home in 1728 when she was 14, having arrived as a chambermaid, later becoming Carriera's student.[38] During the 13 years she lived and worked with Carriera, Sartori received a sound artistic education and also found a place where she felt at home: she could go about her work and improve her skills by learning from the Venetian painter and copying oil paintings of seventeenth- and eighteenth-century artists.[39] This training formed the basis of her future successful career: she was the only artist in Carriera's studio to

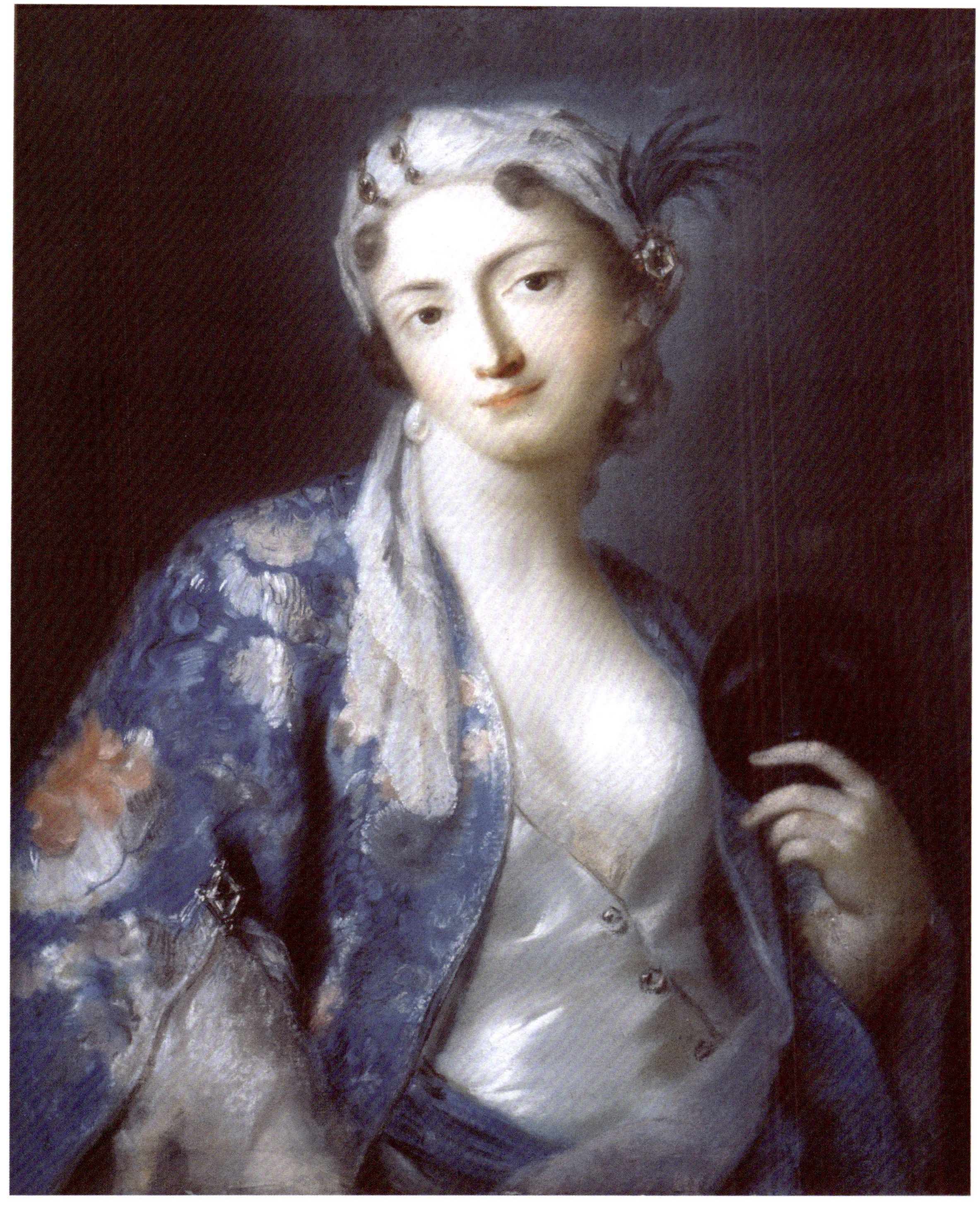

53 Rosalba Carriera, *Portrait of Felicita Sartori*, *c.*1739, pastel on paper, 70 × 55 cm (27⅝ × 21⅝ in), Gallerie degli Uffizi, Florence

rise above the anonymous status of assistant, and later became a respected court artist in Dresden.[40]

Carriera painted the portrait around 1739, the year Franz Joseph von Hoffmann (1696–1749), Privy Councillor to the Saxon Prince and Polish King August III, reappeared on the scene in Venice. On this trip, he was part of the entourage of Prince Frederick Christian of Saxony, whose portrait was discussed earlier. Hoffmann's visit was to be a turning point in Sartori's life. The Councillor purchased additional pastel paintings by Carriera for August III, one of her major customers, but he also bought a few miniatures that had been executed by her pupil whom he met at Carriera's house. August III was so delighted with some of her works that he invited Sartori to his court in Dresden.[41] Hoffmann and Sartori began to correspond and he soon asked her to come to Germany, but she delayed her decision. In May 1741, Sartori received an official invitation from Hoffmann to serve as a court painter in Dresden, and he soon asked her to marry him. Although Carriera did not personally accompany her protégé to Germany, she took care of the details of Sartori's trip to Dresden, and made sure she had an honourable companion for the journey. At the end of July 1741, the couple married in Germany.

The strong emotions that linked the two women find their clearest expressions in the way their feelings of loss are described in surviving documents and by Sartori's somewhat odd gesture of sending Carriera a piece of her wedding garter. On the one hand, this gift could be seen as emphasising and respecting the close affective ties between the women, but it is telling that Carriera was given something so very intimate from Sartori's private sphere – an object associated with the bride's loss of virginity – as though she, Carriera, were the parent who had given Sartori to her husband and to the consummation of the marriage, or as if she, perhaps unconsciously, were associated with her friend's defloration. With this gift, Carriera is symbolically involved in the bodily effects of her beloved friend's marriage and invited to conserve the proof of such effects in the form of a tangible item. Likewise, when Carriera referred to the piece of garter as a *reliquia* (relic), i.e. something belonging to a saint or someone deceased, it also implied that it came from someone who was no longer physically present in Carriera's life. At any rate, and maybe not truly by coincidence, the gift to Carriera was certainly highly symbolic.

Turning again to the portrait, one realises that, apart from the protagonist, the painting's most interesting object is arguably the mask. In a thematically and stylistically similar artwork by Carriera in Dresden, *Portrait of a Turk*, the male sitter is, like Sartori, depicted in exotic attire (fig.54). Turbaned and looking directly at the observer, the mysterious blond man with a handlebar moustache holds a coffee cup, an object unmistakably associated with Turkish culture. Apart from the moustache, which is likely artificial, there is no other object alluding to disguise, concealment or masquerade. Instead, Carriera decided to include a mask in her student's portrait, an article that had been connoted as feminine since the seventeenth century[42] – but it was not an item that would suggest a Turkish woman.

In 2011, Johnson offered a new interpretation of a *Woman Holding a Mask and a Pomegranate* by the Florentine artist Lorenzo Lippi (1606–65). Within the context, James H. Johnson suggested the mask was 'a version of the honest mask that hides all things securely within the heart', an instrument of virtue, a symbol of 'a modus vivendi, intended to preserve rather than disrupt'.[43] This pronouncement offers an interesting key to a better understanding of Carriera's portrait. In both Lippi's and her painting, the sitters cover the mask's mouth with a finger, Sartori tellingly with her index finger, the one typically placed on one's lips to indicate silence. Such interpretation would be compatible with the way the *moretta* was worn: it had no bands or strings, and it was held in place by a button that the masked lady had to clench in between her teeth. Consequently, any speech was effectively precluded.[44] It might well be, therefore, that Carriera,

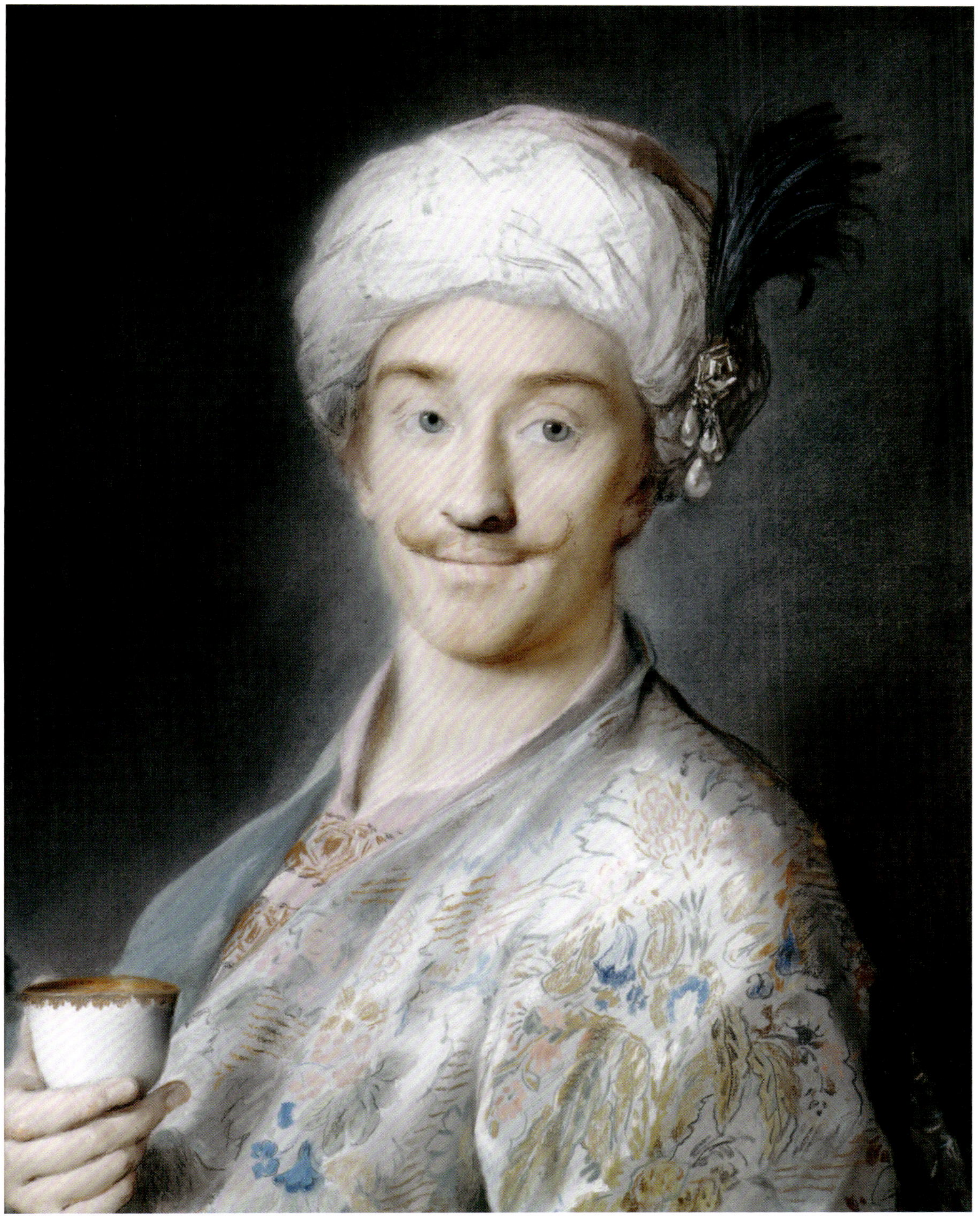

54 Rosalba Carriera, *Portrait of a Turk*, undated, pastel on paper, 56.5 × 44 cm (22 ¼ × 17 ¼ in), Staatliche Kunstsammlungen, Gemäldegalerie Alte Meister, Dresden

who entertained a close, intimate relationship with her student, was either trying to include a warning against feigning and falsehood, or aiming at reinforcing their close ties by showing her dearest friend as one who keeps the secrets of the heart. The portrait could thus be also understood as a token of trust, mutual agreement or a secret arrangement. In Carriera's rather sensual work, Sartori's seductive pose, her languid glance and the mask in her hand intrinsically link the friends together; the artist is symbolically present not only as the creator of the painting but also in a more subtle manner as one of the recipients of Sartori's glance. Her gesture of covering the mask's mouth, the indication of keeping silent, is open to interpretation.

EROTICISM IN CARRIERA'S PASTELS

A particularly stunning painting of Carriera's is her *Young Lady with a Parrot* at the Art Institute of Chicago (fig.55). The pastel, dated *c.*1720–30, shows an unknown, young, elegant woman who, with the hint of a smile on her bright red lips, looks directly at the spectator. The alluring lady is depicted with cascades of reddish, bejewelled hair swathing her back and her shoulders, a hairstyle that represents a notable exception to Carriera's typical rendering of women. Fashion and societal norms would have prescribed a more contained, controlled hairstyle.[45] A blossoming rose and some smaller flowers at ear height adorn the right side of her head. The woman wears an ornate blue silk dress that is open almost to her waist, with more jewellery attached to the sleeves. She invites the onlooker's gaze to linger freely on the broad expanses of her soft, naked flesh. Further escalating the painting's erotic charge, a long string of pearls is wound around the woman's neck and emerges descending and crossing in the middle of her chest before being attached to a pink and white bow at her left breast. A mischievous parrot perched on two fingers of her left hand holds in its beak one hem of her bodice, attempting to strip it away to reveal yet more of her bosom. From a purely aesthetic point of view, the exotic bird enhances the colour scheme's elegant balance – its green-blue plumage beautifully matches the young woman's silk dress. As for the interpretation of the pastel, Cesare Ripa and his *Iconologia* – which, as indicated already, Carriera used as a textual resource for symbolic meaning in a number of her paintings – provides little meaningful insight for understanding the parrot's significance. Ripa linked this specific bird primarily to the figures of 'Quiescence', 'Docility' and 'Eloquence'.[46] Most likely, however, Carriera's decision to include a parrot stemmed from the notion of this exotic bird being directly associated with lust, sensuality and eroticism, as can be observed in other eighteenth- and nineteenth-century paintings.

At the Ashmolean Museum in Oxford, a painting by Giovanni Battista Tiepolo, dated 1760–61, for example, depicts a female figure holding a parrot. De Grazia interprets the Tiepolo painting as a depiction of a Venetian courtesan, evidenced by typical attributes such as the roses in her hair, a yellow dress, costly pearls and the macaw as a symbol of lust.[47] In this painting, possibly of a prostitute, the interpretation of the same exotic bird flanking an exposed breast is a convincing symbol of longing, libido and sensuality. Paintings by French artists, including *Woman with a Parrot* by Eugène Delacroix (1798–1863), dated 1827, and similarly titled works by Gustave Courbet (1819–77) and Edouard Manet (1832–83), both executed in 1866 and residing today in the Metropolitan Museum in New York, are evidence of the further development of an unequivocally erotic theme that Carriera's pastels importantly conveyed as early as 1720 and 1730.

Carriera's *Young Lady with a Parrot* features several aspects that Filippo Pedrocco has described as being part of the typical iconography of Venetian courtesans in the sixteenth century and later: the full crimson lips, a wild rose in sinuous reddish-blonde curly tresses that carefully drape the shoulders, and two strings of pearls that lie crossed upon the partly

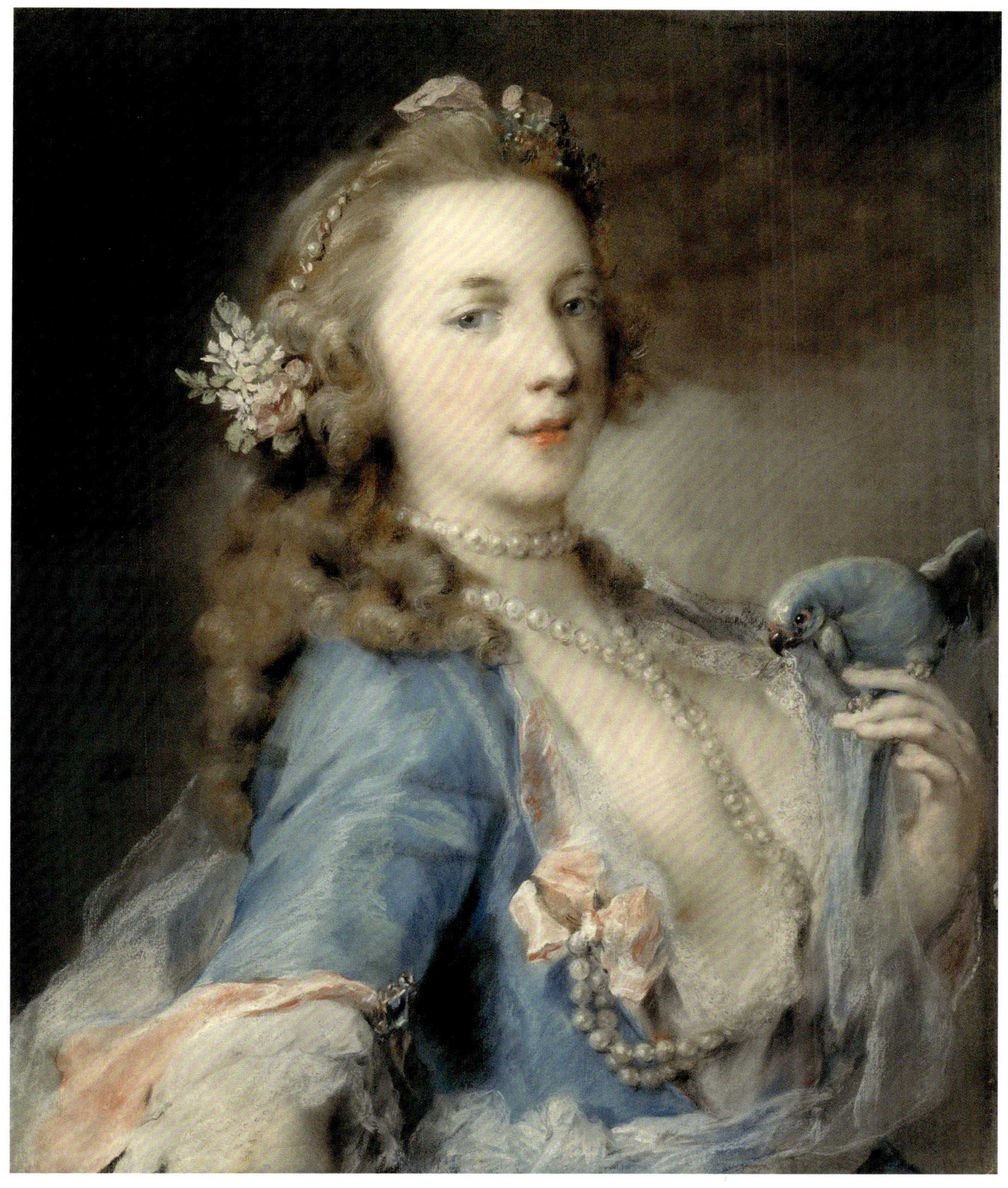

55 Rosalba Carriera, *A Young Lady with a Parrot*, c.1720–30, pastel on paper, 60 × 50 cm (23 ⅝ × 19 ¾ in), The Art Institute, Chicago, IL

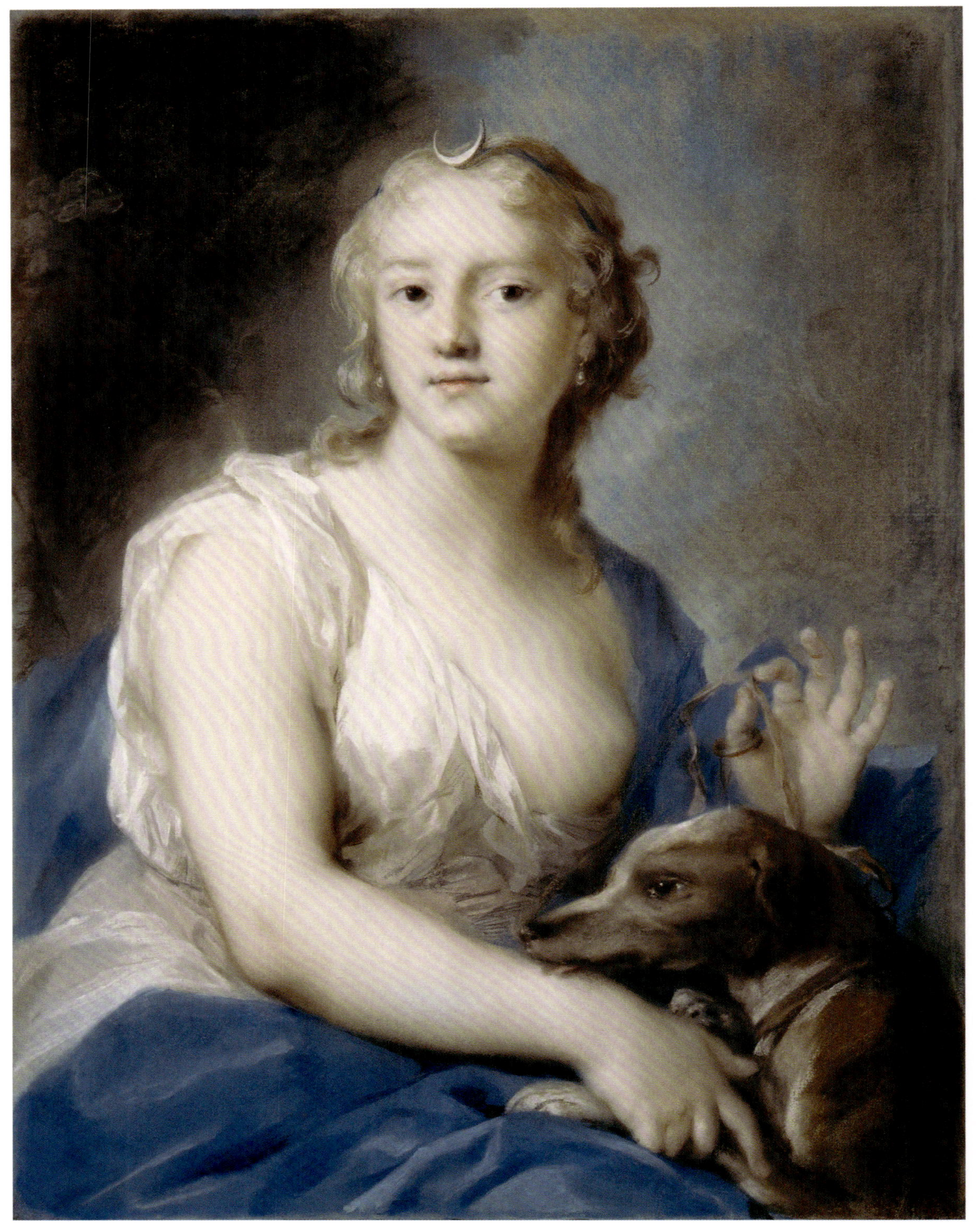

56 Rosalba Carriera, *Diana*, 1740–46, pastel on paper, 67 × 52 cm (26⅜ × 20½ in), The State Hermitage Museum, St Petersburg

exposed chest and tie diagonally across the dress.[48] Notably, in eighteenth-century England, hair, and especially curls, could function as a fetish with a variety of sexually charged associations.[49] Since Carriera's oeuvre contains no other image of a woman presented with long curly hair, as in the pastel in Chicago, I argue that the artist depicted the sitter in this manner to accentuate the painting's eroticism. And maybe it is no coincidence either that both Tiepolo's woman and Carriera's wear a clearly visible rose in their hair. While flowers often decorated the heads of women in the eighteenth century, the choice of the rose was surely not accidental, especially considering the sexual connotations of roses in courtly literature, and the association of roses with Venus, the goddess of sexual desire. The combination of the rose and the parrot opening up the sitter's blouse are significant facets of Carriera's presentation of a flamboyant, eroticised subject.

Mythological characters were an often-requested theme, with Diana being the most popular, and they lent themselves particularly well to the depiction of eroticism. Numerous letters and diary entries by Carriera confirm that she regularly worked on different versions of the hunting goddess, especially during the 1730s. The images of the chaste deity that conform with the eighteenth-century fashion of alluring pastoral scenes and historiated portraits were perfect examples of an erotically coded role model which offered collectors, or spectators in general, the opportunity to identify with her, as is obvious in Carriera's works portraying women dressed as Diana. The Hermitage in St Petersburg holds an outstanding pastel by Carriera showing a *Diana* with other sensual and more explicit erotic elements (fig.56). This pastel and the pendant piece of *Apollo* were originally part of the collection of Robert Walpole, Britain's first Prime Minister, and were hung in the great middle room of his mansion in Downing Street (fig.57).[50]

The goddess, half-dressed in a flimsy white tunic underneath a bright blue mantle, is framed at three-quarter length. The delicate half-moon on her head and the presence of a hunting dog leave no doubt about her identity. Carriera has projected an aura of sensuality through the alluring glance of the almond-shaped dark brown eyes and the exposure of the porcelain-white left breast that beautifully contrasts with the brilliant blue shoulder mantle. Judging from the way she looks directly at the spectator, she seems rather nonchalant about the prospect of losing her virginity, and perhaps, she is indeed anticipating the joy of seduction. With her right hand, Diana holds her canine companion's left phallic leg on her lap while the dog licks her forearm. With her left index finger and thumb, she pinches the part of the dog's leash next to her exposed breast. It is one of the gestures in Carriera's works that 'when present, are active but often ambiguous'.[51] Hands were often understood as potential signifiers of erotic love starting in the early Renaissance. As one of the few areas of flesh visible on the Renaissance body, hands were repeatedly celebrated in Petrarchan poetry. When hand gestures are complemented by glancing eyes and a playful smile, the externalisation of desire aligns with the conventional imagery of the Petrarchan lover.[52] In Carriera's case, the erotic charge also materialises in other details of the pastel. The leash fashioned of a material softer than leather, the pinching fingers, the breast, and the licking dog are all placed around Diana's lap; their positioning epitomises the painting's thinly veiled eroticism.

At the same time, Carriera's intention is witty: the goddess, who had Actaeon killed by his own hunting dogs to protect her chastity and to punish him for his forbidden voyeurism, is touting herself as available, with hardly anything concealed from anyone. Although not a ferocious animal, the dog is present to dissuade any imagined transgression on the part of the spectator, beguiled with the sexual allusions. The goddess's body and the conspicuous sexual innuendo turn the spectator who lingers over the image into a participant in a potentially dangerous game of glances. It is an encounter of the two: the onlooker is Actaeon enchanted by the naked beauty of the goddess but, unlike the hunter, he/she is fully aware of the titillating fatality of the enchanting vision.

In the pendant piece (fig.57), the figure of Apollo is depicted as the usual half-figure, almost perfectly mirroring Diana's pose. A laurel crown sits atop his blond curly hair and he holds a lyre in front of his torso, which is only slightly covered by a brown cape. Apollo's eyes are not directed towards the onlooker but towards the top right corner of the painting. Unusually for Carriera's pastels, the background is not simply anonymous, but it features bushes and trees. This pastel is the only one in Carriera's oeuvre to focus on an almost nude male figure, and it is hardly a coincidence that she depicted Apollo in this manner. She aptly chose a personage who did not require the representation of a virile masculine physique. With the sun god's iconography justifying an effeminate body, Carriera could avoid being criticised for her lack of male anatomy studies. Her knowledge of the female body was sufficient for this pastel, and indeed, if one compares Apollo's body with those of *Winter* or the *Personification of Autumn*, both in the Royal Collections in Windsor, the *Muse Clio*, once part of the Dresden collection, or *Poetry* in Karlsruhe (fig.58), just to name a few, it is evident that the anatomy in all of them is basically the same, with the breasts only slightly more developed in the female figures.

Carriera elected to paint both the god of youth, music, healing and prophecy and Diana as her subjects were twins who loved to go hunting together. Apollo is depicted alone, ostentatiously displaying his lyre, a reference to the musical contest between him and the satyr, Marsyas. According to the tale recounted by Ovid in his *Metamorphoses* and *Fasti*, Marsyas, in a fit of pride and presumption, challenged the mythic god of poetry and music. The satyr played the double-reed wind instrument that Minerva had invented and thrown away, and Apollo defeated him with his lyre. As reward, the winner could choose the loser's punishment, and the temperamental Apollo decided to have Marsyas flayed. Interestingly, Carriera did not highlight the competition between satyr and god: she did not allude to the judgement of their respective merits or, like Ovid, to the brutal punishment. She depicted an intermediate, undefined phase which is open to interpretation. The entire story is implied through the presentation of the lyre, the deity's sidelong glance, and his positioning outdoors, close to trees, which might refer to the spot where Marsyas was bound to a tree to be flayed. At the same time, the sensuality of the god's body, and his perfect, white, smooth skin do not go unnoticed. The satyr's death embodies the end of dark, low, uncontrollable instincts and passion. Marsyas's base sexuality eventually gives way to Apollonian purity. Like in various of her other works, Carriera cleverly combined different layers of meaning in these two pastels. The onlooker can focus on a moral reading of her artworks, while they can also easily indulge in the pleasures of erotically charged images. Both pastels feature deities who torture and eventually kill an intruder or rival. Neither sexual transgression nor hubris remains unpunished.

Carriera's rendering of the temperamental musician is also noteworthy for another aspect. With his curly, round mop of hair, his perfectly straight nose, and the shape of his eyebrows, he has an astonishing resemblance to Antinous (*c.*110–30 CE), a young Greek man favoured by Hadrian who suffered a premature death and was later deified by the Roman Emperor. Considering the effeminised looks, Apollo's classicising features, the marble-like skin and melting gaze, it seems feasible that Carriera drew on the ancient image. Reproductions and prints of Antinous were widespread, and, since the Renaissance, numerous artists had included adaptations of the beautiful youth in their paintings or sculptures.[53] At least one bust of the young man was on display in Venice during Carriera's lifetime, and is today kept in the Palazzo Grimani in Venice (fig.59). What is certain is that the exposed chest, the emasculation of the arm muscles and, in particular, the hair and straight nose are all elements to suggest a link between Carriera's Apollo and the famous Antinous.

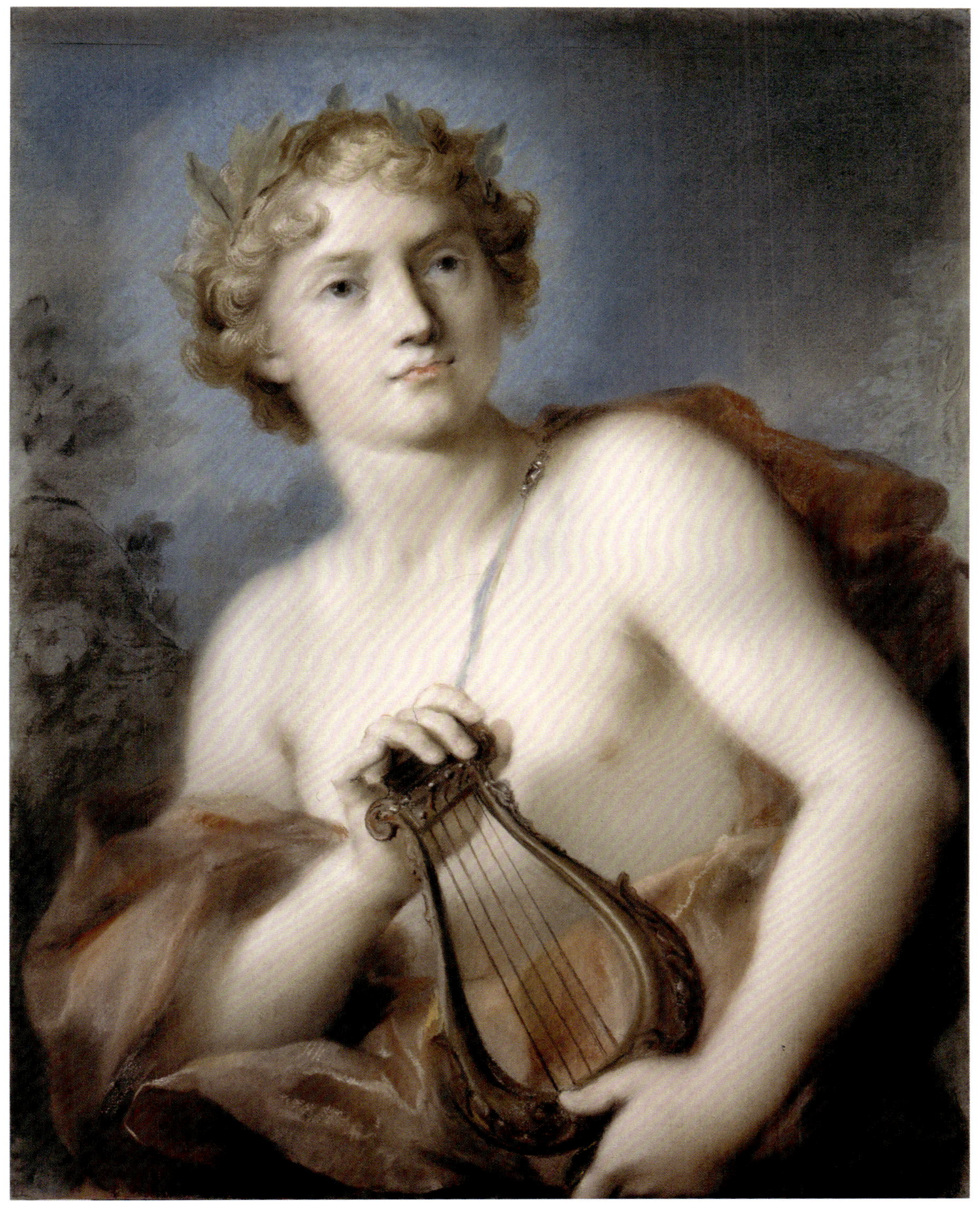

57 Rosalba Carriera, *Apollo*, 1740–46, pastel on paper, 67 × 52 cm (26 ⅜ × 20 ½ in), The State Hermitage Museum, St Petersburg

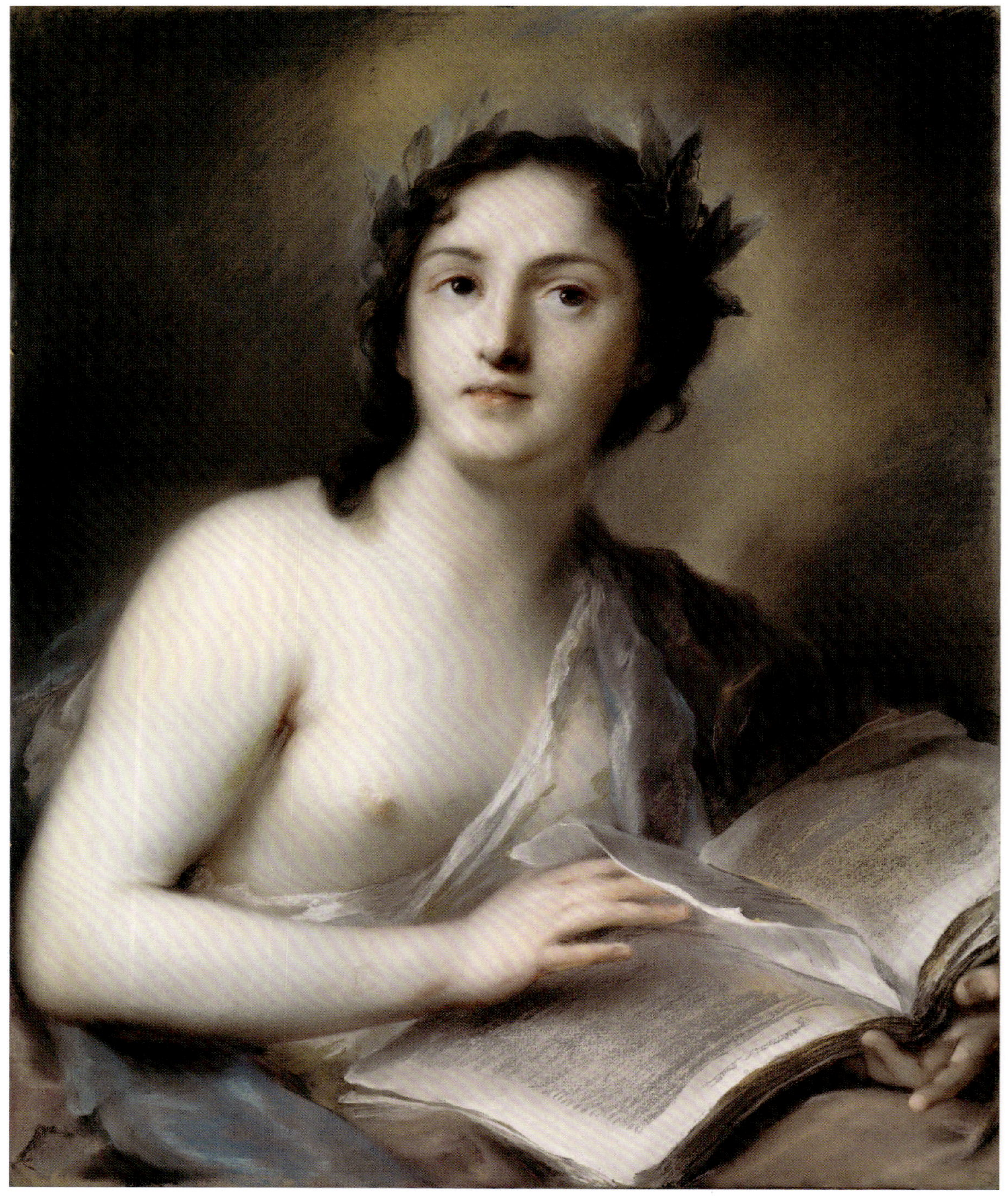

58 Rosalba Carriera, *Poetry*, around 1740, pastel on paper, 63 × 50 cm (24 ¾ × 19 ¾ in), Staatliche Kunsthalle Karlsruhe

Indeed, the two characters show analogies: both were known as beautiful youths, both were hunters, and both (eventually) were divinities. Even if Carriera was unaware of their overlapping stories, or about the tradition since antiquity of linking the two figures, she could have easily created an analogy on her own, drawing on their exceptional beauty and their youth. Again, Carriera proved herself to be a widely versed and well-informed painter whose artistic taste was not only highly refined but also innovative. And with this pastel, in particular, she heralded a return to classical art on the part of the next generation of artists.

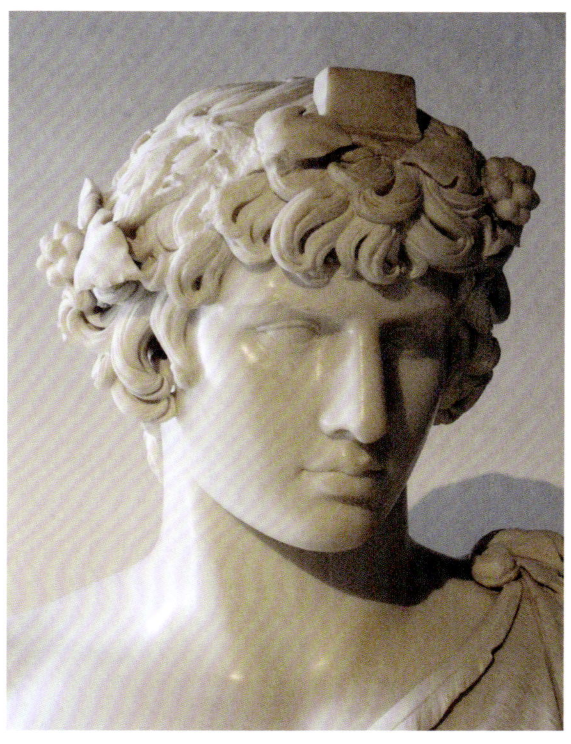

59 Bust of Antinous, marble, second century CE, height 80 cm (31½ in), Museo Archeologico Nazionale – Museo di Palazzo Grimani, Venice

CARRIERA'S FINANCIAL SUCCESS

It remains quite extraordinary that Carriera became the most internationally famous Venetian painter in her lifetime. How was such unprecedented success for any woman in the arts possible? As mentioned earlier, among the various factors that advanced her career was her recognition and exploitation of two artistic niches, miniature and pastel painting, which allowed her enormous personal, artistic and commercial liberties. The lack of rivals was also advantageous.

Furthermore, it is impressive that Carriera managed to keep her prices on a par with those of the officially recognised local painters. The combination of extremely refined artistry and shrewd tactics in publicising herself and her art made her a real attraction not so much to Venetians but to the foreigners who poured into Venice. And when compared to Venetians, her foreign clientele, especially the French and the English, showed a more profound appreciation of her miniature and pastel portraits. It would appear that Carriera was more successful than her contemporary colleagues in capitalising on the potential of a foreign clientele. She knew how to profit from their presence in the city, cultivating special relationships with the transient foreigners, and with intellectuals and artists, aristocrats and rich rulers and their agents.

Her immense success is further apparent in financial terms; her accounts show she managed to sell her work for considerable sums, with most of her collectors ultimately accepting almost astronomical prices for her paintings. Carriera was able to secure average prices for her miniatures that were almost twice those she later received for her pastel paintings.[54] Haskell quotes prices of 50 zecchini for the miniatures, while her customers paid around 20–30 zecchini on average for a pastel painting after 1725, depending on whether one or two hands were included.[55] According to Del Negro, half of her pastel works sold for 8–12 zecchini during the first years of their production. Between 1723 and 1725, the median price for one of her pastels increased steadily, going from 12 zecchini in 1723 to 18 in 1724, and about 21 in 1725. By 1726, the price had reached an average of 34 zecchini, sliding back to 24 in 1727. In 1728 it rebounded to 28, and from 1730 on, the price of a Carriera pastel settled at 30 zecchini. For her popular *Four Seasons* sets, she commanded the princely sum of 240 zecchini.[56] The trend in the prices for Carriera's works corresponds to the general development of the Venetian art market in those years. Sohm pointed out that the average prices for paintings jumped by 85 per cent in the 1720s, and then was surpassed by a stunning 121 per cent in the 1730s. This phenomenon went hand in hand with a self-proclaimed renaissance led by Sebastiano Ricci, Carriera's brother-in-law Giovanni Antonio Pellegrini, Giovanni Battista Piazzetta and Giovanni Battista Tiepolo.[57] Carriera managed to continue working frenetically until the 1740s, before problems with her eyesight forced her to slow down and eventually stop painting, even though demand for her works remained robust.

The minimum annual cost of living in Venice in the eighteenth century is estimated to have been around 15 zecchini. Considering that Piazzetta's average annual income was about 150 zecchini, and Canaletto's pricing of 120 zecchini for a painting was seen as exorbitant around that time, one gets a clearer impression of the generous income Carriera earned from her miniatures and later from her pastels.[58] Carriera unquestionably lived in Venetian society as a fairly wealthy woman, and, for an artist, her earnings were surprisingly high. Additionally, her own art production was not her only source of income. Painters could also earn money by copying works by earlier renowned artists, an activity that reflected a changing art market and a new appreciation of private collections. Collecting art in the seventeenth century had become a way for ambitious individuals to legitimise their social status, emulating the patriciate and the ruling nobility. The consequent more pronounced demand for Renaissance paintings made it increasingly more difficult to find original artworks, which led to the commissioning of copies, a market that had been booming since the seventeenth century.[59] Carriera, too, benefited from this opportunity, as shown by various letters in which her clients asked, for example, for a copy of a Veronese.

Artists also sourced income from offering services as appraisers, collecting fees for their expertise, a job that was paid well and brought with it considerable social cachet.[60] Carriera's correspondence proves that she also acted as a 'painter-consultant'.[61] More than once she was asked to lend her expert eye in valuing a potential acquisition. Occasionally she was also hired as an expert to restore paintings, including oil paintings. Diversifying her sources of earnings was one way to protect herself in a relatively uncertain profession, and safeguard her standard of living against unpredictable fluctuations in the economy. Clever investments in charitable institutions such as the Scuola Grande di San Rocco, the Arte de' Testori di Panna da Seta (the Venetian silk weavers' guild) or the Zecca (the Mint) are evidence of Carriera's astute capacity for supervising and organising her finances.[62] Altogether, it is estimated that these investments alone yielded her an annual income of at least 233 zecchini between 1720 and 1728. In 1741, she earned at least 690 zecchini, and shortly before she died, she lived on 918 zecchini, a sum 12 times the amount of rent she had to pay each year. Considering that state notaries in Venice in the seventeenth century earned around 200 zecchini a year,[63] Carriera's income takes on yet another dimension. Moreover, the calculation of investment income excludes the interest she earned from a private loan to her brother-in-law Pellegrini (which in 1741 amounted to 1,000 zecchini[64]), and the money she made by selling her art.

In Carriera's post-mortem inventory, which is kept in the state archive in Venice and was published in 2011 by Lino Moretti, she had total assets of 24,556 zecchini at the time of her death, including her investments.[65] Heiner Krellig compares this sum to the amount of money other Venetian artists left behind at their deaths, which provides a better gauge of the extent of wealth Carriera accumulated as an artist: Canaletto left 2,588 zecchini when he died; Sebastiano Ricci, 7,196; and Pellegrini, 18,967. Carriera's estate was surpassed only by the 32,000 zecchini left by Johann Carl Loth (1632–98), who seems to have been by far the richest painter working in Venice during the seventeenth century.[66]

Research during the last 15 years has yielded an unprecedented amount of fundamental data regarding the economics of the production, marketing and sale of art in five major Italian cities, including Venice. The recent data make it possible to examine Carriera's position in her home city as an independent woman artist in a bigger context, and to analyse her career in more depth.

In 1679, the painters' guild, the Arte de' Depentori, launched a campaign and made a formal request to break away from the larger community of artisans and form a new institution, the Collegio de' Pittori (College of Painters), which was officially founded on 31 December 1682. The idea was to follow the model of the more organised art academies, where a specialised faculty could teach future artists following a specific curriculum and accordingly improve the quality of painting and subsequently the conditions of the painters in the city. There was no mention of an academy but the Collegio was a professional union that replaced the numerous private academies whose teaching was done in individual artists' houses.[67] Still, the general situation of the local art scene did not seem to recover. The responsibility for the dismal state of artists in Venice was attributed not only to the plague of 1631 but more specifically to the fact that local painters were unable to make a decent living, and were forced to work for patrons abroad. At the same time, the increasing number of foreign artists in the lagoon took over a threatening number of commissions. The seventeenth century was indeed an era when more and more foreigners made Venice their home for short or long periods of time, turning the city – much more than in the Renaissance – into a truly cosmopolitan centre of artistic exchange.

During the first half of the eighteenth century, Venetians generally viewed the realm of art in their home city as decayed and impoverished, even though the development of prices for artworks in Venice and the careers of painters like Pietro Bellotti, Pellegrini, Sebastiano Ricci, Tiepolo, Piazzetta and especially the miniaturist Carriera seemed to prove the opposite. Nevertheless, it is true that a painter who aimed to have a secure, guaranteed income was obliged or was thought to be obliged to travel, creating a talent drain in the city.[68] However, unlike many of her illustrious male colleagues who went to work abroad, Carriera managed to stay and work most of her life in Venice, making much more than just a living, which is even more impressive when considering some additional facts.

The frequently invoked deterioration of the Venetian art market was, according to some experts of the time, a sign of despicable practices whereby art had sunk to the lowest level of commerce: painters had started to sell their art in shops. The age-old concern about money corrupting art was confirmed by the painters' guild in 1679 when it criticised the same aspects of art production in Venice. These vivid sentiments led not only to the foundation of the Collegio de' Pittori but also to a clear and official distinction between painters, who were considered part of the liberal arts, and those considered mere craftsmen. Those other artisans included 'gilders (*doratori*), decorative and house painters (*dipintori*), painters of musical instruments (*cimbanari*), stationers (*cartolari*), miniaturists (*miniatori*), leather painters (*coridori*), painters of wax fruit, and still life painters (*naranzeri*, *fruttarioli*)'.[69] Thus Carriera was not considered to be a painter, and was part of the socially (and artistically) inferior group of artisans. Under the influence of local politics, guilds and academies often regulated the pricing and the commercial conduct of their members, and officially recognised painters (*pittori*) earned far more per capita than other craftsmen. Though this lack of recognition was demeaning to Carriera, and presented an objective difficulty, it also meant that she did not have to face the problems of membership, fees and commitments inherent in the classification. In being denied the status of an official painter, Carriera automatically achieved what many of the 'real' artists only gained by deliberately rejecting any affiliation with a guild or academy: she escaped jurisdictional control. Thus, she could work and pursue her profession with more freedom in her home.

Given all the concerns and the rhetoric of bad times, and the actual difficulties and real problems that artists had to face during the seventeenth century and the beginning of the eighteenth century, Carriera's achievements are even more impressive.

6

An Exceptional Life Comes to an End

The sojourn in Austria was Carriera's last experience outside of Venice. For the rest of her days, the artist stayed in her own city, working and intensely corresponding with her clients and friends all over Europe. Her life had been and continued to be centred in her hometown, where she had created an advantageous situation and exceptional position for herself. Nevertheless, during the last 20 years of her life, she had to cope with a number of painful and dramatic events.

On 9 May 1737, Giovanna, Carriera's sister and closest confidante, died, bringing the artist to the brink of collapse with severe depression. Although she decided to take in Angioletta, the younger sister of her former student and close friend Felicita Sartori, Rosalba did not experience the kind of relief she had hoped for. Giovanna could simply not be replaced by another 'younger sister'. The artist never recovered from her sister's death and, in the end, she only had one last request: 'After my death, I want to be buried in the vault of my family chapel [...] where my sister Giovanna has been buried.'[1]

That same year, she lost her friend and colleague, Nicolas Vleughels. In 1738, on 20 June, she endured the painful death of her mother. The loss of her good friend Pierre Crozat in May 1740 was a further blow, and when her brother-in-law, Pellegrini, died in November 1741, she had lost almost her entire family. Her youngest sister, Angela, the only member of her immediate family still living, took care of the discouraged and ailing artist.

Earlier, in 1724, Carriera began experiencing problems with her vision that would grow increasingly worse and plague her for the rest of her life. As early as 1727, she wrote a letter to Pierre-Jean Mariette in which she expressed how very difficult it was for her ('*una difficoltà ben grande*') to continue making miniatures. Her daily struggle is also revealed in a letter she sent from Vienna in 1730 asking her mother to write larger to make it easier for her to read the correspondence. And, in 1731, the artist had to explain once more that it was extremely stressful for her to produce miniatures as her output might not exhibit the same quality as before.[2]

Nonetheless, between 1744 and 1746 Carriera accepted a commission from Augustus III in Dresden to paint allegories of the *Four Elements* (figs 60–63). The first pastels she sent to Dresden must have been *Earth* and *Fire*, for in a letter sent to Venice on 18 April 1746, the agent insisted that she execute *Air* and *Water* while also reminding her of the pastels' measurements. Carriera's delay in delivering the commission no doubt reflected the problems caused by her degenerating eyesight. The longer-than-usual timespan between the execution of the first two and last two elements could also explain why the figures

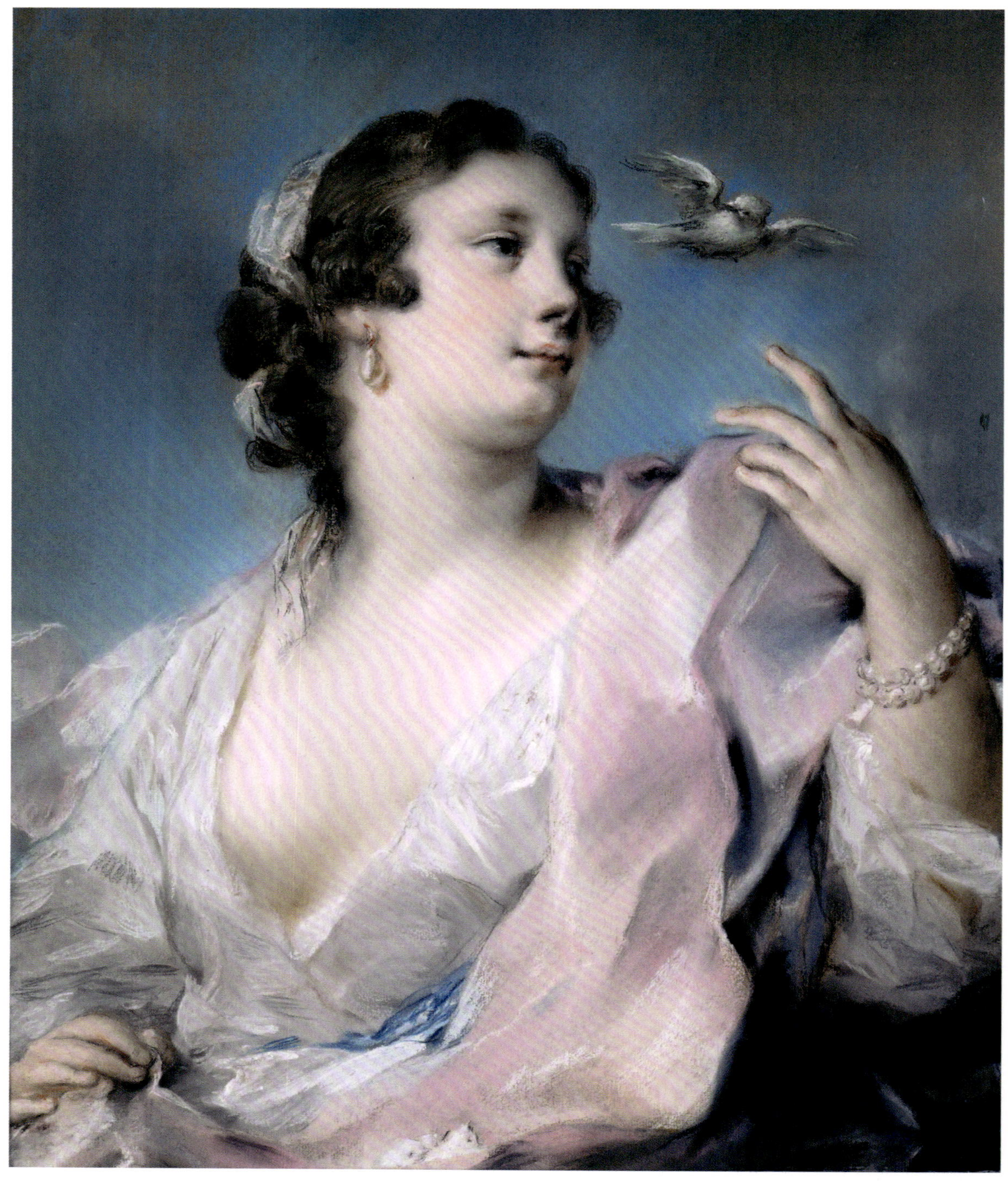

60 Rosalba Carriera, *Air*, 1744–6, pastel on paper, 56 × 46 cm (22 × 18 ⅛ in), Staatliche Kunstsammlungen, Gemäldegalerie Alte Meister, Dresden

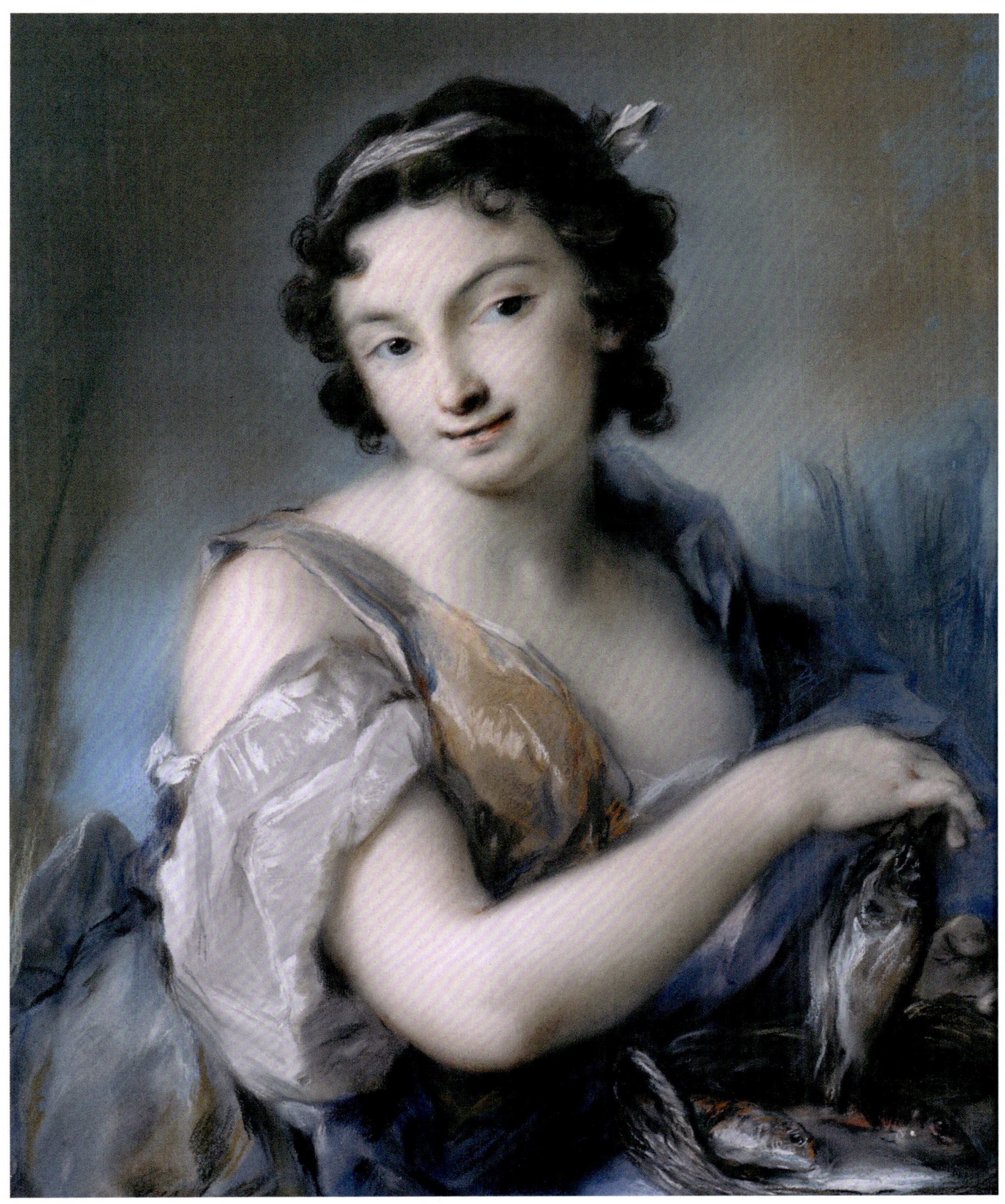

61 Rosalba Carriera, *Water*, 1744–6, pastel on paper, 56 × 46 cm (22 × 18 ⅛ in), Staatliche Kunstsammlungen, Gemäldegalerie Alte Meister, Dresden

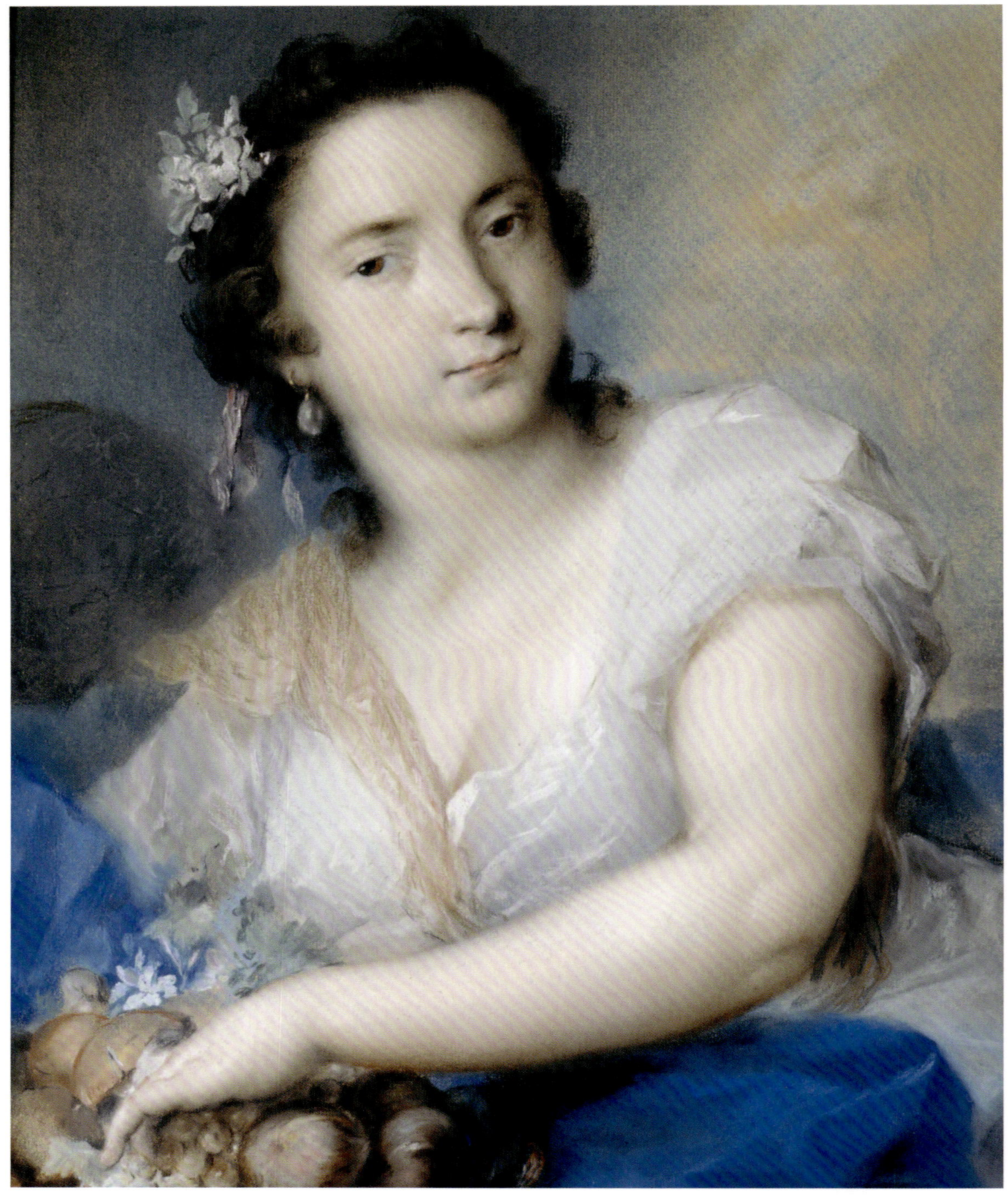

62 Rosalba Carriera, *Earth*, 1744–6, pastel on paper, 56 × 46 cm (22 × 18⅛ in), Staatliche Kunstsammlungen, Gemäldegalerie Alte Meister, Dresden

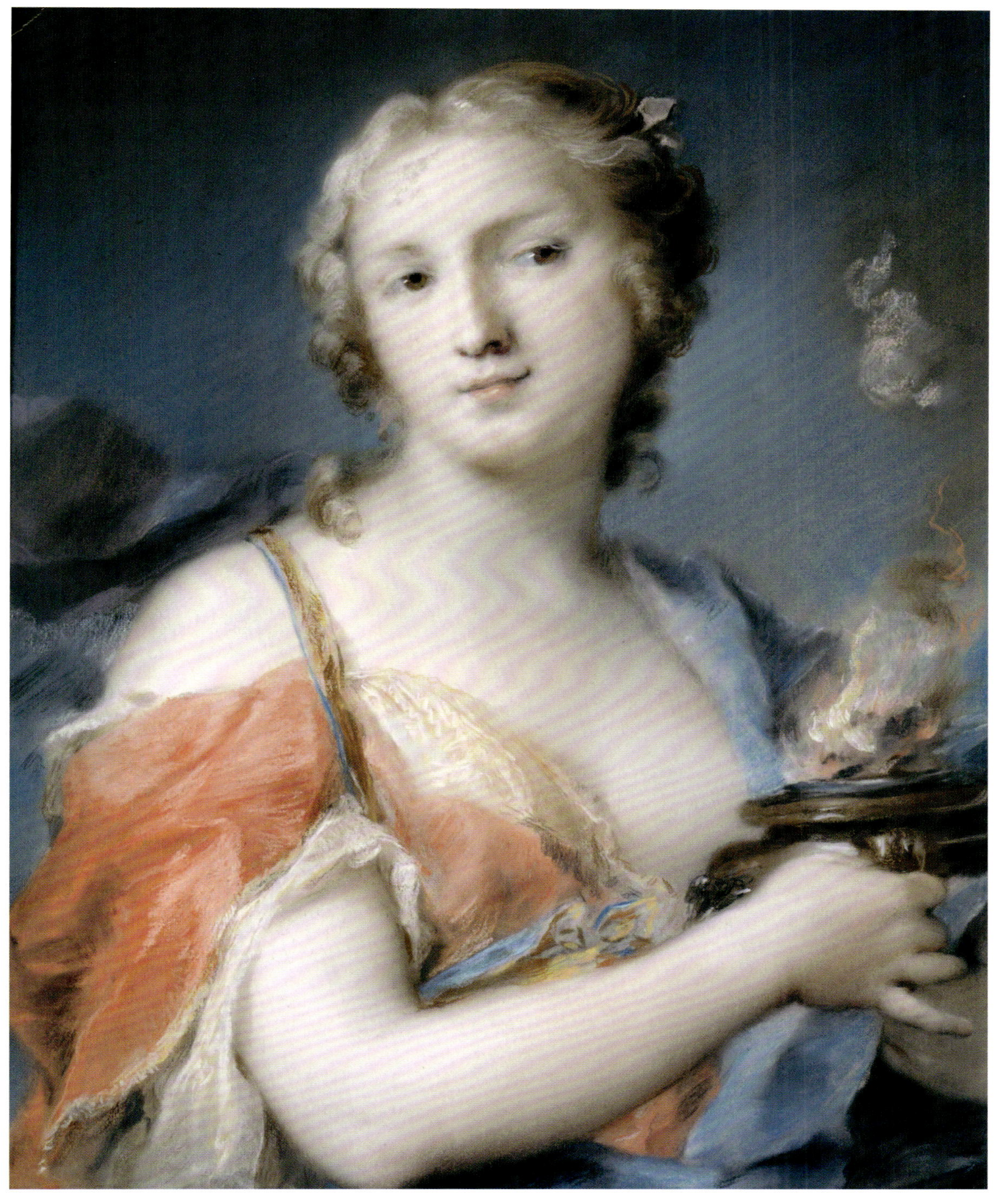

63 Rosalba Carriera, *Fire*, 1744–6, pastel on paper, 56 × 46 cm (22 × 18⅛ in), Staatliche Kunstsammlungen, Gemäldegalerie Alte Meister, Dresden

are of different sizes, with *Water* and *Air* being slightly smaller.[3]

Each allegorical topic is associated with a specific material object or attribute: *Earth* is shown as a dark-haired woman, dressed in blue and white, who seems to be picking mushrooms from a basket, while *Fire* is clothed in a bright orange and blue dress, holding a metal vase in her right hand. The red, orange and yellow flames that produce smoke disappearing in the air pick up the hues of her clothes. *Air* is represented by a woman who has just released a little bird that looks back at her while flying away. *Water* shows a smiling woman with dark, curly hair holding two fish above a basket placed on her lap. *Water* is the only pastel of the four that has a detailed background, with the reed hinting at the meaning of the personification. The four elements for Dresden belong to the last group of paintings Carriera executed in her life, and the commission was most likely one of the most challenging she had ever accepted, given her poor state of health. With the extreme popularity of this subject matter during Carriera's lifetime, she was able to command a noticeably higher price for such artworks, more than twice the average price of her other pastels.

Soon afterwards, for three years beginning in 1746, her cataracts nearly or fully blinded her. In the summer of 1746, Carriera underwent an operation that initially seemed to provide relief. This period is likely when Carriera made her last self-portrait, which is today housed in the Accademia in Venice (fig.64). It shows the artist at a time when she was over 70 years old, wearing simple, brown clothes. Her thin white hair is crowned with laurel, while her face has a sad, tired and pensive expression. The artist looks to her right side, avoiding direct eye contact with the spectator. She has no direct communication with the outside world; it is the onlooker who scrutinises her.

Even though this self-portrait has been, and still is, referred to as a depiction of *Tragedy*, Cesare Ripa's *Iconologia* and his description of 'Old Age' (*Vecchiezza*) and, especially, of Melancholy (*Malinconia*) as states of being offer a different reading of the portrait. Ripa recommends depicting Old Age as a pale, thin, white-haired woman with wrinkles on her face, clothed in the colour of withered leaves, and without any ornamentation. He held that cold blood caused human bodies to deteriorate during any age between 50 and 70 years and that weakening senses induced difficulties with physical effort and mental exercises. Old Age, he added, diminished eyesight, strength and ambition, while also crushing beauty and hope. Its colours resemble late autumn leaves, or the pit into which one will fall after death.[4] Ripa's reference to vision problems is noteworthy considering that Carriera executed this self-portrait as she was slowly turning blind. Even more striking is the artist's depiction of different coloured eyes, which most likely was the result of her cataracts as cataract-stricken blue eyes can look brownish. It is also possible that the effect of two different colours was emphasized by siderosis after her first surgery using the traditional couching procedure. Among the documents edited by Bernardina Sani is an undated record describing the state of the cataracts which at that point were disturbing her vision, especially in her right eye, although her left eye was already suffering as well.[5] As she had hardly ever done in other portraits, Carriera placed a special emphasis on her eyes by zooming in on her face, at a moment when her eyesight had practically left her. She might have been compelled to move the mirror so near to her eyes that she saw herself at close range, or she may have deliberately chosen to focus on the essence of a visual artist: the act of seeing, the act of observing and transforming the scrutinised object onto paper.

Reading Ripa's description of 'Melancholy' (*Malinconia*), the analogies are even more compelling. Again, the author talks about an old woman, sad and sorrowful, poorly dressed without any ornament. Melancholy, according to Ripa, has the same effects on human beings as winter has on trees and plants. Wind, low temperatures and snow make them look dry, sterile, naked and of little value. The author

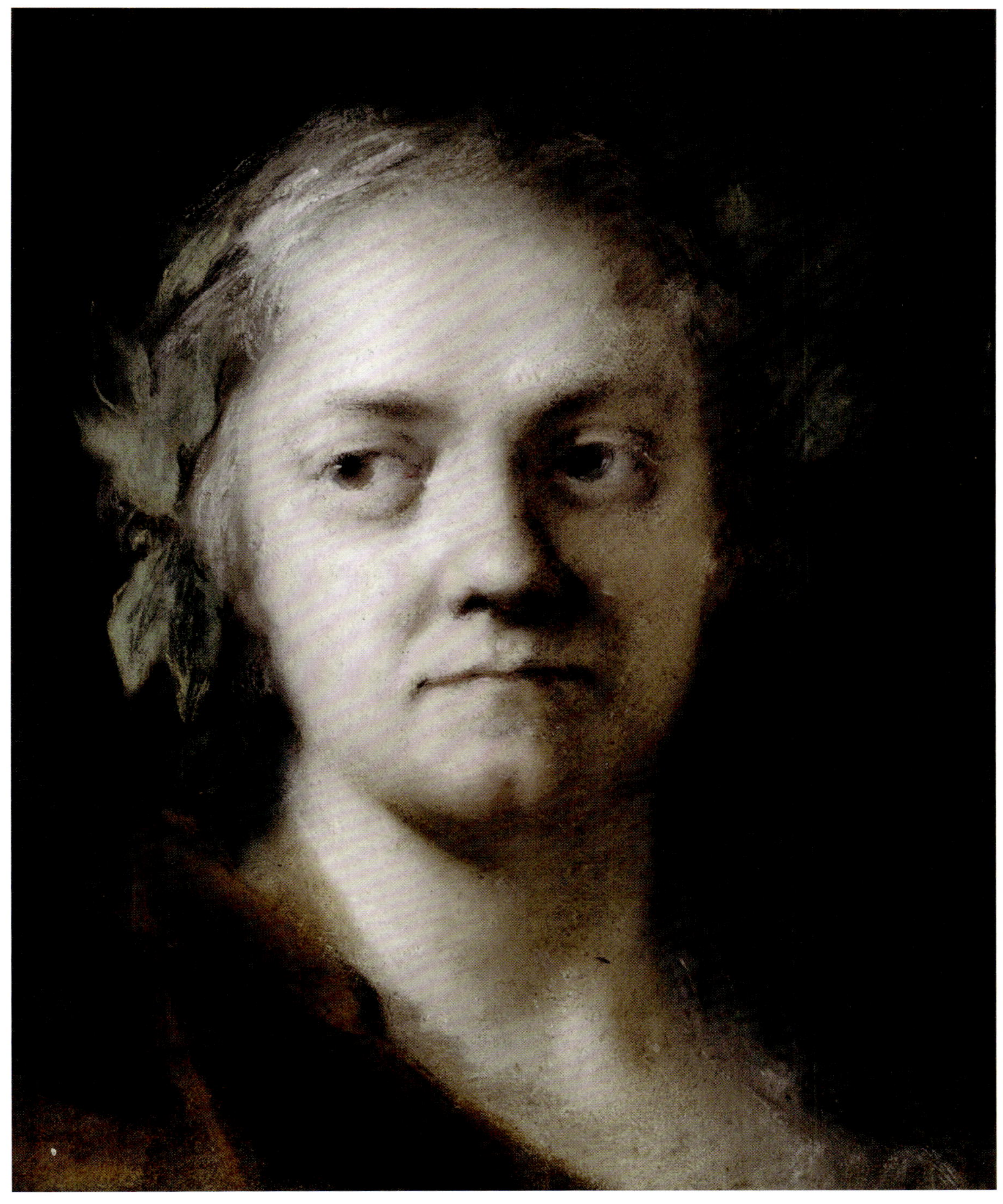

64 Rosalba Carriera, *Self-portrait*, *c.*1746, pastel on paper, 31 × 25 cm (12 ¼ × 9 ¾ in), Gallerie dell'Accademia, Venice

states that melancholic human beings always think of difficult things which, they force themselves to believe, are present and real, causing them sadness and pain. Their simple, plain clothes, he repeats, resemble trees without leaves or fruit. But, he adds at the end, melancholics are endowed with great experience and wisdom, which transforms them into individuals with an enormous capacity for judgement.[6] In fact, since the Renaissance, the melancholic (male) artist has been associated with an intellectual, art-stimulating, positive force that was recognised as the main characteristic of a 'genius'.[7] Looking again at the pastel in Venice and considering the reflections above, one can reasonably assume that Carriera depicted herself as a representation of both Ripa's Old Age and Melancholy, portraying an accurate image of what she was enduring at that time.

One last aspect is worth mentioning. Carriera had previously represented the laurel wreath of fame as an attribute in her depictions of poetry[8] and her series of Muses, like the one held by the J. Paul Getty Museum (fig.65).[9] In the late self-portrait, the wreath signifies her professional achievement and success as an internationally renowned artist, as well as an attribute of divine origin. It encompasses the capacities gained in old age, the life of an accomplished painter, and the wisdom and acuity described by Ripa. Most likely Carriera mingled her artistic and creative inspiration with her professional and personal triumph in this image as final proof of self-realisation and self-glorification. She clearly shows her suffering, but she still manages to crown herself while simultaneously crowning her melancholy and old age.

In April 1749, Carriera underwent a second operation that she hoped would further improve her condition.[10] In August 1750, the surgeons made a third attempt to remove her cataracts, but on 2 January 1751 she admitted, resignedly, to Mariette: '[…] I can no longer see anything, as though I were in the darkness of the night'.[11] Nonetheless, Carriera lived six more years and eventually died on 15 April 1757, at the age of 84. She was buried according to her wishes at the church of Santi Vito e Modesto. Unfortunately, the Carriera family tomb, which lay in front of the altar of the Holy Virgin, was demolished when the church was largely destroyed at the beginning of the nineteenth century.[12] However, it is known that Carriera ordered the following text for a tombstone when Giovanna died: 'To the greatest and the best God. For Giovanna Carriera and for themselves, Carriera, her living sister, and Alba, their mother, prepared this tomb in the year of the Lord 1738.'[13]

It is therefore not her tomb but her art that is kept alive in Venice today. Numerous museums all over the world keep examples of her outstanding interpretations of the sphere around her. Hopefully, with this book and other research on the artist, she will regain the fame she experienced during her lifetime when she was praised as 'an ornament of Italy and Europe's foremost female artist'.[14]

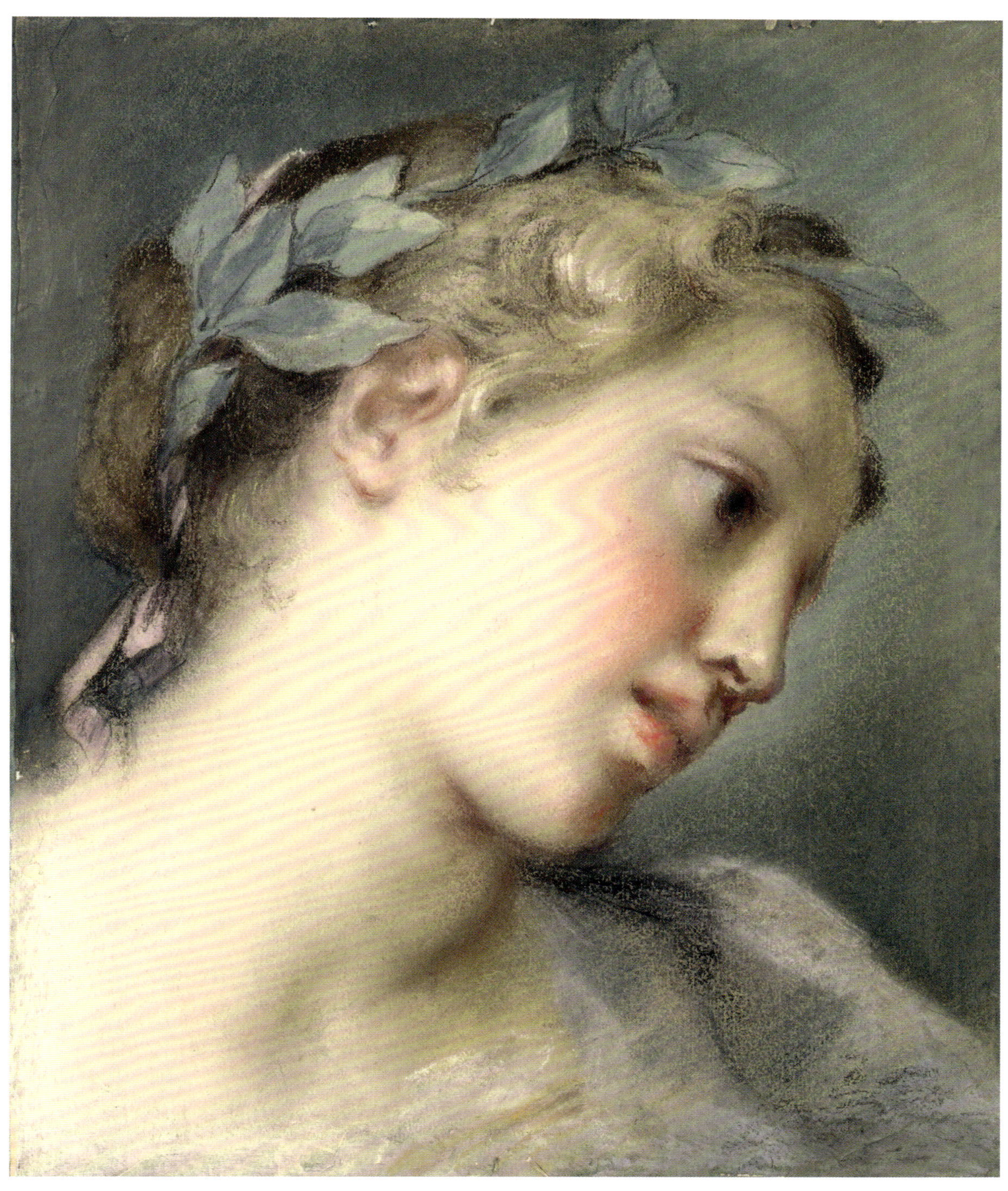

65 Rosalba Carriera, *A Muse*, mid-1720s, pastel on paper, 31 × 26 cm (12 3/16 × 10 1/4 in), J. Paul Getty Museum, Los Angeles, CA

Notes

PREFACE

1 De Girolami Cheney et al., 2009, p.68.
2 ibid., p.98.
3 Sani, 1985, vol.I, p.89.
4 Pavanello, 2007a, p.57.
5 Abate N.N., 1843 [1755], p.21.
6 Mehler, 2006, p.5; Cochin, 1773, 160.
7 Sani, 1988, 2007.

INTRODUCTION

1 Steward, 1996, p.16.
2 Zanini-Cordi, 2013, p.27.
3 Findlen, 2009, p.14.
4 Findlen, 2009. See also Julien, 2019, pp 62–84.

CHAPTER 1

1 Del Negro, 2007, p.34.
2 Zava Boccazzi, 1981, p.217.
3 Translation by Dabbs, 2008, p.35.
4 Dabbs, 2008, pp 35–6.
5 Pointon, 2014, p.17.
6 Pointon, 2001, p.53.
7 Favilla and Rugolo, 2007, p.17.
8 Coronelli, 1697, p.23.
9 Vogtherr, 2010, pp 19–20.
10 Rossi, 1996, p.426.
11 Owens, 2018, p.39.
12 Falconi, 2008, p.14.
13 Sani, 1985, vol.I, p.58.
14 Vogtherr, 2010, p.17.
15 See Sheriff, 1990, pp 105–7.
16 See, for example, Czerny, 2013, p.453.
17 Boose, 1975, p.362.
18 ibid.
19 Ripa, 1613, pt 1, pp 32–5.
20 De Girolami Cheney et al., 2009, p.73.
21 Shefer, 1991, p.447; Grieco, 2010; Alberti et al., 2014, p.201.
22 The Ovid Collection, Metamorphoses, trans. A.S. Kline, Book 10, https://ovid.lib.virginia.edu/trans/Metamorph10.htm (accessed on 14 March 2019).
23 Shefer, 1991; Grieco, 2010.
24 See Georgievska-Shine, 2016, p.65.
25 Kandeler and Ullrich, 2009.
26 Sheriff, 1990, p.192.
27 ibid., p.92.
28 Oberer, 2021.
29 See picture in ibid., p.3.
30 Simons, 1994, p.86.
31 ibid., p.94.
32 Traub, 1996, pp 25–8.
33 Pointon, 2001, p.68.
34 ibid., pp 63–6.
35 Lajer-Burcharth, 2001, pp 56–8.
36 Sani, 1985, vol.II, p.750.
37 Whistler, 2009, p.182; Spence, 1966, p.605; and Sani, 1985, vol. II, p.749.
38 Johns, 2003, pp 33–4.
39 Benton, 1996, pp 22–5.
40 Johns, 2003, p.33.
41 ibid.
42 Sheriff, 1996, p.111.
43 ibid., ch.3.
44 Sama, 2009, p.126.
45 Johns, 2003, pp 20, 32.
46 Sani, 1985, vol.I, p.95, n.5.
47 ibid.

CHAPTER 2

1 Ward, 2018, p.236.
2 Borzello, 2000, pp 65–73.
3 ffolliott, 2016, p.19.
4 Dézallier d'Argenville, 1762, p.314, translation by Dabbs, 2009, p.344.
5 ibid.
6 Pavanello, 2007a, p.57.
7 G. Zanetti, 1818, pp 18–19.
8 Pallucchini, 1970, p.161.
9 Greer, 2001 [1979], p.278.
10 Dabbs, 2008, pp 29–30; Dabbs, 2009, p.340.
11 Greer, 2001 [1979], p.75.

12 Rogers, 1982, p.216.
13 ffolliott, 2013, p.425.
14 Malamani, 1910, p.96; Dézallier d'Argenville, 1762, p.316.
15 Cochin, 1773, p.160.
16 West, 1999, pp 49, 52.
17 De Girolami Cheney et al., 2009, pp 68–9.
18 Dézallier d'Argenville, 1762, p.314, translation by Dabbs, 2009, p.344.
19 Dabbs, 2009, p.340.
20 Sani, 1985, vol.II, p.541.
21 Hoerschelmann, 1908, p.15.
22 Sani, 1985, vol.II, pp 559–60.
23 Goodman, 1989, p.332.
24 Murphy, 2007, pp 28–9.
25 Sani, 1985, vol.I, p.357.
26 Rosenthal, 1997, p.147.
27 Anon., 1737.
28 Rosenthal, 1997, p.148; and Anon., 1737, p.86.
29 ffolliott, 2013, p.428.
30 Spence, 1820, pp 246–7.
31 Rosenthal, 1997, p.154.
32 Johns, 2003, pp 28–9.
33 Pallucchini, 1970, p.161.
34 Sheriff, 1994, p.14.
35 Rosenthal, 1996, pp 308–11.
36 Sani, 1985, vol.II, p.648. See also Sama, 2009, p.129.
37 Borzello, 1998, p.30; Modesti, 2014, p.33.
38 Johns, 2003, p.27.
39 Limentani Virdis, 1996, p.22.
40 See Chambers-Schiller, 1984.
41 Del Negro, 2009, pp 66–73.
42 Moore, 2011, p.11.
43 Plebani, 2003, pp 47–8; Sama, 2008; Sama, 2009. See also Oberer, 2014, pp 63–8.
44 See Lanaro, 1991, p.129.
45 Bergalli, 1726, pp 224–5.
46 Molmenti, 1908, vol.III, pp 456–70.
47 Lanser, 1998–9, p.180.

CHAPTER 3

1 Jeffares, 2022b, p.7; and Burns, 2002a, pp 13–15.
2 McCullagh, 2006, pp 74–5; Sauvage, 2015, p.126.
3 Burns, 2007, pp 72, 105–11.
4 Monnier, 1984, pp 6, 241.
5 Burns, 2007, pp 19–21, 80–81.
6 Whistler, 2009, p.197.
7 Jeffares, 2022b, p.26.
8 Carriera, 2022, pp 14–15.
9 Sani, 1985, vol.I, p.10; Sani, 1988, p.13; Sani, 2007, p.11, and cat. no.1, p.59.
10 Bettagno, 1969, pp 20–26; Bettagno, 1994, pp 122–3; Lucchese, 2015.
11 Sani, 1985, vol.I, p.9.
12 Henning and Marx, 2007, pp 27–8; Sani, 2007, cat.no.23, p.75.
13 Schulze Altcappenberg, 1997, cat.no.53, p.86, fig.50.
14 Reynolds and Peter, 2016, p.15.
15 Ripa, 1603, p.404; Krellig, 2017, p.91.
16 Pasian, 2007, p.86.
17 ibid.
18 Langedijk, 1992, p.88.
19 Mehler, 2006, p.72.
20 Rosenthal, 2006, p.85; Modesti, 2014, p.77.
21 De Gaetani, 2015, p.69.
22 Sutherland Harris and Nochlin, 1976, p.162.
23 Rosenthal, 1996, p.307.
24 Oberer, 2020, pp 169, 171.
25 Burns, 2002b, p.18.
26 Burns, 2007, p.87.
27 Burns, 2002b, pp 19, 21.
28 Burns and Saunier, 2016, p.19.
29 Solkin, 1986, p.42.
30 Oberer, 2020, pp 173–6.
31 Breen, 1990, p.343.
32 Oberer, 2020, pp 128–33.
33 Welch, 2009, p.256.

CHAPTER 4

1 Del Negro, 2009, p.73.
2 Sani, 1985, vol.I, p.97.
3 Marx, 2010, p.17.
4 See Becker et al., 1994, p.50.
5 Cassidy-Geiger, 2018.
6 https://comtedelusace.wordpress.com/1740/04/16/comte-de-lusace-april-1-16-1740-venice/.
7 Henning and Marx, 2007, pp 84–7; Liebsch, 2009, pp 157–9.
8 Cassidy-Geiger, 2018.
9 Walther, 1972–5, p.81.
10 Cassidy-Geiger, 2018.
11 Flathe, 1884.
12 Delau, 2017, pp 92–3.
13 Flathe, 1884.
14 Henning and Marx, 2007, p.65.
15 Riepe, 2006, p.152.
16 Henning and Marx, 2007, p.65. Regarding the painting, see Sani, 2007, cat.no.222, pp 218–19; cat.no.223, p.220.
17 www.grham.hypotheses.org/3157 (accessed on 29 September 2020).
18 Pointon, 1993, pp 112–13.

19 ibid., p.117.
20 Fogelberg Rota, 2015, p.58.
21 ibid., pp 58–9.
22 Fogelberg Rota, 2013, pp 125, 129–32.
23 ibid., p.131.
24 Swinburne, 1686, p.208.
25 Sani, 2007, p.259.
26 Fogelberg Rota, 2015, pp 60–61.
27 Black, 1996, p.532.
28 Levey, 1959, p.144.
29 Russell, 1994, p.57.
30 Quoted in McGeary, 2014, p.118.
31 See Sani, 2007, cat.nos 321–2, pp 288–91.
32 Llewellyn, 2015, p.179.
33 Haskell, 1963, p.299.
34 Jeffares, 2022a, p.2. See also Sani, 2007, cat.no.56, p.91; cat. no.130, p.137; cat.no.179, p.180; cat.no.376, p.331.
35 Razzall, 2017, pp 21–31. See also Cust, 1913, p.151.
36 Whistler, 2009, p.185.
37 Sani, 2007, cat.nos 103–4, p.117; cat.no.300, p.272; cat.no.303, p.275; cat.no.304, p.276; cat.no.410, pp 355–6.
38 Whistler, 2009, p.201.
39 Cust and Colvin, 1898, p.4.
40 The painting is kept in a private collection in England, Whistler, 2009, p.192.
41 Whistler, 2009, p.186.
42 ibid., p.195.
43 Sani, 1985, vol.I, p.390, n.1.
44 ibid., vol.I, p.362.
45 Sama, 2009, p.128. See also Graziosi, 2009.
46 De Girolami Cheney et al., 2009, p.97.
47 Hoerschelmann, 1908, pp 15, 163; Ziskin, 2012, pp 70, 149, 152–4.
48 Dabbs, 2009, p.337.
49 Sani, 2007, p.9.
50 See Becker et al., 1994, p.47.
51 The full title is: Abecedario de P.-J. Mariette, et autres notes inédites de cet amateur sur les arts et les artistes. Carriera is mentioned among the artists discussed; see Mariette, 1851–60, vol.I (1851), pp 329–33.
52 Hagen and Hagen, 2003, p.272; Marx, 2010, p.15.
53 Jeffares, 2022a.
54 See Sani, 1985, vol.I, p.21.
55 Carriera, 2022.
56 Hoerschelmann, 1908, p.96.
57 Henning and Marx, 2007, p.33.
58 Carriera, 2022, p.20.
59 Walther, 1972–5, pp 71–2.
60 Kwass, 2006, pp 645–56.
61 Henning and Marx, 2007, p.30.
62 Sani, 1985, vol.II, pp 777–8.
63 Carriera, 2022.
64 Sani, 1985, vol.II, pp 456–7; West, 1999, p.49.
65 Carriera, 2022, p.20. See also Sani, 2007, p.53, and 2012, pp 298–9.
66 Henning and Marx, 2007, p.32.
67 Sani, 1985, vol.I, p.359.
68 Zava, 2007, p.20.
69 Adamczak, 2014, p.177 and p.189, n.58.
70 Sutherland Harris, in Sutherland Harris and Nochlin, 1979, p.35.
71 Montaiglon, 1881, p.302.
72 Sheriff, 1996, p.79; Von Fellenberg, 2017, pp 113–14.
73 De Girolami Cheney et al., 2009, pp 101, 99.
74 Montaiglon, 1881, p.303.
75 ibid., p.304.
76 Haskell, 1980, p.284.
77 Levey, 1959, p.170.
78 Nicholson, 2019, p.175.
79 Sani, 1985, vol.I, p.407, translation by Nicholson, 2019, p.175.
80 See Brylowe, 2019, p.14.
81 Sheriff, 1996, p.120.
82 Steele, 1997, pp 491–2.
83 Maral, 2017, pp 44–5.
84 See also Hyde, 2000, p.471.
85 See also Rosenthal, 1996, p.43.
86 Sani, 1985, vol.I, pp 415–16.
87 Malamani, 1910, p.60.
88 Henning and Marx, 2007, p.35.
89 Sani, 1985, vol.I, p.440.
90 Sagarra, 2009, p.26.
91 Braubach, 1977; and Mutschlechner, n.d.
92 Sagarra, 2009, p.26.
93 Wollenberg, 1991, p.232.
94 See Becker et al., 1994, pp 46–8.
95 BLKÖ, 1860.

CHAPTER 5

1 Dabbs, 2012, p.8.
2 ibid.
3 ibid., p.2.
4 Woods Marsden, 1998, p.3.
5 Jeffares, 2015, p.27.
6 Sohm, 2007, p.21.
7 ibid., pp 21–6.
8 Dabbs, 2017, p.24.
9 Campbell, 2010, p.830.
10 ibid., p.843.
11 Dabbs, 2012, p.15.

12 Levey, 1994, p.23.
13 Sohm, 1990, p.89; Zarrillo, 2016, p.11.
14 Zarrillo, 2016, pp 11–12.
15 Levey, 1994, p.24.
16 See also Robinson, 1994, pp 13–18.
17 Zarrillo, 2016, p.11.
18 Steward, 1996, p.18.
19 Jeffares, 2016, p.2.
20 ibid., pp 3–4.
21 Gabel, 2013, p.41.
22 Mandelli, 2017, p.602.
23 Giacometti, 1997, p.357.
24 Mandelli, 2017, p.602.
25 Henning and Marx, 2007, p.93.
26 Plebani, 2004, p.157.
27 Campbell, 2010, p.824.
28 Avery, 2000, p.4.
29 Emerson, 2005, p.68.
30 Avery, 2000, p.4.
31 Perego, 2020, pp 14–16.
32 Ascarelli, 1974.
33 Perego, 2020, pp 108–13.
34 Ascarelli, 1974.
35 ibid.
36 Perego, 2020, p.135.
37 Lee, 2002, pp 37–44, 65–71.
38 Dézallier d'Argenville, 1762, p.316. See also Sani, 1985, vol.II, pp 499, 519.
39 Sani, 2003, pp 495–7.
40 Puhlmann, 2003, p.1.
41 ibid., p.10.
42 Trauth, 2009, pp 34–8.
43 Johnson, 2011, pp 97, 101.
44 Steward, 1996, pp 20–21.
45 Rosenthal, 2004.
46 Johns, 2003, p.38; Sani, 1991, p.81; Ripa, 1603, p.128.
47 De Grazia, 1996, pp 256–7.
48 Pedrocco, 1990, p.82.
49 Perry, 2004, p.150.
50 Sani, 2007, cat.no.413, p.358.
51 Burns, 2007, p.98.
52 Welch, 2009, p.260; and Elston, 2018, p.29.
53 Vout, 2005, p.83; and Mambella 2008, pp 263–5.
54 Mehler, 2006, p.19. See also Moücke, 1762, p.241.
55 Haskell, 1980, p.262; Sani, 2007, p.18; Baetjer and Links, 1989; p.87, Knox, 1983, p.17.
56 Del Negro, 2009, p.80; and Jeffares, 2022a.
57 See Sohm, 2010b, p.210.
58 Knox, 1983, p.18; Haskell, 1980, p.262.
59 Sohm, 2010b, p.210; and Goldthwaite, 2010, p.286.
60 Ago, 2010, p.267.
61 Goldthwaite, 2010, p.293.
62 Krellig, 2017, pp 97–8.
63 Sohm, 2010a, p.23.
64 Krellig, 2017, pp 98–9.
65 Moretti, 2011, p.308.
66 Krellig, 2017, p.101.
67 Nepi Sciré, 1994, p.60.
68 Sohm, 2010b, p.220.
69 ibid., p.214.

CHAPTER 6

1 Sani, 1985, vol.II, p.735.
2 ibid., vol.II, pp 466, 516, 558.
3 Henning and Marx, 2007, pp 94–5.
4 See the original text in Ripa, 1603, pp 493–4.
5 Sani, 1985, vol.II, pp 715–16.
6 See the original text in Ripa, 1603, p.303.
7 Klibansky et al., 1964.
8 Sani, 2007, cat.no.419, p.366; cat.no.374, p.331; cat.no.376, p.331.
9 ibid., cat.no.254, p.242; cat.no.255, p.242.
10 Zava Boccazzi, 1981, pp 219–20.
11 Sani, 1985, vol.II, p.725.
12 Urban, 1994–5, pp 200–1.
13 Zava Boccazzi, 1981, p.221, n.13; and Mehler, 2006, p.32.
14 Sani, 1985, vol.I, p.89.

Bibliography

Adamczak, Audrey (2014). 'Présence du pastel au Salon: étude sur l'émergence d'un art', in Isabelle Pachet, ed., *Le Salon de l'Académie royale de peinture et de sculpture: archéologie d'une institution*. Paris: Hermann, 172–94.

Ago, Renata (2010). 'Five Industrious Cities', in Spear and Sohm, eds, *Painting for Profit*, 254–73.

Alberti, Francesca, Nikolaus Manuel Deutsch and Urs Graf (2014). 'Cuckolds, Impotence and Sex Workers in Swiss Renaissance Art (c.1510–1517)', in Sara F. Matthews-Grieco, ed., *Cuckoldry, Impotence and Adultery in Europe (15th–17th century)*. London/New York: Ashgate, 183–213.

Anon. (1737). *The Whole Duty of a Woman or, an Infallible Guide to the Fair Sex*. London: T. Read.

Ascarelli, Alessandra (1974). 'Campanini, Barbara', in *Dizionario Biografico degli Italiani*, 17. Online version: www.treccani.it/enciclopedia/ricerca/Campanini-Barbara/ (accessed on 15 April 2021).

Avery, Charles (2000). 'Giuseppe Broccetti's Medal of the Singer Faustina Bordoni', *The Medal*, 36: 3–7.

Baetjer, Katharine, and J.G. Links, eds (1989). *Canaletto*, exh. cat., New York, Metropolitan Museum of Art, 30 October 1989–21 November 1990. New York: Abrams.

Banta, Andaleeb Badiee, ed. (2016). *The Enduring Legacy of Venetian Renaissance Art*. London/New York: Routledge, Taylor & Francis.

Becker, Christoph, Axel Burkarth and August Bernhard Rave (1994). 'The International Taste for Venetian Art: The Habsburg Empire', in Martineau and Robinson, eds, *Glory of Venice*, 45–54.

Benton, Michael G. (1996). 'Education and Sister Arts', *Journal of Aesthetic Education*, 30(1): 19–38.

Bergalli, Luisa (1726). *Componimenti poetici delle più illustre rimatrici d'ogni secolo raccolti da Luisa Bergalli*. Venice: Antonio Mora.

Bettagno, Alessandro, ed. (1969). *Caricature di Anton Maria Zanetti*, Cataloghi di Mostre, Istituto di Storia dell'Arte 29, exh.cat., Venice, Fondazione Giorgio Cini, Centro di Cultura e Civiltà, San Giorgio. Venice: Neri Pozza.

— (1994). 'Rococo Artists', in Martineau and Robinson, eds, *Glory of Venice*, 113–38.

Black, Jeremy (1996). 'Italy and the Grand Tour: The British Experience in the Eighteenth Century', *Annuali d'Italianistica*, 14, 'L'Odeporica / Hodoeporics: On Travel Literature': 532–41.

BLKÖ (1860). 'Habsburg, Amalie Wilhelmine von Braunschweig-Lüneburg', *Biographisches Lexikon des Kaiserthums Österreich*, 6: 147. Online version: https://de.wikisource.org/wiki/BLK%C3%96:Habsburg,_Amalie_Wilhelmine_von_Braunschweig-L%C3%BCneburg (accessed on 16 December 2019).

Boose, Lynda E. (1975). 'Othello's Handkerchief: "The Recognizance and Pledge of Love"', *English Literature Renaissance*, 5(3), 'Studies in Shakespeare': 360–74.

Borzello, Frances (1998). *Seeing Ourselves: Women's Self-Portraits*. London: Thames & Hudson.

— (2000). *A World of Our Own: Women as Artists*. London: Thames & Hudson.

Braubach, Max (1977). 'Karl VI.', *Neue Deutsche Biographie*, 11: 211–18. Online version: www.deutsche-biographie.de/pnd118560107.html#ndbcontent (accessed on 20 June 2018).

Breen, Timothy H. (1990). 'The Meaning of "Likenesss": American Portrait Painting in an Eighteenth-Century Consumer Society', *Word and Image*, 4(4): 325–50.

Brylowe, Thora (2019). *Romantic Art in Practice: Cultural Work and the Sister Arts, 1760–1820*. Cambridge/New York: Cambridge University Press.

Burns, Thea (2002a). 'Distinguishing between Chalk and Pastel

in Early Drawings', in Stratis and Salvesen, eds, *The Broad Spectrum*, 12–15.
— (2002b). 'Making Up the Face: Technique and Meaning in the Pastels of Rosalba Carriera', in Stratis and Salvesen, eds, *The Broad Spectrum*, 17–22.
— (2007). *The Invention of Pastel Painting*. London: Archetype.
Burns, Thea, and Philippe Saunier (2016). *The Art of the Pastel.* New York: Abbeville Press.
Campbell, Erin J. (2010). 'Saints, and Matriarchs: Portraits of Old Women in Early Modern Italy', *Renaissance Quarterly*, 63(3): 807–49.
Carriera, Rosalba (2022). 'Rosalba Carriera's Journal', in Neil Jeffares, *Pastels & Pastellists*, www.pastellists.com/Essays/Carriera_journal.pdf (accessed on 20 July 2022).
Cassidy-Geiger, Maureen (2018). *Die Grande Kur – Prinz Friedrich Christian von Sachsen auf der Suche nach Heilung und Kultur in Italien, 1738–1740*, exh.cat., Residenzschloss Dresden, 9 May–19 August 2018. Dresden: Staatliche Kunstsammlungen.
Chambers-Schiller, Lee Virginia (1984). *Liberty, a Better Husband: Single Women in America; The Generation of 1780–1840*. New Haven, CT/London: Yale University Press.
Cochin, Charles-Nicolas (1773). *Voyage d'Italie, ou recueil de notes*, vol.III. Paris: Jombert.
Coronelli, Vincenzo (1697). *Viaggio d'Italia in Inghilterra*. Venice: Tramontino.
Cust, Lionel (1913). 'Notes on Pictures in the Royal Collections – XXV: The Paintings Bought for George III in Italy, Consul Smith, and Antonio Canale – I', *Burlington Magazine for Connoisseurs*, 23(123): 150–55, 157, 160–62.
Cust, Lionel, and Sidney Colvin (1898). *History of the Society of Dilettanti*. London/New York: Macmillan.
Czerny, Ilonka (2013). 'Am Anfang war der Paradies-Apfel – zum Symbol- und Darstellungsgehalt einer Frucht', in Johanna Aufreiter, Gunther Reisinger, Elisabeth Sobieczky and Claudia Steinhardt-Hirsch, eds, *Kunst Kritik Geschichte: Festschrift für Johann Konrad Eberlein*. Berlin: Reimer, 443–69.
Dabbs, Julia Kathleen (2008). 'Anecdotal Insights: Changing Perceptions of Italian Women Artists in Eighteenth-Century Life Stories', *Eighteenth-Century Women*, 5: 29–51.
— (2009). *Life Stories of Women Artists, 1550–1800: An Anthology*. Farnham: Ashgate.
— (2012). 'Vision and Insight: Portraits of the Aged Woman Artist, 1600–1800', *Occasion: Interdisciplinary Studies in the Humanities*, 4 (14 June): 1–15.
— (2017). 'Making the Invisible Visible: The Presence of Older Women Artists in Early Modern Artistic Biography', in Cathy McGlynn, Margaret O'Neill and Michaela Schrage-Früh, eds, *Ageing Women in Literature and Visual Culture: Reflections, Refractions, Remainings*. Cham: Springer, 23–30.
De Gaetani, Elisa (2015). 'Die Künstlerinnen in der Selbstporträtsammlung der Uffizien in Florenz – eine Auswahl', Master's thesis, Graz University.
De Girolami Cheney, Liana, Alicia Craig Faxon and Kathleen Lucy Russo (2009). *Self-Portraits by Women Painters.* Washington, DC: New Academia Publishing.
De Grazia, Diane (1996). 'Tiepolo and the "Art" of Portraiture', in Keith Christiansen, ed., *Giambattista Tiepolo, 1696–1770*. New York: Metropolitan Museum of Art, 255–61.
Del Negro, Piero (2007). 'Rosalba Carriera: la famiglia e la società veneziana', in Pavanello, ed., *Rosalba Carriera 'prima pittrice de l'Europa'*, 33–40.
— (2009). 'Le relazioni di Rosalba Carriera e della sua famiglia con il patriziato veneziano', in Pavanello, ed., *Rosalba Carriera 1673–1757: Atti del Convegno*, 45–96.
Delau, Reinhard (2017). *August der Starke und seine Mätressen*. Dresden: Saxophon.
Dézallier d'Argenville, Antoine-Joseph (1762). *Abrégé de la vie des plus fameux peintres*. Paris: De Bure l'aîné.
Dizionario biografico degli Italiani (1960–2017), ed. Alberto M. Ghisalberti, 90 vols. Rome: Istituto della Enciclopedia Italiana.
Elston, Miranda L. (2018). 'Hilliard's Impassioned Miniatures: Enacted Desire within the Elizabethan Court', in Pappe and Schmieglitz-Otten, eds, *Portrait Miniatures*, 26–33.
Emerson, Isabelle (2005). *Five Centuries of Women Singers.* Westport, CT: Greenwood.
Falconi, Bernardo (2008). 'Rosalba Carriera (1673–1757) und die Miniaturmalerei auf Elfenbein', in Bernd Pappe, Juliane Schmieglitz-Otten and Birgitt Schmedding, eds, *Miniaturen des Rokoko aus der Sammlung Tansey*. Munich: Hirmer, 14–23.
Favilla, Massimo, and Ruggero Rugolo (2007). '"Tant plus petit, tant plus beau": i ritratti in miniature dal Settecento all'Ottocento dei Musei Civici Veneziani', *Bollettino dei Musei Civici Veneziani*, 3: 8–91.
ffolliott, Sheila (2013). 'Early Modern Women Artists', in Allyson M. Poska, Jane Couchman and Katherine A. McIver, eds, *Ashgate Research Companion to Women and Gender in Early Modern Europe*. Farnham: Ashgate, 423–43.
— (2016). '"Più che famose": Some Thoughts on Women Artists in Early Modern Europe', in Sheila Barker, ed., *Women Artists in Early Modern Italy: Careers, Fame, and Collectors*. London: Harvey Miller, 15–27.
Findlen, Paula (2009). 'Introduction: Gender and Culture in Eighteenth-Century Italy', in Findlen et al., eds, *Italy's Eighteenth Century*, 1–33.
Findlen, Paula, Wendy Wassyng Roworth and Catherine M.

Sama, eds (2009). *Italy's Eighteenth Century: Gender and Culture in the Age of the Grand Tour*. Stanford: Stanford University Press.

Flathe, Heinrich Theodor (1884). 'Lubomirska, Ursula Katharina Fürstin von', *Allgemeine Deutsche Biographie*, 19: 333–4. Online version: www.deutsche-biographie.de/pnd137875258.html#adbcontent (accessed on 15 September 2020).

Fogelberg Rota, Stefano (2013). 'Education, Pilgrimage and Pleasure. The Rhetorical Strategies in the Writings of Three Eighteenth-Century Swedish Travellers to Italy', *Acta ad archaeologiam at atrium historiam pertinentia. Institutum Romanum Norvegiae, Universita Osloensis*, 26: 123–38.

— (2015). 'La Roma aracde del senatore svedese Nils Bielke', in Sabrina Norlande Eliasson and Stefano Fogelberg Rota, eds, *City of the Soul. The Literary Making of Rome*. Stockholm: Svenka Institutet i Rom, 57–71.

Gabel, Esther (2013). 'The Sisters Sagredo: Passion and Patronage in Eighteenth-Century Venice', in Nebahat Avcioğlu and Emma Jones, eds, *Architecture, Art and Identity in Venice and its Territories*. Burlington, VT: Ashgate, 33–48.

Georgievska-Shine, Anita (2016). 'A Beautiful Woman Should Break Her Mirror Early', in Banta, ed., *The Enduring Legacy of Venetian Renaissance Art*, 61–72.

Giacometti, Margherita (1997). 'Carriera, Rosalba', in Delia Gaze, *Dictionary of Women Artists*, 2 vols. London/Chicago, IL: Fitzroy Dearborn, vol.I, 354–9.

Goldthwaite, Richard A. (2010). 'The Painting Industry in Early Modern Italy', in Spear and Sohm, eds, *Painting for Profit*, 274–301.

Goodman, Dena (1989). 'Enlightenment Salons: The Convergence of Female and Philosophical Ambitions', *Eighteenth-Century Studies*, 22(3): 329–50.

Graziosi, Elisabetta (2009). 'Revisiting Arcadia: Women and Academies in Eighteenth-Century Italy', in Findlen et al., eds, *Italy's Eighteenth Century*, 103–24.

Greer, Germaine (2001 [1979]). *The Obstacle Race: The Fortunes of Women Painters and their Work*. London: Secker & Warburg.

Grieco, Allen J. (2010). 'From Roosters to Cocks: Italian Renaissance Fowl and Sexuality', in Sara F. Matthews-Grieco, ed., *Erotic Cultures of Renaissance Italy*. Farnham: Ashgate, 89–140.

Hagen, Rose Marie, and Rainer Hagen (2003). 'A Morning at the Art Dealer's: Antoine Watteau; Shop-sign for the Art Dealer Gersaint, 1720', in Rose Marie Hagen and Rainer Hagen, *What Great Paintings Say*, 2 vols. Cologne: Taschen, vol.II, 268–73.

Haskell, Francis (1963). *Patrons and Painters: A Study in the Relations between Italian Art and Society in the Age of Baroque*. London: Chatto & Windus.

— (1980). *Patrons and Painters: A Study in the Relations between Italian Art and Society in the Age of Baroque*, rev. edn. New Haven, CT/London: Yale University Press.

Henning, Andreas, and Harald Marx (2007). *Das Kabinett der Rosalba: Rosalba Carriera und die Pastelle der Dresdner Gemäldegalerie alte Meister*. Munich/Berlin: Deutscher Kunstverlag.

Hoerschelmann, Emilie von (1908). *Rosalba Carriera die Meisterin der Pastellmalerei: Studien und Bilder aus der Kunst- und Kulturgeschichte des 18. Jahrhunderts*. Leipzig: Klinkhardt & Biermann.

Hyde, Melissa (2000). '"The Makeup" of the Marquise: Boucher's Portrait of Pompadour at Her Toilette', *Art Bulletin*, 82: 453–75.

Jeffares, Neil (2006). *Dictionary of Pastellists before 1800*. London: Unicorn Press. Online version, regularly updated: Neil Jeffares, *Pastels & Pastellists*, www.pastellists.com.

— (2015). 'Liotard and the Medium of Pastel', in Christopher Baker, William Hauptman and Mary Anne Stevens, eds, *Jean-Etienne Liotard 1702–1789*, exh.cat., Scottish National Gallery, Edinburgh, 4 July–13 September 2015, Royal Academy of Arts, London, 24 October 2015–31 January 2016. London: Royal Academy of Arts, 26–33.

— (2016). 'Rosalba Carriera, *Gustavus, Viscount Boyne*', in *Pastels & Pastellists*, www.pastellists.com/Essays/Carriera_Boyne.pdf, updated 27 August 2016 (accessed on 15 July 2022).

— (2022a). 'Carriera, Rosalba', in *Pastels & Pastellists*, www.pastellists.com/articles/Carriera.pdf, updated 8 September 2022 (accessed on 13 September 2022).

— (2022b). 'Prolegomena', in *Pastels & Pastellists*, www.pastellists.com/misc/prolegomena.pdf, updated 28 June 2022 (accessed on 17 August 2022).

Johns, Christopher M.S. (2003). '"An Ornament of Italy and the Premier Female Painter of Europe": Rosalba Carriera and the Roman Academy', in Melissa Hyde, ed., *Women, Art and the Politics of Identity in Eighteenth-Century Europe*. Aldershot: Ashgate, 20–45.

Johnson, James H. (2011). *Venice Incognito: Masks in the Serene Republic*. Los Angeles, CA: University of California Press.

Julien, Albane (2019). *Rosalba Carriera. Une vénitienne dans l'Europe des Lumières. Entre peinture et écriture (1673–1757)*, Biographies Série XVIIe–XVIIIe siècle. Paris: L'Harmattan.

Kandeler, Riklef, and Wolfram R. Ullrich (2009). 'Symbolism of Plants: Examples from European-Mediterranean Culture presented with Biology and History of Art: MAY:

Columbine', *Journal of Experimental Botany*, 60(6): 1535–6.
Klibansky, Raymond, Erwin Panofsky and Fritz Saxl (1964). *Saturn and Melancholy. Studies in the History of Natural Philosophy, Religion and Art*. London: Nelson.
Knox, George, ed. (1983). *Piazzetta: A Tercentenary Exhibition of Drawing, Prints and Books*, exh.cat., Washington, DC, National Gallery of Art, 20 November 1983–26 February 1984. Washington, DC: National Gallery of Art.
Krellig, Heiner (2017). 'Rosalba Carriera: Neue Quellen und Erkenntnisse zu den Lebensumständen der "ersten Malerin Europas"', in Münch et al., eds, *Künstlerinnen*, 89–110.
Kwass, Michael (2006). 'Big Hair: A Wig History of Consumption in Eighteenth-Century France', *American Historical Review*, 111: 631–59.
Lajer-Burcharth, Ewa (2001). 'Pompadour´s Touch: Difference in Representation', *Representations*, 73(1): 54–88.
Lanaro, Anna (1991). 'Luisa Bergalli Gozzi', in Antonia Arslan, Adriana Chemello and Gilberto Pizzamiglio, eds, *Le stanze ritrovate: antologie di scrittrici venete del Quattrocento al Novecento*. Venice: Eidos, 127–38.
Langedijk, Karla (1992). *Die Selbstbildnisse der holländischen und flämischen Künstler in der Galleria degli Autoritratti der Uffizien in Florenz*. Florence: Edizioni Medicea.
Lanser, Susan S. (1998–9). 'Befriending the Body: Female Intimacies as Class Acts', *Eighteenth-Century Studies*, 32(2), 'Politics of Friendship': 179–98.
Lee, Carol (2002). *Ballet in Western Culture. A History of its Origins and Evolution*. New York: Routledge.
Levey, Michael (1959). *Painting in XVIII Century Venice*. London: Phaidon.
— (1994). 'Introduction to 18th-Century Venetian Art', in Martineau and Robinson, eds, *Glory of Venice*, 22–43.
Liebsch, Thomas (2009). ‚Catalogue number 6, Rosalba Carriera, Kurprinz Friedrich August II. von Sachsen (1696–1763)', in Harald Marx, ed., *Sehnsucht und Wirklichkeit: Wunschbilder. Malerei für Dresden im 18. Jahrhundert*. Cologne: König, 157–9.
— (2010). '"… una picciola e scelta raccolta di quadri moderni": Francesco Algarottis Gemäldeauftrag an zeitgenössische Maler in Venedig', in Marx and Henning, eds, *Venedig–Dresden*, 217–39.
Limentani Virdis, Caterina, ed. (1996). *Le tele svelate: antologia di pittrici venete dal Cinquecento al Novecento*. Mirano: Eidos.
Llewellyn, Tim (2015). 'Owen McSwiny: Impresario of Printmakers', in Bozena Anna Kowalxzyk, ed., *Venezia Settecento: Studi in memoria di Alessandro Bettagno*. Milan: Cinisella Balsamo, 179–87.
Lucchese, Enrico (2015). *L'Album di caricature di Anton Maria Zanetti alla Fondazione Giorgio Cini*. Venice: Lineadacqua.
McCullagh, Suzanne Folds (2006). '"A Finesse of the Crayon": Eighteenth-Century French Portraits in Pastel', *Art Institute Chicago Museum Studies*, 32(2), 'Old Masters at the Art Institute of Chicago': 72–87, 96.
McGeary, Thomas (2014). 'British Grand Tourists Visit Rosalba Carriera, 1732–41. New Documents', *The British Art Journal*, 15(1): 117–19.
Malamani, Vittorio (1910). *Rosalba Carriera*, 2nd edn. Bergamo: Istituto Italiano d'Arti Grafiche.
Mambella, Raffaele (2008). *Antinoo: 'Un Dio malinconico' nella storia e nell'arte*. Rome: Editore Collombo.
Mandelli, Vittorio (2017). 'Sagredo, Caterina', in *Dizionario biografico degli Italiani*, vol.LXXXIX, 601–3.
Maral, Alexandre, ed. (2017). *Apollo Served by the Nymphs: The Masterpiece of the Gardens of Versailles*. Paris: Artlys.
Mariette, Pierre-Jean (1851–60). *Abecedario de P.-J. Mariette, et autres notes inédites de cet amateur sur les arts et les artistes*, ed. Charles Philippe de Chennevières-Pointel and Anatole de Montaiglon, 6 vols. Paris: Dumoulin.
Martineau, Jane, and Andrew Robinson, eds (1994). *The Glory of Venice: Art in the Eighteenth Century*. New Haven, CT: Yale University Press.
Marx, Barbara (2010). 'Diplomaten, Agenten, Abenteurer im Dienst der Künste: Kunstbeziehungen zwischen Dresden und Venedig', in Marx and Henning, eds, *Venedig–Dresden*, 10–67.
Marx, Barbara, and Andreas Henning, eds (2010). *Venedig–Dresden: Begegnung zweier Kulturstädte*. Dresden: E.S. Seemann.
Mehler, Ursula (2006). *Rosalba Carriera 1673–1757: die Bildnismalerin des 18. Jahrhunderts*. Königstein: Ortensia.
Modesti, Adelina (2014). *Elisabetta Sirani, 'Virtuosa': Women's Cultural Production in Early Modern Bologna*, Late Medieval and Early Modern Studies 22. Turnhout: Brepols.
Molmenti, Pompeo (1908). *La storia di Venezia nella vita privata dalle origini alla caduta della Repubblica*, 3 vols. Bergamo: Istituto Italiano d'Arte Grafiche.
Monnier, Geneviève (1984). *Pastels from the 16th to the 20th Century*. New York: Rizzoli International.
Montaiglon, Anatole de (1881). *Procès-verbaux de l'Académie Royale de peinture et de sculpture (1648–1793), publiés pour la Société de l'Histoire de l'Art Français d'après les registres originaux conserves à l'Ecole des Beaux-Art*, IV. Paris: Charavy Frères, Libraires de la Société.
Moore, Lisa (2011). *Sister Arts: The Erotics of Lesbian Landscape*. Minneapolis, MN/London: University of Minnesota Press.
Moretti, Lino (2011). 'Rosalba Carriera: l'inventario dei suoi beni e alcune minuzie marginali', *Arte Veneta*, 68: 308–19.
Moücke, Francesco (1762). *Serie di ritratti degli eccellenti pittori*

dipinti di propria mano che esistono nell'Imperial galleria di Firenze, IV. Florence: Nella Stamperia Moückiana.
Münch, Birgit Ulrike, Andreas Tacke and Markwart Herzog, eds (2017). *Künstlerinnen: neue Perspektiven auf ein Forschungsfeld der Vormoderne*. Petersberg: Michael Imhof.
Murphy, Caroline (2007). 'The Economics of the Woman Artist', in Vera Fortunati Pietrantonio, Jordana Pomeroy and Claudio M. Strinati, eds, *Italian Women Artists from Renaissance to Baroque*. Milan/New York: Skira, 23–30.
Mutschlechner, Martin (n.d.). 'Charles VI: The Last Habsburg', in *The World of the Habsburgs*, www.habsburger.net/en/chapter/charles-vi-last-habsburg (accessed on 20 June 2018).
N.N., Abate (1843 [1755]). *Memorie intorno alla vita di Rosalba Carriera, celebre pittrice veneziana, raccolte dall'Abate N.N., MDCCLV*, ed. Giovambattista Valeri. Padua: Coi Tipi di A. Sicca.
Nepi Sciré, Giovanna (1994). 'Aspects of Cultural Politics in 18th-Century Venice', in Martineau and Robinson, eds, *Glory of Venice*, 60–67.
Nicholson, Kathleen (2019). 'Having the Last Word: Rosalba Carriera and the *Académie Royale de Peinture et de Sculpture*', *Eighteenth-Century Studies*, 52: 173–88.
Oberer, Angela (2014). *Rosalba Carriera e le sue sorelle*, Storie del Mondo 17. Florence: Pagliai.
— (2020). *The Life and Work of Rosalba Carriera (1673–1757) – The Queen of Pastel*. Amsterdam: Amsterdam University Press.
— (2021). 'Rosalba Carriera's Miniature of Françoise Marie de Bourbon as Amphitrite: From a Marine Thiasos to a Happy Threesome', *arthistorcium.net*, http://archiv.ub.uni-heidelberg.de/artdok/volltexte/2021/7226 (accessed on 8 January 2021).
Owens, Eloise (2018). 'The Hand Behind the Likeness: Women's Practice as Professional Miniaturists in Eighteenth-Century England', in Pappe and Schmieglitz-Otten, eds, *Portrait Miniatures*, 34–42.
Pallucchini, Rodolfo (1970). 'Per la conoscenza di Giulia Lama', *Arte Veneta*, 24: 161–72.
Pappe, Bernd, and Juliane Schmieglitz-Otten, eds (2018). *Portrait Miniatures: Artists, Functions and Collections*. Petersberg: Michael Imhof.
Pasian, Alessio (2007). 'Catalogue number 3, Rosalba Carriera, Autoritratto', in Pavanello, ed., *Rosalba Carriera 'prima pittrice de l'Europa'*, 86–7.
Pavanello, Giuseppe (2007a). 'Rosalba 1757–2007', in Pavanello, ed., *Rosalba Carriera 'prima pittrice de l'Europa'*, 56–79.
—, ed. (2007b). *Rosalba Carriera 'prima pittrice de l'Europa'*, exh.cat., Venice, Palazzo Cini a San Vio, 1 September–28 October 2007. Venice: Marsilio.
—, ed. (2009). *Rosalba Carriera 1673–1757: Atti del Convegno internazionale di studi*, 26–8 April 2007, Venice, Fondazione Giorgio Cini, Chioggia, Auditorium San Niccolò. Venice: Scripta Edizioni.
Pedrocco, Filippo (1990). 'Iconografia delle cortigiane di Venezia', in Doretta Davanzo Poli, ed., *Le cortigiane di Venezia dal Trecento al Settecento: il gioco dell'amore*, exh. cat., Venice, Casino Municipale, Ca' Vendramin Calergi, 2 February–16 April 1990. Milan: Berenice, 81–93.
Perego, Andrea (2020). *Barbara – Un affare di Stato*. Venedig: Supernova.
Perry, Gill (2004). 'Staging Gender and "Hairy Signs": Representing Dorothy Jordan's Curls', *Eighteenth-Century Studies*, 38: 145–63.
Plebani, Tiziana (2003). 'La civiltà della conversazione a Venezia (XVII–XVIII secolo)', in *Memorie di lei: corsi di storia delle donne*, January–April 2003. Venice: Provincia di Venezia, Commissione Pari Opportunità, Assessorato alle Pari Opportunità, 38–52.
— (2004). 'Socialità, conversazioni e casini nella Venezia del secondo Settecento', in Maria Luisa Betri and Elena Brambilla, eds, *Salotti e ruolo femminile in Italia: tra fine Seicento e primo Novecento*. Venice: Marsilio, 153–76.
Pointon, Marcia (1993). *Hanging the Head: Portraiture and Social Formation in Eighteenth-Century England*. New Haven, CT/London: Yale University Press.
— (2001). '"Surrounded with Brilliants": Miniature Portraits in Eighteenth-Century England', *Art Bulletin*, 83(1): 48–71.
— (2014). 'The Portrait Miniature as an Intimate Object', in Bernd Pappe, Juliane Schmieglitz-Otten and Gerrit Walczak, eds, *European Portrait Miniatures: Artists, Functions and Collections*. Petersberg: Michael Imhof, 16–26.
Puhlmann, Helga (2003). 'Eine Karriere im Schatten von Rosalba Carriera – Felicita Sartori/Hoffmann in Venedig und Dresden', *Zeitenblicke*, 2(3), www.zeitenblicke.de/2003/03/pdf/Puhlmann.pdf (accessed on 10 August 2022).
Razzall, Rosie (2017). 'Consul Smith and his Circle', in Rosie Razzall and Lucy Whitaker, eds, *Canaletto and the Art of Venice*. London: Royal Collection Trust, 21–33.
Reynolds, Anna, and Lucy Peter (2016). 'Producing and Collecting Portraits of Artists', in Anna Reynolds, Lucy Peter and Martin Clayton, eds, *Portrait of the Artist*, exh. cat., Queen's Gallery, London, 11 May 2016–17 April 2017. London: Royal Collection Trust, 8–91.
Riepe, Juliane (2006). '"Essential to the Reputation and Magnificence of Such a High-Ranking Prince": Ceremonial and Italian Opera at the Court of Clemens August Elector of Cologne, and other German Courts',

in Melania Bucciarelli, Norbert Dubowy and Reinhard Strohm, eds, *Italian Opera in Central Europe. Institutions and Ceremonies*. Berlin: Berliner Wissenschaftsverlag, 147–76.

Ripa, Cesare (1603). *Iconologia, overo, Descrittione di diverse imagini cavate dall'antichità, & di propria inventione*. Rome: Lepido Faeÿ.

— (1613). *Iconologia di Cesare Ripa perugino, cavr. de sti Mauritio, e Lazzaro: nella quale si descrivono diverse imagini di virtù, vitii, affetti, passioni humane, arti, discipline, humori, elementi, corpi celesti, province d'Italia, fiumi, tutte le parti del mondo, ed altere infinite materie; opera utile ad oratori, predicatori, poeti, pittori, scultori, disegnatori, e ad ogni studioso, per inventar Concetti, Emblemi, ed Imprese, per divinare qualsivoglia apparato nuttiale, funerale, trionfale; per rappresentar poemi drammatici, e per figurare co'suoi propri simboli ciò, che può cadere in pensiero humano; ampliata ultimamente dallo stesso autore di C.C. imagini, e arricchita di molti discorsi pieni di varia eruditione; con nuovi intagli, e con indici copiosi nel fine; dedicata all'illustrissimo Signor Filippo Salviati*. Siena: Appresso gli Heredi di Matteo Florini.

Robinson, Andrew (1994). 'The Glory of Venice', in Martineau and Robinson, eds, *Glory of Venice*, 13–21.

Rogers, Katherine M. (1982). *Feminism in Eighteenth-Century England.* Chicago, IL/London: University of Illinois Press.

Rosenthal, Angela (1996). *Angelika Kauffmann: Bildnismalerei im 18. Jahrhundert*. Berlin: Reimer.

— (1997). 'She's Got the Look! Eighteenth-Century Female Portrait Painters and the Psychology of a Potentially "Dangerous Employment"', in Joanna Woodall, ed., *Portraiture: Facing the Subject*. Manchester/New York: Manchester University Press, 147–66.

— (2004). 'Raising Hair' *Eighteenth-Century Studies*, 38: 1–16.

— (2006). *Angelica Kauffmann: Art and Sensibility.* New Haven, CT/London: Yale University Press.

Rossi, Patrizio (1996). 'Il carnevale di Venezia e i viaggiatori del Settecento', *Annali d'Italianistica*, 14: 425–36.

Russell, Francis (1994). 'The International Taste for Venetian Art: England', in Martineau and Robinson, eds, *Glory of Venice*, 56–9.

Sagarra, Eda (2009). *Social History of Germany, 1648–1914*. New Brunswick/London: Transaction Publishers.

Sama, Catherina M. (2008). 'Luisa Bergalli e le sorelle Carriera: un rapporto d'amicizia e di collaborazione professionale', in Adriana Chemello, ed., *Luisa Bergalli: poetessa drammaturga traduttrice critica letteraria: atti del convegno*. Mirano-Venice: Eidos, 59–75.

— (2009). '"On Canvas and on the Page": Women Shaping Culture in Eighteenth-Century Italy', in Findlen et al., eds, *Italy's Eighteenth Century*, 125–50.

Sani, Bernardina (1985). *Rosalba Carriera: lettere, diari, frammenti*, 2 vols. Florence: Leo S. Olschki.

— (1988). *Rosalba Carriera*. Turin: Umberto Allemandi & Co.

— (1991). 'Rosalba Carriera's *Young Lady with a Parrot*', *Art Institute of Chicago Museum Studies*, 17(1): 74–87, 95.

— (2003). 'Note sulle cerchie artistiche e intellettuali intorno a Rosalba Carriera e Felicita Sartori Hoffmann', *Arte Documento*, 17–19: 494–9.

— (2007). *Rosalba Carriera 1673–1757: maestra del pastello nell'Europa 'ancien régime'*. Turin: Umberto Allemandi & Co.

— (2012). 'Raccolte di stampe tra Parigi e Venezia nella corrispondenza di Rosalba Carriera e Hyacinthe Rigaud', *Arte Veneta*, 68: 297–307.

Sauvage, Leila (2015). 'Jean-Étienne Liotard und Karoline Luise von Baden – eine Geschichte der Pastelle', in Christoph Frank and Wolfgang Zimmermann, eds, *Aufgeklärter Kunstdiskurs und höfische Sammlerpraxis: Karoline Luise von Baden im europäschen Kontext*. Berlin: Deutscher Kunstverlag, 124–31.

Schulze Altcappenberg, Hein-Thomas (1997). *Eine unbekannte Sammlung italienischer Zeichnungen aus Berliner Privatbesitz: Neuerwerbungen des Kupferstichkabinetts der Kunstbibliothek; Begleitbuch zur Ausstellung, im Kupferstichkabinett 1997–1998*. Berlin: Staatliche Museen zu Berlin, Preussischer Kulturbesitz.

Shefer, Elaine (1991). 'The "Bird in the Cage"', *Journal of the History of Sexuality*, 3: 'History of Sexuality: Sir John Everett Millais and William Holman Hunt', 446–80.

Sheriff, Mary D. (1990). *Fragonard: Art and Eroticism*. Chicago, IL/London: University of Chicago Press.

— (1994). 'Woman? Hermaphrodite? History Painter? On the Self-Imaging of Elisabeth Vigée-Lebrun', *The Eighteenth Century*, 35(1): 3–27.

— (1996). *The Exceptional Woman: Elisabeth Vigée-Lebrun and the Cultural Politics of Art.* Chicago, IL/London: University of Chicago Press.

Simons, Patricia (1994). 'Lesbian (In)Visibility in Italian Renaissance Culture: Diana and Other Cases of donna con donna', *Journal of Homosexuality*, 27: 81–122

Sohm, Philip (1990). 'The Critical Reception of Paolo Veronese in Eighteenth-Century Italy: The Example of Giambattista Tiepolo as Veronese Redivius', in Jürg Meyer zur Capellen and Bernd Roeck, eds, *Paolo Veronese: Fortuna Critica und Künstlerisches Nachleben*. Sigmaringen: Thorbecke, 87–107.

— (2007). *The Artist Grows Old: The Ageing of Art and Artists in Italy, 1500–1800.* New Haven, CT/London: Yale University Press.

— (2010a). 'Introduction', in Spear and Sohm, eds, *Painting for Profit*, 1–32.

— (2010b). 'Venice', in Spear and Sohm, eds, *Painting for Profit*, 205–54.

Solkin, David (1986). 'Great Pictures or Great Men? Reynolds, Male Portraiture, and the Power of Art', *Oxford Journal*, 9: 42–9.

Spear, Richard E., and Philip Sohm, eds (2010). *Painting for Profit: The Economic Lives of Seventeenth-Century Italian Painters*. New Haven, CT: Yale University Press.

Spence, Joseph (1820). *Observations, Anecdotes and Characters of Books and Men*. London: W.H. Carpenter.

— (1966). *Observations, Anecdotes and Characters of Books and Men*, ed. James M. Osborn. Oxford: Oxford University Press.

Steele, Brian D. (1997). 'In the Flower of their Youth: "Portraits" of Venetian Beauties ca. 1500', *Sixteenth-Century Journal*, 28: 481–502.

Steward, James Christen (1996). 'Masks and Meanings in Tiepolo's Venice', in James Christen Steward, ed., *Mask of Venice: Masking, Theater and Identity*, exh.cat., Berkeley Art Museum, University of California. Berkeley, CA: Berkeley Art Museum in association with University of Washington Press, 15–33.

Stratis, Harriet K., and Brit Salvesen, eds (2002). *The Broad Spectrum: Studies in the Materials, Techniques, and Conservation of Color and Paper*. London: Archetype.

Sutherland Harris, Ann, and Linda Nochlin, eds (1976). *Women Artists, 1550–1950*, exh.cat., Los Angeles, County Museum of Art, 21 December 1976–31 March 1977. Los Angeles, CA: County Museum/New York: Alfred Knopf.

—, eds (1979). *Le grandi pittrici, 1550–1950*. Milan: Feltrinelli.

Swinburne, Henry (1686). *A Treatise of Spousals, or Matrimonial Contracts wherein all the Questions relating to that Subject are Ingeniously Debated and Resolved*. London: Robert Clavell. Online version: https://quod.lib.umich.edu/e/eebo2/A62036.0001.001?view=toc (accessed on 27 September 2022).

Traub, Valerie (1996). 'The Perversion of "Lesbian" Desire', *History Workshop Journal*, 41: 23–49.

Trauth, Nina (2009). *Maske und Person: Orientalismus im Porträt des Barock*. Berlin/Munich: Deutscher Kunstverlag.

Urban, Lina (1994–5). 'L'Andata dogale a San Vio: rituali, un quadro, una "beata", una chiesa', *Studi Veneziani*, 28: 191–202.

Vogtherr, Christoph Martin (2010). 'Some Aspects of French Eighteenth-Century Miniature Painting', in Stephen Duffy and Christoph Martin Vogtherr, eds, *Miniatures in the Wallace Collection*. London: Wallace Collection, 15–20.

Voltaire (1784). *La vie privée du roi du Prusse ou Mémoires pour serivir à la vie de M. de Voltaire, écrits par lui-même*. Amsterdam: Les Héritiers.

Von Fellenberg, Valentine (2017). 'Die Künstlerinnen an der Académie royale de peinture et de sculpture 1648–1793: eine Analyse im Lichte verschiedener Formen der Kunsttradierung', in Münch et al., eds, *Künstlerinnen*, 111–32.

Vout, Caroline (2005). 'Antinous, Archaeology and History', *Journal of Roman Studies*, 95: 80–96.

Walther, Angelo (1972–5). 'Zu den Werken der Rosalba Carriera in der Dresdener Gemäldegalerie', *Beiträge und Berichte der Staatlichen Kunstsammlungen Dresden*, 65–90.

Ward, Adrienne (2018). 'The Drama of Marriage in Eighteenth-Century Venice: Carlo Goldoni's *La Locandiera*', in David Thatcher Gies and Cynthia Wall, eds *The Eighteenth Centuries. Global Networks of Enlightenment*. Charlottesville, VA/London: University of Virginia Press, 233–63.

Welch, Evelyn (2009). 'Art on the Edge: Hair and Hands in Renaissance Italy', *Renaissance Studies*, 23: 241–68.

West, Shearer (1999). 'Gender and Internationalism: The Case of Rosalba Carriera', in Shearer West, ed., *Italian Culture in Northern Europe*. Cambridge: Cambridge University Press, 46–66.

Whistler, Catherine (2009). 'Rosalba Carriera e il mondo britanico', in Pavanello, ed., *Rosalba Carriera 1673–1757: Atti del Convegno*, 181–206.

Wollenberg, Susan (1991). 'The Austro-German Courts', in Julie Anne Sadie, ed., *Companion to Baroque Music*. Berkeley/Los Angeles, CA: University of California Press, 229–48.

Woods Marsden, Joanna (1998). *Renaissance Self-Portraiture: The Visual Construction of Identity and the Social Status of the Artist*. New Haven, CT/London: Yale University Press.

Zanetti, Anton Maria (1771). *Della pittura veneziana e delle opere pubbliche de' veneziani maestri*, 5 vols. Venice: Stamperia di Giambattista Albrizzi.

Zanetti, Girolamo (1818). *Elogio di Rosalba Carriera scritto da G.Z. a cura di C. Zacco*. Venice: Tipografia di Alvisopoli.

Zanini-Cordi, Irene (2013). 'Botteghe da caffè: Sociability and Gender in Eighteenth-Century Venice', *NeMLA*, 35, 26–50.

Zarrillo, Taryn Marie (2016). 'The Neurosis of Visual Legacy: Seicento Venetian Painters Confront their Past', in Banta, ed., *The Enduring Legacy of Venetian Renaissance Art*, 11–24.

Zava, Franca (2007). 'M.lle Rosalba très vertueuse peintresse', in Pavanello, ed., *Rosalba Carriera 'prima pittrice de l'Europa'*, 15–26.

Zava Boccazzi, Franca (1981). 'Rosalba Carriera e famiglia: nuovi documenti veneziani', *Arte Veneta*, 35, 217–26.

Ziskin, Rochelle (2012). *Sheltering Art. Collecting and Social Identity in Early Eighteenth-Century Paris*. University Park, PA: Pennsylvania State University Press.

Image Credits

The publisher would like to thank the copyright holders for granting permission to reproduce the images illustrated. Every attempt has been made to trace accurate ownership of copyrighted images in this book. Any errors or omissions will be corrected in subsequent editions provided notification is sent to the publisher.

Academia di San Luca, Rome: fig.20

The Art Institute, Chicago: fig.55

Bayerisches Nationalmuseum, München: fig.12

The Cleveland Museum of Art, Cleveland: figs 8, 9, 15

Fondazione Giorgio Cini, Gabinetto dei Disegni e delle Stampe, Venice: fig.21

Gallerie degli Uffizi, Florence: figs 25, 42, 53

Gallerie dell'Accademia, Venice: fig.64

The Hermitage, St Petersburg: figs 56, 57

The Metropolitan Museum of Art, New York: figs 1, 2, 3, 5, 6, 11, 18, 19, 35, 46

Musée du Louvre, Paris: figs 39, 41

Musei Civici di Treviso – Museo di Santa Caterina, Treviso: fig.37

Museo degli Argenti, Palazzo Pitti, Florence: fig.13

Museo del Settecento, Ca´Rezzonico, Venice: fig.48

Museo di Palazzo Grimani, Venice: fig.59

National Gallery of Denmark, Copenhagen: fig.14

National Museum Stockholm: figs 22, 27, 31

Paul J. Getty Museum, Los Angeles: figs 34, 65

Private Collection: fig.32

The Rijksmuseum, Amsterdam: figs 10, 38

Royal Collection Trust: fig.17

Samuel Kress Collection, National Gallery of Art, Washington: fig.4

Staatliche Kunsthalle Karlsruhe: fig.58

Staatliche Kunstsammlungen, Gemäldegalerie Alte Meister, Dresden: figs 16, 23, 26, 28, 29, 30, 36, 43, 44, 45, 47, 49, 50, 51, 52, 54, 60, 61, 62, 63

Staatliche Museen, Preußischer Kulturbesitz, Kupferstichkabinett, Berlin: fig.24

Yale Center for British Art, New Haven: fig.33

Index

Note: italic page numbers indicate figures; Rosalba Carriera is abbreviated to RC in headings and subheadings.